Applied Cyber Threat Intelligence

Applied Cyber Threat Intelligence: From Detection to Disruption is a comprehensive guide for cybersecurity students, analysts, and professionals looking to gain practical, in-demand skills in today's rapidly evolving digital threat landscape. This book bridges the gap between theoretical knowledge and operational expertise, providing readers with a hands-on approach to Cyber Threat Intelligence (CTI), threat hunting, malware analysis, and open-source investigations.

Covering the full CTI lifecycle from intelligence collection and analysis to adversary attribution and takedown, the book offers step-by-step walkthroughs of key tools such as Sysmon-Modular, DeTT&CT, OSSEM, and VirusTotal. Readers will learn how to conduct static and dynamic malware analysis, apply threat frameworks like MITRE ATT&CK and the Diamond Model to perform real-world investigations across surface, deep, and dark web environments.

Designed for both classroom use and professional upskilling, the book includes case studies and lab exercises. Whether you're preparing for a cybersecurity role or enhancing your current capabilities, this book equips you with the analytical mindset, technical skills, and practical tools to proactively detect, understand, and respond to cyber threats with confidence and precision.

Dr Akashdeep Bhardwaj is working as Professor & Director for the Center of Cybersecurity at UPES, Dehradun, and is the Chief Executive Officer (CEO) for Global Cybersecurity Association (GCA). An eminent IT industry expert with around 30 years of experience in areas such as cybersecurity, digital forensics, and IT operations, Dr Akashdeep mentors graduate, masters', and doctoral students and leads several projects.

Dr Akashdeep is a postdoctoral researcher from Majmaah University, Saudi Arabia; holds a Ph.D. in Computer Science from UPES Dehradun; a master's in business administration; and an engineering degree in Computer Science from Pune University. Dr Akashdeep has published over 180 research works including copyrights, patents, and research manuscripts published SCI/WoS/Scopus indexed in highly referred international journals, as well as authored and edited several books and chapters.

Dr Akashdeep worked as a technology leader for several multinational organizations during his time in the IT industry. Dr Akashdeep has expertise in multiple cyber domains, including open-source intelligence, cyber threat intelligence, malware analysis, compliance, web/network/data security, and is certified in several industry certifications from Microsoft, Cisco, CompTIA, EC-Council, and VMware technologies.

Applied Cyber Threat Intelligence
From Detection to Disruption

Dr Akashdeep Bhardwaj

CRC Press
Taylor & Francis Group
Boca Raton London New York

CRC Press is an imprint of the
Taylor & Francis Group, an **informa** business

Designed cover image: Shutterstock ID: 2655768299

First edition published 2027
by CRC Press
2385 NW Executive Center Drive, Suite 320, Boca Raton FL 33431

and by CRC Press
4 Park Square, Milton Park, Abingdon, Oxon, OX14 4RN

CRC Press is an imprint of Taylor & Francis Group, LLC

ISBN: 978-1-041-22088-6 (hbk)
ISBN: 978-1-041-22089-3 (pbk)
ISBN: 978-1-003-73058-3 (ebk)

DOI: 10.1201/9781003730583

Typeset in Sabon
by SPi Technologies India Pvt Ltd (Straive)

To my parents, Late Wg. Cdr. K C Bhardwaj and Usha Bhardwaj, for the foundation
of love and values that made this possible.
To my wife, Archana, my constant strength and inspiration.
And to my daughter, Raavi, my greatest joy and the reason I dream bigger every day.

Contents

AI statement

Generative Artificial Intelligence tools were used in a limited and supportive capacity during the preparation of this manuscript. Specifically, ChatGPT (OpenAI, GPT-4/GPT-4.1) was used to assist with language refinement, paraphrasing, summation of technical concepts, and structural clarity in selected sections of the manuscript.

Chapter 1

Introduction to cyber threat intelligence (CTI)

1.1 DEFINITION OF CYBER THREAT INTELLIGENCE (CTI)

To understand the modern cybersecurity ecosystem, it's helpful to think of it as a vast digital city where countless interactions, signals, and behaviors occur every second. Just as the movement and noise of a city require interpretation to uncover patterns, risks, and anomalies, so too do the streams of data generated by networks and systems. This is where Cyber Threat Intelligence (CTI) [1] becomes indispensable. CTI involves gathering and analyzing raw, unorganized digital data to produce actionable insights. These insights empower security professionals to proactively detect, understand, and respond to potential cyber threats with greater precision and efficiency.

CTI goes beyond basic data monitoring. It allows organizations to build a forward-looking defense strategy by continuously analyzing current and emerging threats. This proactive approach helps businesses avoid being caught off-guard by malicious actors. CTI combines contextual threat data with analytical reasoning to inform strategic and tactical decisions within the security architecture. Rather than merely reacting to incidents, CTI empowers organizations to make informed decisions about where and how to reinforce their digital defenses. Intelligence is generated by analyzing threat behaviors, tracking known attack patterns, and interpreting anomalies from internal and external sources. Common inputs include open-source threat feeds, incident reports, system and application logs, malware repositories, and even content shared across social platforms. When properly processed, this intelligence acts as a force multiplier, shifting the role of cybersecurity from passive defense to active prevention.

By enabling early detection, reducing false positives, and supporting more focused investigation, CTI enhances the organization's ability to guard its assets efficiently. The strength of CTI lies in its capacity to provide timely, relevant, and actionable knowledge, allowing businesses to prioritize threats, allocate resources wisely, and mitigate risks before damage occurs.

1.2 CRITICAL TERMS

Understanding CTI requires familiarity with several foundational terms. These concepts serve as the building blocks for effective threat analysis and communication within cybersecurity teams. Below is an elaboration of key terms, contextualized for real-world relevance.

- Cyber refers to the digital domain encompassing interconnected systems, devices, and networks. While its roots trace back to Norbert Wiener's concept of cybernetics focused on control and communication in systems the term has evolved. Today, "cyber" broadly encapsulates everything from internet browsing and cloud computing to encrypted messaging and data transmission across networks. It symbolizes the entire spectrum of digital interactions, far beyond just the web.

DOI: 10.1201/9781003730583-1

- Threat is any element that poses a potential danger to an information system, its data, or its users. Threats can arise from intentional actors like hackers or from accidental mishandling of resources. Common examples include malware infections, unauthorized system access, phishing campaigns, social engineering tactics, denial-of-service (DoS) attacks, and data exfiltration. Some threats exploit known vulnerabilities, while others, such as zero-day attacks, target previously undiscovered flaws.
- Intelligence in the CTI context is the outcome of processing and analyzing data to derive actionable insights. It turns raw, fragmented information into structured knowledge that informs defensive actions. While data refers to basic facts such as IP logs, file names, or timestamps, intelligence emerges when this information is contextualized and interpreted through a security lens.
- Cybersecurity is the discipline focused on safeguarding digital infrastructure against unauthorized access, tampering, or destruction. This includes measures like encryption, firewall deployment, access control policies, and continuous monitoring. Whether it's securing online banking platforms or enterprise databases, cybersecurity ensures the confidentiality, integrity, and availability of digital assets.
- Event is any observable occurrence within a digital environment, whether benign or potentially malicious. Examples range from routine user logins and file transfers to configuration changes or application crashes. Events alone may not signal a threat, but their context is essential in identifying suspicious behavior.
- Incident differs from an event in that it implies a breach of security policy or an imminent risk. Incidents include unauthorized access attempts, malware outbreaks, or insider threats. They represent situations requiring immediate attention to prevent data loss or operational disruption.
- Asset refers to any resource or piece of information that holds value for an organization. This may include physical devices like servers, digital repositories such as customer databases, or intangible elements like proprietary algorithms. Protecting assets is central to any security strategy.
- Vulnerability refers to a weakness or oversight in a system's architecture, setup, or functioning that can be taken advantage of by malicious actors. These flaws might arise from outdated applications, improperly secured configurations, or insufficient encryption protocols. When left unaddressed, such issues can significantly weaken an organization's security posture.
- Exploit is the technique or mechanism employed to leverage a known vulnerability. It involves using specific knowledge of a system's shortcomings to infiltrate or disrupt it without authorization. Cyber attackers frequently deploy automated programs to detect these weak points and execute precise operations to breach the system or inflict harm.
- Attack is a deliberate action taken by an adversary to compromise a system or network. Whether it's stealing data, disrupting services, or installing malware, attacks are executed with the intent to harm, gain advantage, or cause financial loss.
- Breach occurs when an attack successfully bypasses security mechanisms, resulting in the unauthorized access or disclosure of sensitive information. Breaches often result in reputational damage, legal repercussions, and financial loss for organizations.
- Malware, an abbreviation for malicious software, stands as a constantly changing and enduring challenge within the realm of cybersecurity. While not every attack involves malware, it remains a powerful tool in the hands of adversaries, capable of inflicting significant harm through disruption, data theft, or surveillance. Malware operates through a sequence of stages, and understanding its lifecycle enables security professionals to detect, analyze, and respond to threats more effectively.

The life cycle of malware generally starts with the phase of gaining access to a target system. This is commonly achieved through deceptive means like fraudulent emails, infected file attachments, silent downloads, or visiting websites that have been tampered with. In many cases, an initial program, often disguised as a harmless file, acts as a carrier to introduce the harmful code without drawing attention. For more sophisticated cyber threats, a layered or multistage delivery mechanism may be employed. This approach assembles separate segments of the malware on the victim's machine, helping it bypass early security checks and delay detection.

Next is the execution phase, where the core payload of the malware is activated. This stage determines the intended impact, ranging from system corruption and data theft to establishing backdoor access for remote control. Often, malware will attempt to obfuscate its behavior to avoid detection by antivirus software, using techniques like code scrambling, encryption, or process hollowing. Following execution, malware seeks persistence, ensuring that it remains active even after system reboots or user logouts. This may involve modifying registry keys, injecting code into startup programs, or creating hidden services that launch automatically. Once persistence is secured, the malware may initiate command-and-control (C2) communication [2]. Through C2 channels, attackers can issue commands to the malware, exfiltrate stolen data, update configurations, or download new components. These channels may rely on obscure methods such as DNS queries, social media comments, or even legitimate platforms like GitHub or cloud services to avoid triggering alerts.

An advanced stage in the lifecycle is data exfiltration, where sensitive files, credentials, or system data are transmitted to the attacker's remote server. In some cases, malware may exhibit propagation behavior, attempting to spread laterally across networks by exploiting shared drives or unpatched vulnerabilities, often mimicking worm-like traits. Attackers may also bundle malware with exploit kits, allowing it to target specific software vulnerabilities across multiple endpoints. The final phase is the impact or outcome, which varies based on the malware's purpose. It may involve deleting files, encrypting data for ransom, hijacking user credentials, or deploying spyware to monitor user behavior. Some malware focuses on denial of service, overwhelming resources to disrupt operations, while others specialize in espionage, gathering intelligence over extended periods without detection.

Modern malware often includes advanced capabilities such as polymorphism, where the code alters itself to bypass signature-based detection, or metamorphism, where it rewrites its own structure entirely to remain elusive. Additionally, stealth techniques such as disabling security tools, running in memory only, or hiding in legitimate processes that allow it to operate without drawing attention.

Malware is not a singular entity; it comes in various forms, each serving specific objectives.

- Worms replicate across networks without user intervention
- Trojans disguise themselves as benign applications to bypass security.
- Rootkits are embedded into system processes, masking the presence of other malicious tools.
- Ransomware locks users out of their systems or encrypts files until a ransom is paid, often in cryptocurrency.
- Keyloggers silently record user keystrokes to capture sensitive data like passwords.
- Other variants include adware, which bombards users with unwanted ads, spyware, which monitors user activity, and scareware, which deceives users into thinking their system is infected.
- Some threats even involve backdoors, which provide attackers ongoing remote access, or wipers, designed to irreversibly destroy data.

- Exploit kits serve as malicious toolkits capable of identifying vulnerabilities in targeted systems and deploying appropriate malware payloads accordingly. In many cases, malware samples are grouped into families, clusters of variants that share common traits, often attributed to the same author or hacker group. Open-source malware tools can further blur attribution, as these are used and repurposed by multiple actors, both state-sponsored and criminal.

Malware family refers to a collection of malicious programs that exhibit similar traits and are often attributed to the same developer or origin. In certain instances, these families can be linked to specific threat actors. However, it is also common for various cybercriminal groups to use the same malware or tools, especially when those tools are open-source and easily accessible. By utilizing publicly available malware, attackers can obscure their identities and make attribution more challenging.

1.2.1 Hashes

These are digital fingerprints used for verifying the integrity of data. Even small change in the original data (text, code, image, content) will completely alter the hash value. Example Hash Online value calculator [3] or the MD5 Hash value calculator [4]. This is useful when for file downloads to ensure that it is not corrupted or changed during the transfer. There are different hashing algorithms like MD5 or the SHA (1, 256).

1.2.2 IoC and IoA

Indicators of Compromise (IoC) and Indicators of Attack (IoA) are both crucial for detecting and responding to cyber threats. While they both provide valuable information, they differ in their focus, purpose, and the stage of an attack they address as shown above. By combining IoCs and IoAs, security teams access the comprehensive threat landscape. IoC are behavior or data that shows a breach, intrusion, cyberattack has occurred. Presence of IoC indicates vulnerability within the infra, system, app, or the network. Primary purpose of IoCs is to identify, analyze security events after they have occurred, Post Event Analysis/Post Attack investigations. IoCs help identify systems that need remediation as per three conditions:

1. Observability – display a sign that a malicious event has transpired
2. Context – artifact must fit the specific context – Phishing → suspicious URLs/Email attachment
3. Metadata – info that helps make sense of that IoC – Source data, Date of occurrence, files

Types of IoCs:

- Network-based: analyze network traffic across different infra devices to find malicious data
- File-based: IoCs attached to files within a host system – hashes, file name, IP address
- Behavioral-based: observe patterns within a system/network to indicate malicious activities

Table 1.1 presents the IoC and IoA, which describe the behaviors to identify a Cyberattack that is in progress, which identifies the intent, techniques to carry out the malicious activity.

Table 1.1 Difference between IoC and IoA

	Indicators of compromise or IoC	*Indicators of attack or IoA*
Focus	Evidence of past compromise – artifacts/proof left behind after a breach.	Signs of ongoing or imminent malicious activity.
Purpose	Identify a system or network that has already been compromised	Detect and prevent an attack before it compromises a system.
Time-based	Lookback at evidence	Dynamic info for handing ongoing
Nature	Post event analysis, allows you to respond to a crime after it has been carried out.	Empowers you with just enough info to stop an attack before the situation worsens.
Nature	Static data, Confirmed info. Have a format that can be classified/compared with past info.	Dynamic Patterns/Techniques that hint at an ongoing event – not forensic info. Unpredictable, change based on intent of attack's goal/malware propagation.
Examples	• Malicious files: Unexplained executables, scripts, or data archives on a system. • Suspicious network activity: Unusual data transfers, connections to unknown IP addresses, or unauthorized access ➔ C2 attempts. • Registry key changes: Modifications to system configuration settings often associated with malware installation. • Stolen data: Loss of sensitive information like customer records or financial data. • CCTV recording after a crime • Repeated login failures – Brute Force password cracking • Access Database by unknown accounts with increase in read/write volumes • Geographical Irregularities – violate rules that allow access from specific IPs – Impossible Travel Time Violation! • Access at different times – outside office hours, weekends, early morning • Unexpected Software/OS update • Suspicious Registry changes	• Unusual login attempts: Multiple failed logins from unexpected locations or times. • Suspicious email activity: Phishing attempts with generic greetings, typos in domain names, or unsolicited attachments. • Anomalous network traffic: Spikes in traffic volume, attempts to exploit known vulnerabilities, or connections to command-and-control servers. • System resource depletion: Unusual spikes in CPU or memory usage, suggesting malware or resource-intensive processes.

Real-life examples

1. IC3 RagnarLocker Ransomware Alert [5]: The FBI and CISA jointly issued a security notice warning about the RagnarLocker ransomware, which has been actively targeting multiple industries since April 2020. As of early 2022, the malware had affected over 50 organizations spanning critical infrastructure sectors such as energy, finance, government, and technology. RagnarLocker cleverly uses tools like VMProtect and UPX to conceal its code and sometimes operates within a virtualized Windows XP shell. It ... certain system directories and halts its activity in machines located ... pean regions. The ransomware also disables backup services and ... ption keys tied to infected systems.

   ... Trends [6]: ANY.RUN, a cloud-based malware analysis service, ... ights into malware activity from its live sandbox environment. ... four million executed samples, its annual report for 2024 shows ... re the most frequently detected malware type, followed by loaders and remote access tools (RATs). Some of the most active malware strains included Lumma Stealer, AsyncRAT, and Agent Tesla. ANY.RUN provides investigators with detailed intelligence, including IoC like hashes, IP addresses, and domains. These features help analysts track threats, understand behavior patterns, and improve detection and prevention strategies in real time.

3. BlackBerry Threat Research & Intelligence Repository [7]: BlackBerry's open-access GitHub repository is a rich resource for cybersecurity professionals, offering threat intelligence reports, detection rules, and incident analysis tools. This well-structured collection features original blogs, YARA signatures, and contextual data useful for identifying and understanding various cyber threats. It supports security teams in activities such as threat hunting, malware analysis, and digital forensics. The repository encourages collaborative defense efforts and is available under an open-source license, allowing researchers to adapt and apply the shared content. BlackBerry's contributions underscore the importance of transparency and knowledge-sharing in staying ahead of rapidly evolving cyberattacks.

1.2.3 Zero-day exploit

This technique involves exploiting a security flaw that is either newly discovered or previously unknown in a system's software, hardware, or firmware. The phrase "zero-day" highlights the fact that the vulnerability is not yet recognized by the software creator, vendor, or end user, meaning they have had zero days to address or patch the issue with a security solution. Only the attackers know about this discovery. This makes zero-day exploits particularly dangerous because there's no patch available to protect systems from being compromised as:

1. Unknown vulnerability: The vulnerability being exploited is new and hasn't been publicly disclosed. This gives attackers a significant advantage as most security software wouldn't be able to detect or block the exploit.
2. Rapid attacks: Hackers who discover a zero-day vulnerability often try to exploit it as quickly as possible before the software vendor becomes aware of it and releases a patch.
3. High risk: Because there's no patch available, zero-day attacks are highly likely to succeed, allowing attackers to gain unauthorized access to systems, steal data, or disrupt operations.

Zero-day exploits are powerful tools that can be used by different types of threat actors for various malicious purposes. Cybercriminals often leverage these unknown vulnerabilities to gain unauthorized access to systems, allowing them to steal sensitive data such as financial records, personal details, or proprietary information, as illustrated in Figure 1.1. State-sponsored groups may use such exploits to conduct espionage or cyber sabotage, as seen in incidents involving surveillance tools like Pegasus. Meanwhile, hacktivists exploit zero-day flaws to disrupt digital infrastructure and draw attention to their social or political causes. These attacks often occur before any patch or defense mechanism can be deployed.

Although it is impossible to guarantee complete protection against zero-day exploits, certain measures can significantly reduce the risk. Keeping all software, hardware, and firmware updated ensures known vulnerabilities are patched promptly. Utilizing trusted security solutions can help detect and prevent some types of attacks, including unknown ones. Promot cybersecurity awareness among users is essential, and encouraging caution with susp emails, links, and attachments helps prevent accidental exposure. Additionally, orga can benefit from subscribing to threat intelligence services, which provide timely i emerging threats and vulnerabilities, allowing for proactive defense strategies tial cyberattacks before they can be exploited.

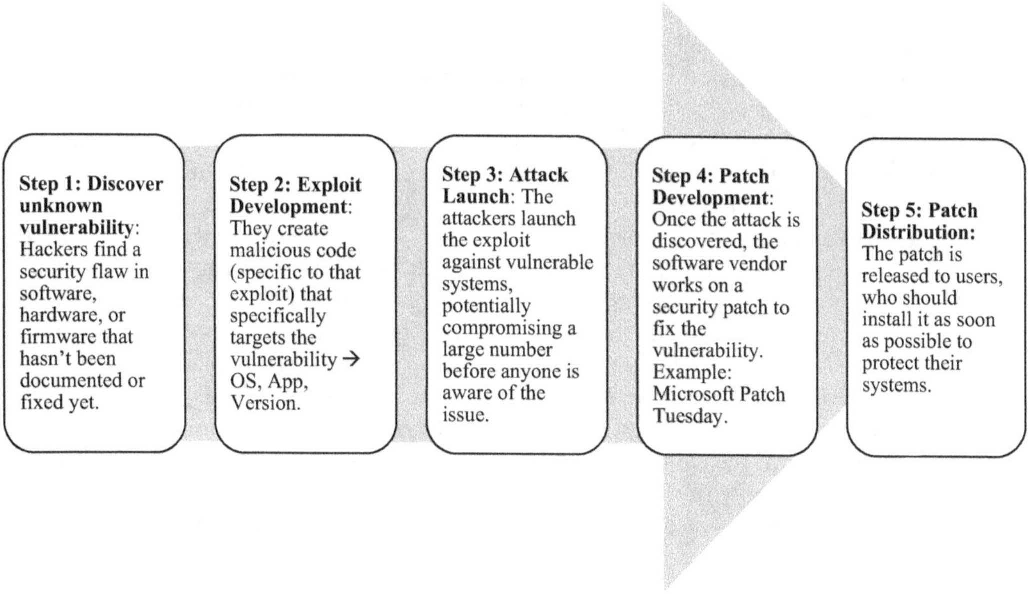

Step 1: Discover unknown vulnerability: Hackers find a security flaw in software, hardware, or firmware that hasn't been documented or fixed yet.

Step 2: Exploit Development: They create malicious code (specific to that exploit) that specifically targets the vulnerability → OS, App, Version.

Step 3: Attack Launch: The attackers launch the exploit against vulnerable systems, potentially compromising a large number before anyone is aware of the issue.

Step 4: Patch Development: Once the attack is discovered, the software vendor works on a security patch to fix the vulnerability. Example: Microsoft Patch Tuesday.

Step 5: Patch Distribution: The patch is released to users, who should install it as soon as possible to protect their systems.

Figure 1.1 Zero-day exploits lifecycle.

1.2.4 Sandbox

Sandboxes are crucial tools in cybersecurity used to analyze potentially malicious files or behaviors in an isolated environment, preventing them from affecting real systems. There are primarily two types: appliance-based sandboxes using virtual machines (VMs) and cloud-based sandboxes. Appliance-based sandboxes operate on local infrastructure, typically using dedicated physical or VMs to simulate user environments. These VMs mimic real operating systems, allowing security analysts to safely execute and observe suspicious files or applications. Since the analysis is performed locally, it offers full control, customization, and data privacy, making it ideal for organizations with strict compliance or offline environments. However, this setup often requires substantial hardware resources, regular maintenance, and skilled personnel to manage.

Cloud-based sandboxes leverage remote servers managed by third-party vendors to perform malware analysis. These sandboxes provide scalability, faster updates, and minimal setup costs. They are ideal for organizations looking for rapid deployment and real-time threat intelligence without investing in extensive infrastructure. Cloud sandboxes often integrate with threat intelligence feeds, automating detection and response processes. However, concerns related to data confidentiality, vendor reliability, and internet dependency may limit their use in sensitive sectors. Both types play complementary roles, and many organizations adopt a hybrid model to maximize threat detection capabilities while balancing control and scalability. These are isolated and controlled environments to dynamically analyze malware pieces, specifically threats that have not been seen before or match any known malware on file. In a sandbox, the suspected malware piece is executed, and its behavior is recorded.

A sandbox environment typically comprises several critical components that enable safe testing and analysis of potentially harmful software. One essential element is the VM, which replicates a full computing system within an isolated environment. This ensures that any code or application tested within it cannot affect the host system, making it ideal for security and development tasks. Another vital component is the emulator, which imitates specific hardware or software configurations. Emulators are useful for examining how software behaves under particular conditions, allowing more precise targeting during tests. In some setups, a system-level sandbox is deployed, offering complete system isolation. These are particularly beneficial when scrutinizing code that might interact with low-level system operations, such as kernel processes or drivers. On the other hand, application-level sandboxes impose constraints on what resources an application can access. These are designed to allow enough functionality for observing behavior without letting potentially malicious actions spread beyond the sandboxed instance.

To evaluate suspicious code, cybersecurity experts apply several analytical techniques. One of the primary approaches is static analysis, which involves reviewing the code without executing it. This technique helps quickly identify common malicious patterns or known threat signatures embedded in the code. In contrast, dynamic or runtime analysis focuses on observing how the code behaves during execution within a controlled sandbox. This method is particularly useful for detecting threats that activate only under certain runtime conditions. Another advanced technique involves analyzing memory dumps generated during the sandbox session. By examining the contents of system memory, analysts can uncover malware that operates only in memory and avoids leaving evidence on the file system. This memory-centric analysis plays a critical role in identifying stealthy, in-memory threats that are otherwise difficult to detect.

1.3 DIKW PYRAMID (DATA, INFORMATION, KNOWLEDGE, WISDOM)

Figure 1.2 outlines the progression from raw data to actionable wisdom using the DIKW pyramid. This demonstrates how data evolves through various stages, beginning as unprocessed facts and gradually transforming into meaningful insights. The foundational layer consists of data, which lacks context but holds potential. When this data is organized and given relevance, it becomes information. Further interpretation and contextual understanding of this information lead to knowledge. At the pinnacle of the pyramid lies wisdom, where knowledge is applied judiciously to make sound decisions.

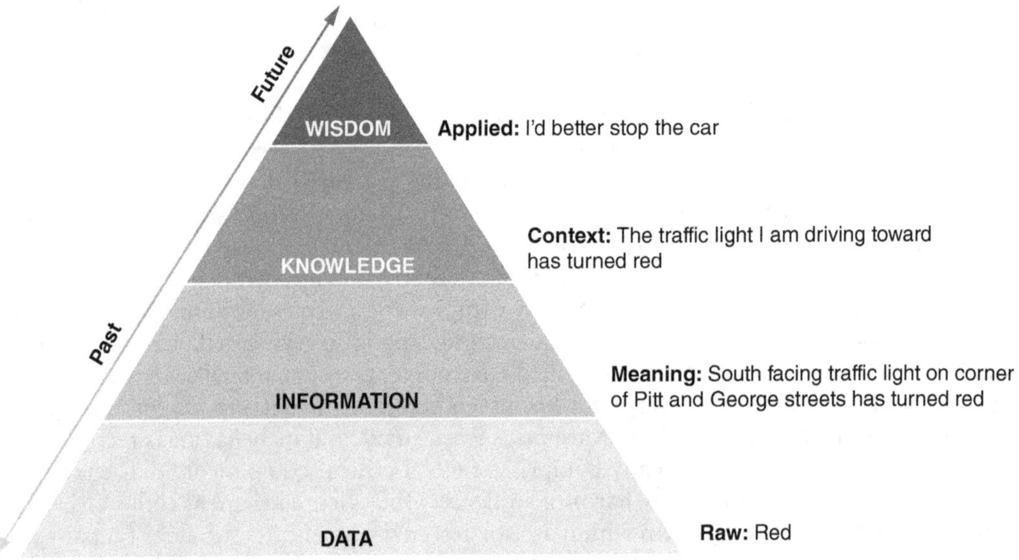

Figure 1.2 DIKW pyramid.

Each level in this hierarchy addresses a specific aspect of the original data, enhancing its value and purpose. By systematically adding context, structure, and meaning to raw data, we convert it into a resource that supports deeper understanding and practical application. As we climb from data to wisdom, we enable more accurate analysis, stronger insights, and smarter, evidence-based decision-making. This structured transformation helps organizations and individuals move from simply having data to truly leveraging it for strategic advantage.

Gaining a clear understanding of the DIKW (Data, Information, Knowledge, Wisdom) hierarchy enables us to systematically convert unstructured network data into meaningful and practical intelligence. This structured approach helps in recognizing emerging security threats early on and taking timely actions to prevent any major impact or disruption. Through this transformation process, raw data is elevated into valuable insights that enhance our ability to anticipate and mitigate cyber risks proactively.

1.3.1 DIKW from cybersecurity perspective

1.3.1.1 Raw data

Unorganized facts in form of logs from different digital devices and numbers, characters from network devices, OS system, and apps like Apache, FTPD, or Samba services, Oracle Database server, Web Portal apps as displayed in Figure 1.3.

These logs are difficult to decipher and offer minimal security value. Imagine you're a network security analyst tasked with monitoring the network for suspicious activity. The primary source of data is network traffic logs viewed individually on each device or system. These logs contain a wealth of information which will contain a massive amount of data, including –

- IP addresses (source and destination)
- Port numbers
- Time stamps
- Packet sizes
- Protocol types (e.g., HTTP, HTTPS, FTP)
- 07011991 → sequence of numbers

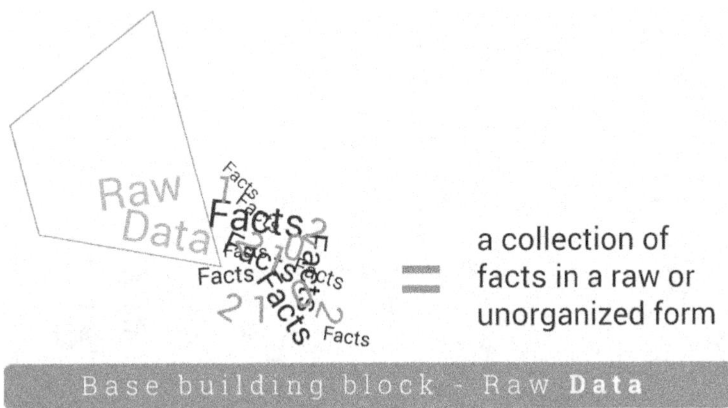

Figure 1.3 Raw data.

1.3.1.2 Information

To extract meaningful insights from raw data, it must first undergo a process of measurement, analysis, and visualization. This transformation enables organizations to better understand and interpret system behaviors and potential threats. Tools such as Security Information and Event Management (SIEM) platforms play a pivotal role in this context. These systems collect log data from a wide array of sources across the IT infrastructure and bring them together into a unified dashboard. By consolidating these disparate logs, SIEM solutions offer a centralized perspective on system activities, making it easier for security teams to monitor, investigate, and respond to incidents effectively as presented in Figure 1.4, example:

- Total number of connections per hour
- Most frequently accessed destinations
- Types of protocols used.
- Unusual spikes in traffic volume
- 07011991 → sequence of numbers → 07 = date, 01 = month and 1991 = year

Data to Information allows security analysts to identify patterns and anomalies, such as a surge in login attempts from unusual locations or scanning attempts by attackers. This is the process of organizing the raw data. Security software can aggregate logs from various devices, providing a consolidated view of network activities.

1.3.1.3 Knowledge

This is where the real magic happens. Analysts leverage their knowledge, threat intelligence feeds, and threat hunting techniques to analyze the information, asking questions (*who, what, when, where*) to derive valuable info as shown in Figure 1.5.

They correlate events, check patterns, identify IOCs – signs of malicious activity – and assess the potential risk – what can be the impact, what to protect first, who is responsible, and where is that device.

- 07011991 → sequence of numbers → 07 = date, 01 = month and 1991 = year → Birth date!
- Why is there a sudden surge in traffic from an unknown IP address?
- Which are the connections to suspicious websites or ports typically used for remote access?
- Why was there a significant increase in traffic outside of school hours?

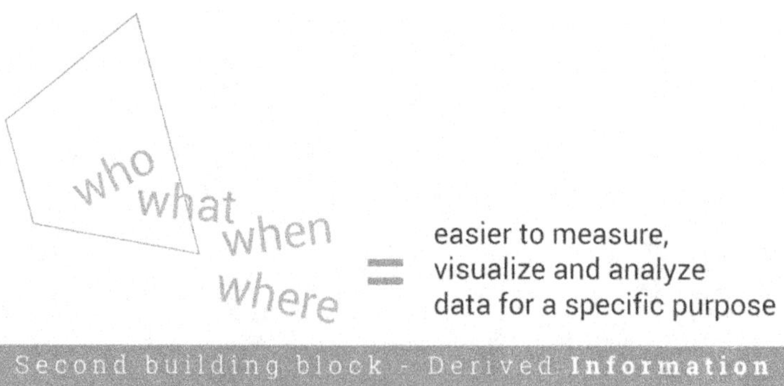

Figure 1.4 Information.

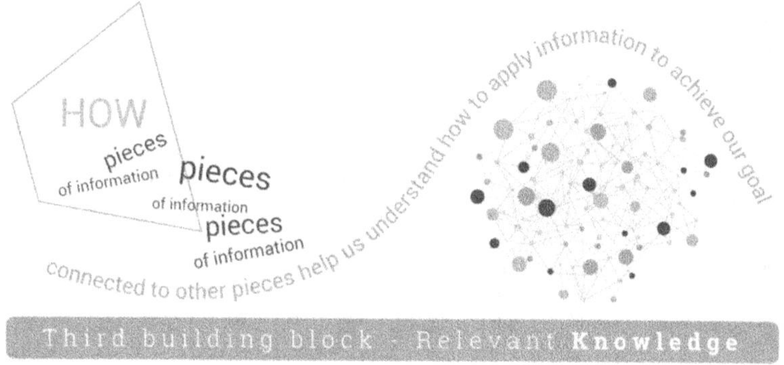

Figure 1.5 Knowledge.

1.3.1.4 Intelligence

By critically examining data and leveraging expert insights, raw information can be converted into meaningful and operational intelligence. This refined output sheds light on the identities and behaviors of threat actors, outlining their specific tactics, techniques, and procedures (TTPs). Additionally, it provides a clearer understanding of the systems or entities that may be at risk, enabling more focused and strategic security responses. It empowers security teams to:

- Prioritize actions: Focus resources on the most critical threats based on their likelihood and potential impact.
- Improve defenses: Identify vulnerabilities and implement mitigation strategies like patching systems or adjusting firewall rules.
- Proactive threat hunting: Look for hidden threats based on the intelligence gathered, rather than waiting for them to strike.
- The unusual traffic could be a potential denial-of-service attack (DoS) aimed at disrupting school network access.
- The suspicious website connection could indicate malware infection on a student device.
- The late-night traffic might be unauthorized access by a hacker.

1.3.1.5 Wisdom

This is the pinnacle of the pyramid, where knowledge is applied to make informed decisions to take actions as shown in Figure 1.6.

Figure 1.6 Wisdom.

With actionable intelligence in hand, analysts perform steps to decide and mitigate the threat. Based on the analysis, the analyst might conclude:

- Block the malicious IP address.
- Identify and isolate the infected device.
- Implement stricter access controls for after-hours network usage.

1.3.1.6 DIKW use cases

Use Case #1: Analyzing network logs

- Company's network logs show a spike in login attempts from a foreign IP address - This is raw data.
- SIEM system aggregates these logs – this provides information about the source and frequency of attempts.
- Analysts look at the dashboard (rows and columns) then analyze this information.
- Analysts consider current threat scenarios, reports about ongoing phishing campaigns (attacks), identify specific IOCs associated with that campaign, such as malicious URLs or login credentials. Analysts apply knowledge.
- This analysis transforms information into actionable intelligence, allowing the security team to block the suspicious IP address, warn employees about the phishing attempt, and update login protocols for stronger protection. This could also indicate that employees need cyber training.

Use Case #2: Cyberattack on bank

- Data (D): Imagine you're a security analyst at a prominent bank. Your team receives a constant stream of data from various sources, including:
  - Customer Login Attempts: Timestamps, usernames, IP addresses, login success/failure flags.
  - Email Logs: Incoming and outgoing emails with details like sender, recipient, subject line, and attachments.
  - Website Traffic Logs: User activity on the bank's website, including page visits, login attempts, and downloads.
  - Network Traffic Logs: Information about data flowing across the bank's network, like IP addresses, ports used, and data size.
- Information (I): This is where the raw data gets some structure. Security software aggregates and analyses this data, providing insights like:
  - Number of logins attempts per hour: Identifying unusual spikes.
  - Geographic distribution of login attempts: Highlights logins from unexpected locations.
  - Commonly accessed website page: Focusing on login attempts from non-bank websites.
  - Suspicious attachments in emails: Identifying potential malware attempts.
- Knowledge (K): Security analysts leverage their expertise and threat intel feeds and reports to interpret the information and find some IoCs. They ask questions like:
  - Does the login attempt pattern resemble known phishing campaigns?
  - Are there logins from previously compromised IP addresses?
  - Do the email attachments have characteristics of malware often used in phishing attacks?

- Sudden surge in login attempts from a foreign country with a history of phishing attacks is a red flag.
- Login attempts from a known malicious IP linked to phishing campaigns raise serious concerns.
- Emails with generic greetings and attachments with suspicious file extensions suggest a potential phishing attempt.
- Wisdom (W): This is where the "aha" moment happens. Analysts combine knowledge with the information gleaned from data to make informed decisions and take preventive measures:
  - Alerting customers: The bank can send out warnings about a potential phishing campaign targeting their login credentials.
  - Blocking suspicious IP addresses: This prevents unauthorized access attempts from known malicious sources.
  - Enabling multifactor authentication (MFA) enhances security by introducing additional verification steps beyond the traditional username and password login.

By effectively using the DIKM framework, the bank can proactively defend against phishing attacks.

- Reduced Risk of Fraud: Identifying and thwarting phishing attempts protects customer accounts and financial information.
- Improved Customer Trust: Taking swift action against cyber threats builds trust and confidence in the bank's security measures.
- Enhanced Security Posture: The DIKM framework allows for continuous monitoring and adaptation to evolving cyber threats.

Effective cybersecurity requires constant vigilance and a data-driven approach. The DIKM framework empowers security teams to transform raw data into actionable insights, safeguarding valuable information and financial assets. CTI is the cornerstone of a proactive cybersecurity posture. By harnessing the power of data analysis and threat intelligence, organizations can move from reactive incident response to proactive threat prevention. This chapter has laid the groundwork for your deeper exploration into the world of CTI, its various facets, and its importance in today's ever-evolving cyber threat landscape.

1.4 SURFACE, DEEP AND DARK WEB

The structure of the internet can be compared to an iceberg, where the portion that is visible above the waterline signifies only a tiny fragment of its full mass. This metaphor effectively illustrates how the digital realm is layered, with different levels of accessibility and visibility. At the top lies the surface web, the part of the internet easily accessible and indexed by traditional search engines. Beneath this layer exist the deep web and dark web, each requiring specific tools or permissions to access, and each representing progressively more concealed and complex aspects of online activity. Imagine the internet as an iceberg, as shown in Figure 1.7.

1.4.1 Surface web

The surface web refers to the portion of the internet that is easily accessible and indexed by standard search engines such as Google, Bing, or Yahoo. This includes public websites like news portals, blogs, social media profiles, educational resources, and e-commerce platforms.

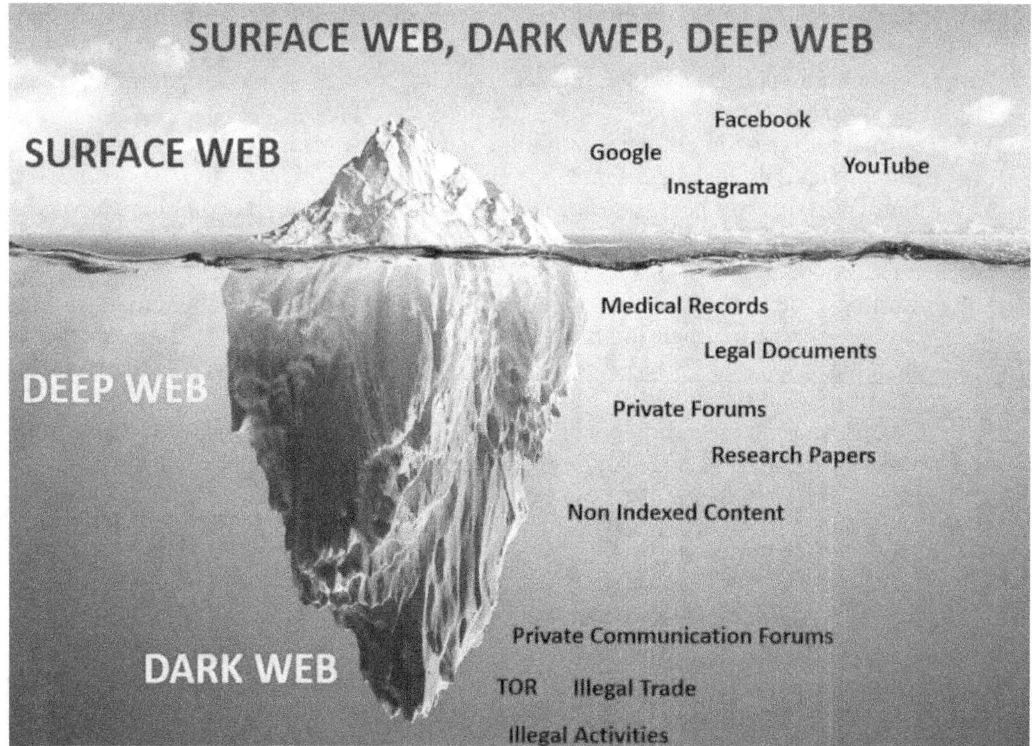

Figure 1.7 Internet levels.

Users can access this content simply by entering a URL or using a search engine. While this layer may seem vast, it represents only a minor fraction of the total content on the internet. Example: www.ndtv.com, www.upes.ac.in, www.bbc.com, www.facebook.com, favorite social media or online stores, and e-commerce portal.

The surface web operates through two principal types of Internet Protocol (IP) addresses: IPv4 and IPv6. These address formats are critical for identifying and connecting devices across the internet. IPv4, or Internet Protocol version 4, is the most widely implemented version to date. It uses a 32-bit address system typically expressed in a dotted-decimal structure, such as 192.168.1.1. Although highly efficient during the early years of the internet, the rapid expansion of online activity and connected devices has significantly depleted the availability of IPv4 addresses, making them a limited resource. In response to the growing demand for more addressable devices, IPv6 or Internet Protocol version 6 was introduced. Unlike its predecessor, IPv6 employs a 128-bit address format written in hexadecimal notation, exemplified by addresses like 2001:0db8:85a3:0000:0000:8a2e:0370:7334. This version vastly increases the number of possible IP addresses and enhances routing efficiency and network security. Although its adoption has been gradual, IPv6 is steadily being integrated into global networking infrastructures to accommodate the ever-increasing number of internet-connected devices.

1.4.2 Deep web

Beneath this lies the deep web, a much larger segment comprising content that is not indexed by conventional search engines. This includes pages behind login forms, databases, academic archives, subscription content, banking portals, government resources, and enterprise intranets. Deep web refers to portions of the internet that are not indexed by standard search engines and therefore remain hidden from general browsing. However, unlike the dark web, the deep web is not associated with illegal activity or secrecy by default. Instead, it includes content that is purposefully kept private for security and privacy reasons. This might include academic databases, private organizational records, subscription-based services, or password-protected platforms. Accessing these areas typically requires some form of authentication, such as a username and password, or a direct URL. Despite being out of reach for the average internet user, the deep web serves a vital function by protecting confidential information. Technically, it operates using standard internet protocols like DNS and either IPv4 or IPv6 addressing, just like any part of the regular internet infrastructure.

1.4.3 Dark web

Beneath the surface of the deep web lies a more concealed segment often referred to as the dark web. To gain entry into this part of the internet is not possible through standard browsers; instead, it demands the use of specific technologies. One of the most prominent tools used for this purpose is the Tor browser. This software enables users to browse anonymously by channeling internet traffic through several encrypted layers, effectively obscuring both the identity of the user and the server being accessed. Dark web sites typically use ".onion" addresses and are unreachable through standard browsers. This network infrastructure makes it a haven for users seeking anonymity, including whistleblowers, journalists in oppressive regimes, and activists. However, this same concealment also attracts illicit activity such as drug markets, weapons trafficking, and cybercrime forums.

The dark web should not be confused with the deep web in general. While both are non-indexed, the dark web's reliance on encryption, anonymity tools, and hidden services makes it distinct. Communication across the dark web is designed to obscure IP addresses and metadata, often involving cryptocurrency to further enhance privacy. Servers hosting dark web sites use standard IP addresses, but Tor obfuscates the origin and destination of traffic, creating the illusion of invisibility. To explore the Dark Web, one must utilize a specialized tool known as the Tor Browser. This browser ensures user anonymity by encrypting web traffic and routing it through a decentralized network of relay servers across the globe. With the Tor Browser, users can reach websites that have addresses ending in ".onion," which are not accessible through conventional browsers. Although the Dark Web is often linked to unlawful activities due to the presence of black markets and hidden forums, it is essential to understand that not every website hosted there engages in criminal behavior. The Dark Web also hosts platforms with legitimate and socially valuable purposes. Some common types of sites found within this hidden layer of the internet include:

- Underground Marketplaces: Platforms such as the now-defunct Silk Road, AlphaBay, and Dream Market once facilitated the trade of illegal items like narcotics, counterfeit currencies, digital exploits, and stolen personal data.
- Cybersecurity and Hacking Communities: Forums like Hack Forums serve as hubs for discussions around network security, ethical hacking, and in some cases, unauthorized cyber activities.
- Whistleblowing Portals: Services like SecureDrop and GlobaLeaks enable individuals to anonymously share confidential information, often exposing unethical practices in corporations or government entities.
- Private Communication Tools: Services including TorBox and ProtonMail offer end-to-end encrypted communication channels, allowing users to maintain privacy and secure conversations beyond the reach of surveillance.

The dark web itself doesn't have a specific type of IP address because it's about the content and how it's accessed, not the addresses themselves. Much of the deep web, including hidden sites, still relies on standard IP addresses (IPv4 or IPv6) just like the surface web. The deep web consists of online content that search engines do not index; however, it remains accessible to users who have the appropriate credentials or authorization. Imagine a private social media profile (deep web content) accessible only after logging in. The server hosting that profile would still use a regular IP address. However, there's a crucial distinction for a part of the deep web:

- Dark Web with Tor: The dark web, a small portion of the deep web, uses anonymizing tools like Tor. Tor works by routing traffic through a network of volunteer relays, making it difficult to track the true IP address of the server hosting the dark web content.
- Hidden IP Addresses: When you access a dark web site using Tor, the website itself might have a regular IP address, but Tor obscures it by bouncing your connection through multiple relays. This makes it appear as if the traffic is originating from one of the Tor relays, not your actual device.

1.4.4 Darknet

Darknet is a hidden network built on top of the existing Internet. It uses special software and protocols to anonymize communication and make it difficult to track users. Examples of darknets include Tor, I2P, OneSwarm, RetroShare, and Freenet. This is like a hidden railway system with its own tracks and stations (communication protocols). The darknet provides the infrastructure for the dark web to exist. You need the darknet to access the dark web, but not all darknets host dark web content. Some darknets might be used for legitimate purposes that prioritize anonymity. This uses floating databases of unique base64 address of nodes mapping to human readable URLs within the darknet. Sending anonymous emails without revealing sender IP, destination, or ISP. Uses Bitcoin and other crypto based money for digital footprint anonymity.

1.5 IMPORTANCE AND ROLE OF CTI

1.5.1 Key advantage of CTI

Organizations can gain five key advantages of CTI as cyber threats continue to evolve and become more complex.

- **Proactive approach**
  CTI **empowers** organizations to shift from a reactive posture to a proactive cybersecurity strategy. By leveraging CTI, companies can detect both existing and emerging threats, such as advanced persistent threats (APTs), malware, or targeted attacks that are specific to their industry or region. Rather than waiting to respond after a breach, organizations continuously collect and analyze threat data to anticipate and neutralize potential risks early. This intelligence-driven approach enhances preparedness, enabling swift action to block intrusions before significant damage occurs, and helps security teams make informed decisions that strengthen the overall defense posture of the organization.

- **Custom defense mechanism**
  CTI enables organizations to tailor their security strategies by analyzing threat actors targeting their specific industry or region. This focused approach allows for customized defenses, aligning security protocols with the most relevant risks and improving the effectiveness of protection against likely cyber threats.
- **Data breach prevention**
  CTI strengthens data breach prevention by uncovering vulnerabilities and potential threats before they're exploited. By analyzing global threat patterns, CTI delivers actionable insights into attacker behavior and tactics. This enables organizations to proactively enhance their defenses, address high-risk areas, and reduce breach risks – shifting cybersecurity from a reactive stance to a strategic, forward-looking approach.
- **Regulatory compliance**
  Regulatory authorities often mandate that businesses take proactive measures to protect sensitive data. Adopting a CTI program showcases an organization's commitment to compliance and data security. This not only strengthens cybersecurity posture but also helps avoid potential penalties, legal issues, or sanctions by demonstrating responsible and informed risk management practices.
- **Competitive advantage**
  In competitive industries, robust cybersecurity serves as a key differentiator, showcasing an organization's commitment to data protection. Strong defenses not only build trust among customers and stakeholders but also enhance the company's reputation for reliability and security, offering a strategic advantage in an environment where safeguarding digital assets is increasingly vital.

1.5.2 Who benefits from threat intelligence

Threat intelligence plays a vital role across multiple functions within an organization, offering tailored benefits to each team involved in cybersecurity and risk management. For security and IT analysts, it provides valuable context and actionable insights that enhance both threat prevention and detection efforts, ultimately reinforcing organizational defenses. Security Operations Centre (SOC) teams leverage this intelligence to assess the severity and urgency of incidents, allowing them to prioritize responses and allocate resources efficiently. Similarly, the Computer Security Incident Response Team (CSIRT) utilizes threat intelligence to streamline investigations, enabling rapid identification, containment, and resolution of security incidents. Intelligence analysts use it to profile and monitor threat actors, supporting long-term strategy and adversary tracking. Additionally, executive leadership relies on threat intelligence to gain a clearer view of evolving cyber risks, which informs their strategic decisions regarding investment in cybersecurity infrastructure and risk mitigation. Overall, threat intelligence is a foundational element in maintaining a resilient cyber defense framework.

1.5.3 What does a cyber threat intelligence (CTI) analyst do

A CTI Analyst is essential in safeguarding an organization's digital infrastructure by analyzing vast amounts of security data and converting it into clear, practical intelligence that supports informed decision-making and proactive defense strategies. Rather than responding to incidents after they occur, the CTI analyst enables a proactive security stance by identifying, profiling, and tracking potential threat actors. This early-warning approach helps organizations gain a complete understanding of threat campaigns and prevent attacks before they materialize. The CTI analyst's responsibilities begin with data collection, where intelligence is gathered from diverse sources, including internal logs, private threat databases, and open-source platforms. This raw data is then subjected to analytical processing, where irrelevant noise is filtered out, and potential IoC are identified. In the threat evaluation phase, the analyst studies the origin, nature, and severity of identified threats, estimating their potential impact on the organization's assets and operations. CTI analyst develops intelligence reports, presenting clear, concise findings to decision-makers and security teams. These reports inform cybersecurity strategies, improve incident response plans, and influence risk mitigation policies. Ultimately, the CTI analyst serves as a vital link between threat detection and strategic defense, helping organizations stay ahead of evolving cyber threats in a dynamic digital landscape.

1.5.4 How to become a CTI analyst

Pursuing a career as a CTI Analyst demands a strong combination of technical expertise, investigative thinking, and a solid grounding in cybersecurity principles. Candidates should start with a sound understanding of core technologies such as Linux systems, network infrastructure, and the implementation and configuration of security frameworks. This foundational knowledge is typically developed through academic paths like degrees in cybersecurity, computer science, or related disciplines, and can be further strengthened through industry-recognized certifications. Beyond theoretical learning, practical experience plays a vital role. Familiarity with diverse data sources – including internet scan results, passive DNS records, domain registrations, and malware databases – is essential. Engaging in roles that involve collecting, analyzing, and responding to tactical threat intelligence helps build real-world skills in monitoring and detection.

Hands-on exposure to incident response, threat hunting, intrusion analysis, and enterprise-level security tools significantly enhances a candidate's capabilities. Proficiency in analyzing forensic data, packet captures, system logs, and malware behavior is crucial in identifying potential breaches or vulnerabilities. CTI Analyst is also expected to track APTs, attacker TTPs, and translate raw threat data into actionable intelligence. This includes identifying IOCs, attack vectors, and behavioral patterns – providing insights that help organizations pre-empt cyber risks and fortify their defenses.

1.5.5 CTI training and certification programs

- GIAC Cyber Threat Intelligence (GCTI): Based on the SANS FOR578 curriculum, this credential validates a cybersecurity professional's expertise in handling and utilizing CTI across strategic, operational, and tactical layers. It delves into adversarial behaviors, methodologies, and the processing of intelligence data. The exam is supervised, ensuring candidates possess a well-rounded proficiency in the discipline.
- Certified Threat Intelligence Analyst (CTIA) by EC-Council: Combining both coursework and examination, this certification delivers practical experience alongside theoretical knowledge. It walks participants through the entire lifecycle of threat intelligence, including project planning, collection, analysis, and information sharing.
- CREST Practitioner Threat Intelligence Analyst (CPTIA): Geared toward beginners, this qualification confirms foundational knowledge of CTI and readiness to support operational tasks under guidance. It is ideal for those entering the field and aiming to understand core intelligence workflows.

- CREST Registered Threat Intelligence Analyst (CRTIA): At the intermediate level, this certification is designed for professionals capable of independently managing threat intelligence processes. It emphasizes collecting, interpreting, and delivering actionable intelligence insights.
- CREST Certified Threat Intelligence Manager (CCTIM): Intended for experienced professionals, this credential signifies mastery in leading and directing CTI initiatives. It focuses on team management, strategic oversight, and the development of intelligence capabilities within organizations.
- MITRE ATT&CK Defenders (MAD): Offered by MITRE Engenuity, this dynamic certification evolves with the shifting threat landscape. It emphasizes key areas of cyber defense: adversary intelligence, red/blue team evaluation, and mitigation strategies. Participants can opt for either real-time or on-demand sessions.
- Certified Cyber Threat Intelligence Analyst (CCTIA) by CybersTraining 365: Tailored for threat research specialists, this program equips learners with skills to detect, trace, and locate threat actors. The training enhances threat detection strategies by teaching malware tracing and attacker profiling techniques.
- Certified Cyber Intelligence Analyst: Provided by Treadstone 71, this course offers a rigorous immersion in intelligence practices and methodologies. It includes structured learning on collection techniques and analytical methods, aligning with global standards for entry-level intelligence analysts.
- Certified Threat Intelligence Specialist I (CTIS-I): Designed for those just starting out in the threat intelligence domain, this foundational certification introduces essential concepts such as threat sources, data gathering, basic analysis, and report writing.
- Certified Threat Intelligence Specialist II (CTIS-II): An advanced continuation of CTIS-I, this certification targets professionals with prior experience in the field, enabling them to showcase higher-level competencies in threat intelligence operations and analysis.

1.6 CONCLUSION

CTI has emerged as an essential pillar in the defense architecture of modern organizations. As this chapter has detailed, CTI is not simply about collecting data but about transforming scattered digital footprints into actionable insights that anticipate threats before they escalate into incidents. Through a comprehensive exploration of foundational concepts such as IoCs, IoAs, the DIKW framework, and the malware lifecycle, readers gain clarity on how CTI bridges technical vigilance with strategic foresight. The layered understanding of the surface web, deep web, and dark web further illustrates the diverse channels where threats originate and intelligence is gathered. CTI enables security teams to tailor defenses according to industry-specific risks, promote a proactive security posture, and support regulatory compliance. Moreover, the role of the CTI analyst is pivotal, acting as the translator between threat data and organizational decision-making. From real-time threat detection to long-term adversary profiling, the CTI function ensures that cybersecurity is no longer reactionary but a continuous, informed process. As organizations face increasingly complex threats, CTI provides the clarity and confidence required to stay resilient in a dynamic digital landscape. This chapter sets the foundation for exploring how CTI aligns with other threat detection strategies in subsequent sections.

MULTIPLE CHOICE QUESTIONS

1. A security team notices random login attempts across multiple servers. They collect raw logs from Apache, Samba, and FTP services. Initially, the logs appear disorganized and overwhelming. The CTI analyst explains that meaningful threat insights will only emerge after these logs are contextualized and analyzed systematically. What CTI concept is the analyst referring to?

   A. Event Correlation
   B. DIKW Pyramid
   C. Threat Actor Profiling
   D. Zero-Day Vulnerability

   Correct Answer: B. DIKW Pyramid
   Reason: The scenario describes transforming raw logs → information → knowledge → intelligence. Other options are incorrect:
   - A: Event correlation is part of the process but not the overall model.
   - C: Threat actor profiling happens after intelligence generation.
   - D: Zero-day refers to unknown exploits, irrelevant to the data transformation process.

2. A school's network logs show unusual spikes in traffic late at night. The team wants to determine whether this is normal student activity or a possible intrusion attempt. A CTI analyst aggregates data from SIEM dashboards, compares it with ongoing global threat reports, and investigates suspicious IP origins. What stage of the DIKW model is the analyst primarily engaged in?

   A. Raw Data
   B. Information
   C. Knowledge
   D. Wisdom

   Correct Answer: C. Knowledge
   Reason: The analyst is correlating information with threat intelligence and asking investigative questions. Other options are incorrect
   - A: Raw data was already collected.
   - B: Information is the organized SIEM output, but deeper analysis is happening now.
   - D: Wisdom involves taking final action (e.g., blocking IP), not analysis.

3. An organization finds unexpected executable files and strange registry changes on multiple systems. Forensic analysis shows suspicious outbound connections to unknown IPs. Analysts conclude that the breach has already happened. Which artifact type is being observed?

   A. Indicator of Attack
   B. Indicator of Compromise
   C. Zero-Day Indicators
   D. System Vulnerabilities

Correct Answer: B. Indicator of Compromise

Reason: IoCs are discovered AFTER a breach and include malicious files, registry changes, and suspicious outbound connections. Other options are incorrect:

- A: IoAs indicate *ongoing* or imminent activity.
- C: Zero-day indicators involve unknown vulnerabilities.
- D: Vulnerabilities may enable attacks but are not artifacts of compromise.

4. A company notices multiple failed logins from a foreign IP address, followed by unusual after-hours access attempts on internal apps. No system has been breached yet, but the pattern resembles brute-force and unauthorized access behavior. What are these signs categorized as?

   A. IoCs
   B. IoAs
   C. Data Exfiltration Events
   D. Malware Execution

   Correct Answer: B. IoAs

   Reason: These are signs of *ongoing attack attempts* before damage occurs. Other options are incorrect:

   - A: No confirmed breach yet.
   - C: No data theft is shown.
   - D: No malware presence indicated.

5. A suspicious program is found modifying registry keys to auto-launch every time a system boots. It also hides itself by running inside legitimate processes. Analysts confirm that these actions help it survive reboots. Which malware lifecycle stage is this?

   A. Execution
   B. Persistence
   C. Propagation
   D. Command-and-Control

   Correct Answer: B. Persistence

   Reason: Modifying registry/startup to remain active = persistence. Other options are incorrect:

   - A: Execution is the initial payload run.
   - C: Propagation moves across systems.
   - D: C2 refers to remote communication.

6. A threat intel analyst finds that stolen company data is being sold on a hidden website accessible only via Tor. The site uses a ".onion" domain and relies on anonymous routing. Which part of the internet are they investigating?

   A. Surface Web
   B. Deep Web
   C. Dark Web
   D. Cloud Web

Correct Answer: C. Dark Web

Reason: .onion domains via Tor = Dark Web. Other options are incorrect:

- A: Public, indexed web.
- B: Requires login but not anonymous hidden services.
- D: No such classification.

7. A public university's research database requires login credentials. Some staff believe this is part of the "dark web." A CTI analyst clarifies that although it is unindexed, it is not anonymous or illegal. What part of the internet is being accessed?

    A. Dark Web
    B. Deep Web
    C. Surface Web
    D. Darknet

    Correct Answer: B. Deep Web

    Reason: Password-protected but legitimate content = deep web. Other options are incorrect:
    - A: Dark web requires anonymization like Tor.
    - C: Surface is fully accessible without login.
    - D: Darknet is broader infrastructure of anonymous networks.

8. A cybercriminal discovers an unknown flaw in a widely used banking application. They immediately begin exploiting it before vendors are aware or can release a patch. What type of attack is this?

    A. Known vulnerability exploit
    B. IoC-based attack
    C. Zero-Day Exploit
    D. Misconfiguration attack

    Correct Answer: C. Zero-Day Exploit

    Because: Nobody knows about the flaw except the attacker – no patches. Other options are incorrect:
    - A: Not known.
    - B: IoC is *after* compromise.
    - D: Misconfiguration is unrelated.

9. A security team receives a suspicious email attachment. They execute it inside a VM to observe behavior. The file attempts to contact a remote C2 server and modifies system memory. What analytical method is being used?

    A. Static Analysis
    B. Dynamic Analysis
    C. Reverse Engineering
    D. Threat Modeling

    Correct Answer: B. Dynamic Analysis = executing malware in a sandbox to observe behavior. Other options are incorrect:
    - A: Code review without execution.
    - C: Deep code disassembly.
    - D: Designing attack paths, not analyzing malware.

10. A CTI analyst gathers raw logs, filters noise, correlates threat patterns, identifies malicious IPs, and delivers a report advising firewall changes and mandatory MFA. Which responsibility does this represent?

    A. Incident containment
    B. Patch management
    C. Intelligence reporting
    D. Network administration

    Correct Answer: C. Intelligence reporting
    Because: They prepare actionable threat intelligence for decision-makers. Other options are incorrect:
    - A: Done by IR teams.
    - B: Admin/IT job.
    - D: Network admin work.

11. A healthcare company identifies patient databases, hospital servers, and proprietary algorithms as high-value digital components they must protect. What CTI term refers to these?

    A. IoCs
    B. Assets
    C. Exploits
    D. Vulnerabilities

    Correct Answer: B. Assets
    Correct: Assets = anything of value. Other options are incorrect:
    - A: Breach artifacts.
    - C: Techniques used by attackers.
    - D: Weaknesses.

12. A CTI team monitors an attacker group known for using AsyncRAT and Lumma Stealer. They compare TTPs with global reports and categorize the group as financially motivated cybercriminals. What type of CTI activity is this?

    A. Tactical
    B. Operational
    C. Strategic
    D. Technical

    Correct Answer: B. Operational intelligence = profiling threat actors and campaigns. Other options are incorrect:
    - A: IoC-level intelligence.
    - C: Executive decision-making.
    - D: Low-level data feeds.

13. Employees access news websites, e-commerce portals, and social media during breaks. All these appear in search engines. Which internet layer is being accessed?

    A. Deep Web
    B. Surface Web
    C. Darknet
    D. Dark Web

    Correct Answer: B. Surface Web Indexed and publicly accessible.

14. A CTI analyst reviews intelligence showing repeated brute-force attempts from a known malicious IP. She decides to block the IP and enforce MFA across the network. Which DIKW stage is this?

    A. Data
    B. Information
    C. Knowledge
    D. Wisdom

Correct Answer: D. Wisdom = applying knowledge to make decisions.
Others represent earlier stages.

15. A SOC team receives CTI feeds showing active ransomware campaigns targeting banks. They immediately update detection rules and monitor for suspicious registry changes and unexpected file activities. What CTI advantage is being used?

    A. Competitive Advantage
    B. Custom Defense Mechanisms
    C. Proactive Approach
    D. Regulatory Compliance

Correct Answer: C. Proactive Approach. They defend BEFORE attack occurs.
Other options do not match real-time threat anticipation.

REFERENCES

1. K. Baker, "What is cyber threat intelligence? [beginner's guide] | CrowdStrike," *Crowdstrike.com*, Mar. 4, 2025. https://www.crowdstrike.com/en-us/cybersecurity-101/threat-intelligence
2. "What are command & control (C2) servers?," *SentinelOne*, Sep. 13, 2024. https://www.sentinelone.com/cybersecurity-101/threat-intelligence/what-are-command-control-c2-servers
3. "Hash: online hash value calculator," 2025. https://www.fileformat.info/tool/hash.htm
4. "MD5 file - HTML5 file hash online calculator - MD5, SHA1, SHA2 (SHA-256), SHA-384, SHA-512," 2025. *md5file.com*. https://md5file.com/calculator
5. "FLASH number RagnarLocker ransomware indicators of compromise," 2022. Accessed: Jul. 1, 2025 [Online]. https://www.ic3.gov/CSA/2022/220307.pdf
6. "Malware trends tracker | ANY.RUN," Malware Trends Tracker | ANY.RUN, 2026. https://any.run/malware-trends
7. Blackberry, "Threat research and intelligence," *GitHub*, 2021. Accessed Jul. 1, 2025. https://github.com/blackberry/threat-research-and-intelligence/tree/main/Blogs%20%26%20Reports/Blogs

Chapter 2

Cyber threat landscape

2.1 CURRENT CYBER THREATS

In today's hyper-connected digital ecosystem, cybersecurity has evolved from being a backroom IT function to a central pillar of organizational risk management and strategic planning. Cyber Threat Intelligence (CTI) now plays a vital role in predicting, identifying, and responding to the rapidly changing threat landscape. The trends shaping cybersecurity in 2024 and beyond reflect a shift toward proactive defense, AI-enabled threat detection, zero trust enforcement, ransomware evolution, and the growing integration of geopolitical intelligence into cyber operations. Cyber threats are malicious attempts to gain unauthorized access to a computer system or network. These attacks can be launched by individuals, criminal organizations, or even nation-states.

2.1.1 Rise of AI and ML in threat detection

One of the most transformative trends in cybersecurity is the integration of artificial intelligence (AI) and machine learning (ML) for threat detection and mitigation. Traditional signature-based tools are no longer sufficient to identify novel attacks, especially those involving polymorphic malware and fileless techniques. AI-driven platforms now enable organizations to sift through billions of logs and telemetry data points to detect anomalies and emerging threats. A notable example is Microsoft's Defender platform, which utilizes ML models to monitor behavioral baselines across endpoints and cloud services. In 2023, Microsoft's AI security model [1] helped detect a targeted phishing campaign against hybrid work environments by analyzing subtle deviations in email metadata and login patterns. Similarly, CrowdStrike's Falcon platform uses behavioral AI models to detect threats in real-time, even when adversaries use living-off-the-land binaries (LOLBins) [2] to evade detection. However, attackers are also using AI to their advantage. Deepfake technologies and generative models like ChatGPT clones have been used to craft highly convincing social engineering messages. In January 2024, a Southeast Asian bank reported a CEO fraud incident [3] where a deepfake video was used during a virtual meeting to authorize a fraudulent transfer. This dual-use nature of AI demands continuous evolution in CTI capabilities to identify and counter adversarial AI tactics.

2.1.2 Zero trust architecture becoming the norm

The adoption of Zero Trust Architecture (ZTA) [4] has transitioned from theory to practice, especially in organizations operating under hybrid and remote work models. Zero Trust is no longer just a buzzword but a mandated requirement in several sectors, particularly those handling critical infrastructure and sensitive data. The U.S. federal government's executive

DOI: 10.1201/9781003730583-2

order on improving the nation's cybersecurity has made ZTA a baseline requirement for all federal agencies [5]. Private companies are following suit, driven by the need to reduce the attack surface and protect against lateral movement. Under the Zero Trust model, users, devices, and applications are not automatically trusted, even if they are inside the network perimeter. Every access request is continuously evaluated based on identity, device health, location, and behavior. Real-world deployment is evident in enterprises like Google, which expanded its BeyondCorp model to support full-scale Zero Trust across its infrastructure [6]. In another example, Capital One implemented a Zero Trust strategy [7] combined with micro-segmentation to prevent attackers from moving laterally across its AWS environment during an attempted breach in 2023.

2.1.3 Ransomware-as-a-service and double extortion

Ransomware remains one of the most persistent threats in cyberspace, but its evolution has made it more complex and damaging. The emergence of Ransomware-as-a-Service (RaaS) platforms has lowered the entry barrier for cybercriminals, allowing even non-technical actors to deploy sophisticated attacks. What sets modern ransomware apart is the "double extortion" model, where attackers not only encrypt data but also steal it and threaten to release it publicly if the ransom is not paid. A case in point is the 2023 attack on the City of Oakland, where the Play ransomware group exfiltrated gigabytes of sensitive municipal data before encrypting internal systems [8]. Despite the city refusing to pay the ransom, attackers released employee information, police reports, and financial documents on the dark web. To counter such threats, threat intelligence teams are using dark web monitoring and data leak detection tools to proactively track ransomware group activities. For example, threat analysts at Recorded Future and Intel 471 track ransomware affiliates across forums and marketplaces to identify emerging strains and victim profiles [9]. Organizations are also investing in immutable backups, Endpoint Detection and Response systems, and tabletop exercises to enhance ransomware resilience.

2.1.4 Threat intelligence integration with SOC operations

Security Operations Centers (SOCs) are increasingly integrating threat intelligence feeds into their workflows to enhance detection and response times. Contextual threat data, such as indicators of compromise (IOCs), TTPs (tactics, techniques, and procedures), and threat actor profiles are now being operationalized via SIEM (Security Information and Event Management) and SOAR (Security Orchestration, Automation, and Response) platforms. For example, Elastic SIEM now allows seamless integration of MITRE ATT&CK mappings, enabling threat hunters to create detection rules based on behavioral patterns instead of static signatures. In a case study from a European telecom company, integrating CTI feeds from MISP (Malware Information Sharing Platform) into their SIEM reduced detection time for credential stuffing attacks by 35%. Moreover, platforms like Splunk and IBM QRadar now offer inbuilt threat intelligence apps that correlate incoming events with global threat databases. This not only improves detection accuracy but also aids incident responders in prioritizing alerts based on threat criticality. Real-time enrichment using threat intel from providers like Anomali, Cisco Talos, and ThreatConnect ensures that analysts can respond faster to emerging threats.

2.1.5 Cloud security and API abuse

As businesses shift workloads to the cloud, attackers are evolving tactics to exploit misconfigurations, insecure APIs, and lack of visibility across multicloud environments. Cloud-native threats are now a major concern for CTI teams, especially with the rise of containerized deployments and serverless functions. The 2024 breach of T-Mobile, attributed to API abuse targeting exposed cloud microservices, highlighted the dangers of unmonitored APIs and insufficient access control. Threat actors were able to extract customer metadata by abusing overlooked endpoints that lacked proper authentication. To mitigate such risks, organizations are adopting Cloud Security Posture Management tools and using behavior analytics to detect anomalies across cloud workloads. Security teams are also aligning with the Shared Responsibility Model of cloud providers to ensure that configuration, identity, and runtime protections are regularly audited.

2.1.6 Identity-based attacks and MFA fatigue

Identity is the new perimeter, and attackers are increasingly targeting credentials and authentication mechanisms to bypass security controls. A troubling trend in this domain is "Multifactor Authentication (MFA) fatigue," where attackers flood users with MFA prompts until they inadvertently approve one. Uber breach in late 2022 [10] was a textbook example, where an attacker tricked an employee into approving an MFA request, gaining access to internal systems and even security tools. Since then, many organizations have transitioned to phishing-resistant MFA methods such as FIDO2 security keys, biometric authentication, and adaptive access policies. CTI platforms now routinely track stolen credentials being sold on dark web marketplaces. Integration of credential breach detection into Identity Providers (IdPs) like Okta and Azure AD enables organizations to pre-emptively rotate compromised accounts and block suspicious logins.

2.1.7 Geopolitical threats and state-sponsored attacks

Geopolitical tensions have increasingly spilled over into cyberspace, with state-sponsored threat actors engaging in espionage, sabotage, and influence operations. CTI must now account for geopolitical context when analyzing attack campaigns, especially those originating from Advanced Persistent Threat (APT) groups. Russia-Ukraine conflict continues to illustrate how cyber warfare is used in tandem with kinetic operations. Groups like Sandworm [11] and Gamaredon [12] have launched destructive malware such as WhisperGate [13] and AcidRain [14] to disrupt Ukrainian infrastructure. On the other side, hacktivist groups like the IT Army of Ukraine have retaliated with DDoS and defacement campaigns against Russian websites. In Asia, threat groups linked to China have been observed targeting defense, telecom, and critical infrastructure in Taiwan and India. The Volt Typhoon group, exposed in 2023, used living-off-the-land techniques to maintain stealth and avoid triggering endpoint alerts. Such attacks often bypass traditional detection systems, requiring high-fidelity threat intelligence and behavior-based hunting to uncover.

2.1.8 Insider threats and behavioral monitoring

Insider threats remain a persistent challenge, especially with increased remote work and hybrid environments. Not all threats originate from external actors; some come from within, whether intentional or due to negligence. Recent studies show that insider incidents now account for nearly 25% of security breaches, underscoring the need for continuous user behavior monitoring. In 2023, Tesla faced an insider data leak where a disgruntled employee shared sensitive information with journalists, bypassing internal access controls. This has led to greater emphasis on User and Entity Behavior Analytics (UEBA), which uses ML to establish behavioral baselines and flag deviations such as unauthorized downloads or unusual access patterns. Integrating UEBA with SIEM and DLP (Data Loss Prevention) systems enables organizations to detect insider activity early, while privacy-preserving techniques ensure compliance with data protection laws.

2.1.9 Threat intelligence sharing and collaboration

One of the positive trends in cybersecurity is the increasing collaboration across industries and governments for sharing threat intelligence. Platforms like ISACs (Information Sharing and Analysis Centers), MISP, and the Open Cybersecurity Alliance facilitate real-time exchange of IOCs, malware samples, and adversary techniques. For instance, the Financial Services ISAC (FS-ISAC) has been instrumental in identifying and mitigating fraud campaigns targeting banks across continents. Similarly, JPCERT/CC in Japan collaborates with national and international partners to publish threat bulletins related to emerging malware like Emotet and Qakbot variants. This trend has also been reinforced by a regulatory push. The EU's NIS2 Directive mandates critical infrastructure operators to report incidents and share intelligence to strengthen collective cyber resilience. CTI platforms are becoming more interoperable, supporting standards like STIX, TAXII, and OpenIOC to ensure machine-readable threat sharing.

2.1.10 Cybersecurity skills gap and automation

Despite technological advancements, the cybersecurity workforce continues to face a significant skills shortage. As threats become more complex and frequent, the demand for skilled analysts, incident responders, and CTI professionals is outpacing supply. This gap has driven greater adoption of automation and AI-driven decision support tools. Security automation tools now handle routine tasks such as IOC enrichment, sandbox detonation, and alert triaging. For example, a Fortune 500 company reported a 60% reduction in analyst fatigue after deploying a SOAR system that automated low-priority alert responses. Meanwhile, platforms like MITRE ATT&CK Navigator help analysts map and simulate adversary behavior across their environment, making CTI work more efficient and structured. Upskilling initiatives like Google's Cybersecurity Certificate Program and government-sponsored reskilling programs are also gaining traction to fill the talent gap. However, the long-term solution lies in aligning CTI with automation and building human-machine teaming frameworks that empower analysts rather than replace them.

Some of the most common types of cyber threats are:

- Malicious Software (Malware) refers to any software deliberately designed to harm, exploit, or compromise the integrity of computer systems. These programs can stealthily collect sensitive data, cripple functionalities, or even render systems inoperable. In early 2024, the *Black Basta* ransomware group targeted several healthcare organizations in Europe, encrypting patient records and demanding significant ransom payments in cryptocurrency.
- Social Engineering attack technique relies on psychological manipulation rather than technical exploits. Cyber attackers deceive individuals into revealing private information or performing risky actions like clicking harmful links. In 2023, employees of a prominent U.S. telecom company were tricked by phishing emails that mimicked internal HR communications, leading to credential leaks that enabled further internal access.
- Man-in-the-Middle (MitM) attacks occur when a threat actor secretly intercepts and possibly alters communication between two unsuspecting parties. Public Wi-Fi hotspots are particularly vulnerable to such breaches. In a 2024 incident in Tokyo, attackers intercepted transaction data from customers using an unsecured café Wi-Fi, extracting financial details during mobile banking sessions.

- Denial-of-Service (DoS) attacks aim to overload servers or online platforms with excessive traffic, rendering them inaccessible to genuine users. In March 2024, an online gaming service was overwhelmed by a coordinated botnet attack, causing multihour downtime during a major eSports tournament.
- Zero-Day Exploits involve leveraging unknown software flaws – those that developers haven't yet discovered or patched to execute unauthorized activities. A critical vulnerability in Microsoft Outlook was exploited in early 2024 before a patch could be released, allowing attackers to steal credentials from targeted enterprises globally.
- Password Cracking attacks are attempts to uncover user passwords through various strategies like brute-force attempts, dictionary attacks, or credential stuffing. In 2023, brute-force bots targeted WordPress websites across Europe, systematically attempting millions of password combinations to hijack admin accounts.
- Internet of Things (IoT)-Based attacks impact the growing use of internet-connected devices, attackers increasingly exploit insecure IoT gadgets such as smart locks, security cameras, and home assistants. In 2024, vulnerabilities in a popular brand of smart doorbells were exploited to gain unauthorized entry into home networks, allowing access to personal surveillance footage.
- Injection-Based attacks involve inserting malicious scripts into otherwise trusted web applications or databases. One common form is SQL injection, used to manipulate or extract sensitive backend data. In a 2023 cyberattack on a financial firm, attackers used SQL injection to exfiltrate customer records and transaction histories via a vulnerable feedback form.
- Cryptojacking occurs when malicious code hijacks a user's computing resources to mine cryptocurrency without consent, often resulting in slow performance and high electricity usage. A 2024 study revealed that over 200 mobile apps on unofficial Android stores contained hidden cryptojacking scripts, covertly mining Monero on users' devices.
- Supply Chain Compromise happens when rather than attacking the target organization directly, cybercriminals infiltrate through third-party vendors or service providers with trusted access. The 2024 breach of a major DevOps software vendor allowed attackers to inject backdoors into thousands of enterprise installations globally, including critical infrastructure in Asia.
- Insider Threats, which include employees, contractors, or partners, pose significant risks when they misuse their access for malicious purposes or negligence. In early 2024, a disgruntled IT administrator at a logistics firm in Bengaluru wiped out critical databases before resigning, causing days of operational disruptions.
- Deepfake attacks allow for the generation of synthetic media that convincingly mimics real people, often for deceitful or manipulative purposes. In 2023, a deepfake video of a European politician appeared on social media, falsely portraying them making controversial statements, which sparked political unrest before being debunked.
- Social Media Phishing impacts platforms like Facebook, Twitter (X), and Instagram with frequent phishing scams. Threat actors impersonate friends or trusted pages to lure users into clicking malicious links or entering sensitive data. In 2024, Instagram users were targeted with DMs claiming account verification was pending. Victims who clicked the link were redirected to a counterfeit login page, resulting in widespread account takeovers.

By understanding these different types of cyber threats, you can take steps to protect yourself and your organization from attack.

2.2 THREAT ACTORS

In the ever-evolving world of cybersecurity, various categories of malicious individuals and groups pose substantial threats to digital infrastructure. These entities, commonly referred to as threat actors, differ in terms of their motivations, tactics, and affiliations. Understanding the nature and activities of these adversaries is crucial for organizations and individuals to develop robust cyber defenses. From financially motivated criminals to ideologically driven hackers, the cyber threat landscape encompasses a wide spectrum of actors. It is important to understand the different types of threat actors so that you can take steps to protect yourself and your organization from cyberattacks. To maintain a high level of cybersecurity, it is essential to follow some fundamental safety practices. Keeping your software updated ensures that you have the latest security patches to protect against newly discovered vulnerabilities. Using strong, unique passwords for different accounts and enabling two-factor authentication adds an extra layer of defense against unauthorized access. It's equally important to be mindful of the personal information you share online, as oversharing can make you an easy target for cybercriminals. Always exercise caution when clicking on links or opening email attachments, especially if they come from unknown or unexpected sources. Lastly, any suspicious activity should be promptly reported to your IT security team to mitigate potential threats before they escalate.

One of the most widespread and persistent categories of threat actors are cybercriminals. These individuals or collectives engage in illegal activities online primarily to make money. Their toolkit often includes ransomware, phishing, and various forms of data theft. They target businesses, governments, and private citizens to steal sensitive data such as banking information, login credentials, or proprietary data, which can later be sold on dark web marketplaces or used for extortion. A recent example is the LockBit ransomware group, which in early 2024 claimed responsibility for attacks against government institutions in France and multinational corporations in the United States. These actors often use highly automated and scalable techniques to breach thousands of systems simultaneously, making them a significant and relentless threat to digital ecosystems worldwide.

A more covert yet extremely dangerous category consists of nation-state actors. These are government-affiliated or state-sponsored hacking groups that execute cyber operations aligned with national strategic interests. Their objectives often include intelligence gathering, espionage, cyber warfare, and disruption of adversary infrastructure. These groups are typically very well-resourced and employ APTs that can remain undetected in a system for months. For instance, the infamous APT29, also known as Cozy Bear and linked to Russia, has been repeatedly accused of targeting Western political entities. In 2023, this group reportedly conducted cyber-espionage activities against NATO countries, leveraging zero-day vulnerabilities to infiltrate secure networks. Nation-state actors are increasingly focusing on sectors like energy, telecommunications, and defense, attempting to destabilize adversaries through silent but severe cyber offensives.

Hacktivists, or hacking activists, form another distinct group of cyber actors driven by ideological or political motivations rather than financial gain. These actors aim to bring attention to specific issues or protest against governmental and corporate actions they deem unethical or oppressive. Their arsenal typically includes website defacements, DDoS (Distributed Denial-of-Service) attacks, and data leaks. A recent example is the Anonymous Sudan hacktivist group, which claimed responsibility in 2023 for cyberattacks on Israeli institutions, citing political reasons. Another instance is the Killnet group, a pro-Russian hacktivist collective known for targeting European government websites in response to geopolitical tensions. While these actions may be framed as digital protests, they can still cause major disruptions, reputational damage, and financial losses.

Another often underestimated category includes thrill-seeking hackers, individuals driven more by curiosity and challenge than malicious intent. These actors often explore vulnerabilities for the adrenaline rush and intellectual stimulation, rather than for political or financial gain. However, their activities, even when not intended to be harmful, can have unintended consequences. For instance, in 2022, a teenage member of the Lapsus$ group from the UK was involved in breaches of major tech companies like Microsoft and NVIDIA. Initially perceived as harmless teenage pranks, the breaches turned into severe data leaks affecting millions. Thrill seekers may inadvertently disrupt services, expose sensitive data, or open backdoors that other actors can exploit. The blurred line between ethical hacking and unauthorized probing is what makes this group particularly complex to address.

A more insidious threat often comes from within an organization itself, in the form of insider threats. These are individuals who have legitimate access to an organization's networks, systems, or data but misuse this access either deliberately or accidentally. Malicious insiders may steal intellectual property, sabotage operations, or leak confidential information for personal or political motives. In contrast, unintentional insiders may unknowingly click on malicious links or be manipulated through social engineering attacks. A well-known case involves the Capital One data breach in 2019, where a former employee exploited a configuration vulnerability to access sensitive customer data affecting over 100 million individuals. Insider threats are particularly dangerous because they bypass many traditional security mechanisms that are designed to detect external intrusions, making them harder to identify and stop.

Another emerging and rapidly growing category of cyber threat actors is the Initial Access Brokers (IABs). These cybercriminals specialize in the early stages of cyberattacks, infiltrating networks and then selling this initial access to other cybercriminals, including ransomware gangs. They typically exploit weak credentials, unpatched systems, or phishing campaigns to establish unauthorized entry. Once inside, they perform reconnaissance, establish persistence, and list the compromised access for sale on underground forums. In 2023, cybersecurity firms like Mandiant and Sophos observed a surge in IAB activities tied to the Cactus ransomware group, which purchased initial access from brokers to infiltrate manufacturing and healthcare companies across Europe and North America. The commodification of access has enabled ransomware operators to scale their operations dramatically, reducing the technical barriers to launching sophisticated attacks. As IABs evolve, their role in the cybercrime ecosystem becomes increasingly central, effectively acting as the gatekeepers to digital vaults.

The modern cybersecurity threat landscape is populated by a diverse array of adversaries, each with distinct motives, tools, and impacts. Cybercriminals chase monetary profits through scams and extortion; nation-state actors wage silent cyberwars with geopolitical consequences; hacktivists push ideological agendas by attacking digital symbols of power; thrill seekers tamper with systems for personal challenge; insiders leverage their trusted positions to exploit or accidentally compromise organizational security; and IABs operate as brokers of digital doors, facilitating entry for more targeted and destructive attacks. Each type of actor requires different defense mechanisms and response strategies, making cybersecurity a multidimensional challenge. The increasing sophistication of these actors, coupled with the ever-expanding digital footprint of businesses and individuals, means that vigilance is no longer optional, it is imperative. Awareness of threat actor categories, paired with timely intelligence and tailored countermeasures, forms the bedrock of effective cyber defense. The future of cybersecurity hinges not only on technology but on our collective understanding of the humans, both rogue and righteous behind the code.

2.3 COMMAND AND CONTROL SERVER (C2/C&C)

Command and Control (C2) refers to the framework of technologies, communication methods, and systems that cyber attackers use to direct and manage their malicious operations. It enables persistent connectivity with infected devices, often called bots or zombies allowing attackers to conduct activities such as deploying malware, stealing information, and orchestrating complex cyberattacks. Functioning as the operational hub for both cybercriminals and nation-state adversaries, C2 systems provide continuous oversight and manipulation of compromised networks. These infrastructures are often equipped with stealthy communication channels and advanced evasion techniques, making them increasingly difficult to detect and neutralize. Botnets, which are networks of infected devices, typically operate under a centralized or distributed C2 system. The role of C2 is critical in sustaining cyber intrusions, facilitating data exfiltration, and coordinating successive attack phases, thereby presenting a significant threat to cybersecurity defenses and organizational resilience.

These include the following components:

- Bots: In cybersecurity, a bot refers to an automated software application that performs tasks without human intervention. While bots can be used for legitimate purposes such as indexing websites for search engines or automating customer service, they are often weaponized for malicious activities. In the context of cyber threats, bots are commonly deployed to perform repetitive tasks like credential stuffing, spamming, and scanning for vulnerabilities across vast networks. Unlike botnets, which are large-scale networks of compromised devices, individual bots can act independently or as part of a smaller coordinated attack. Malicious bots are a growing concern due to their ability to operate at scale and speed, bypass security measures, and adapt to changing defenses. They are frequently used in *automated attacks* against web applications, APIs, and authentication systems. Some of the recent examples include:
    - Imperva's 2024 Bad Bot Report revealed that nearly 50% of all internet traffic in 2023 came from bots, with a significant portion being malicious.
    - OpenBullet Tool misuse (2023) – Cybercriminals used bots powered by OpenBullet for large-scale credential stuffing attacks against online banking and e-commerce platforms.
    - Ticketmaster bot attack (2023) – Malicious bots were used to bypass CAPTCHA systems and hoard event tickets, leading to public outrage and policy changes in ticket sales platforms.

    These examples highlight the growing sophistication and threat of bots in modern cybersecurity.
- Botnet refers to a network of compromised devices, often called "zombie systems," that are covertly controlled by an attacker to carry out coordinated malicious tasks. These networks are typically used for illegal activities such as launching DDoS attacks, data theft, or spamming. In today's underground cybercrime economy, it is increasingly common for cybercriminals to offer botnet access as a commercialized service, a model often referred to as "Attack-as-a-Service." Some of the recent examples include:
    - Mozi Botnet (2023) – This IoT-based botnet expanded rapidly by exploiting weak credentials and unpatched vulnerabilities. Despite law enforcement interventions, it continued to evolve, showing how persistent and adaptable such threats can be.
    - Dark Frost Botnet (2023) – Discovered targeting the gaming industry, Dark Frost utilized compromised machines to launch high-volume DDoS attacks on game servers, causing significant disruption and downtime.
    - The 911 S5 Botnet Takedown (2024) – One of the largest residential proxy botnets, 911 S5 was dismantled by global authorities after it was found to be controlling over 19 million IP addresses, used for a variety of fraudulent online activities.

- Zombies refers to a compromised device, typically a computer, server, or IoT device that has been infected with malware and is remotely controlled by an attacker without the user's knowledge. These zombie systems operate silently in the background, often forming the building blocks of larger malicious infrastructures, such as DDoS attacks, spam campaigns, or cryptojacking operations. Unlike traditional hacking, where the goal may be data theft or surveillance, zombie systems are leveraged primarily for their processing power and network access.

  The unique threat of zombies lies in their stealth. Infected devices continue to function normally from a user's perspective, making detection difficult. Cybercriminals use techniques like rootkits and command-and-control (C2) servers to maintain persistent access. Zombies are also instrumental in masking the attacker's identity, as they serve as intermediaries or proxies during an attack. Some of the recent examples include:
  - Dark Frost (2023): This attack campaign leveraged zombie devices from the gaming and streaming communities to launch powerful DDoS attacks against game servers. Many victims were unaware that their systems were participating in the attack.
  - Chaos Malware Variant (2023): This malware transformed infected Windows and Linux machines into zombies for ransomware distribution and DDoS attacks. It specifically targeted unpatched vulnerabilities in enterprise environments.
  - Cloudflare DDoS Report (2024): Cloudflare highlighted a massive DDoS attack powered by over 30,000 zombie devices originating from unsecured routers and IP cameras. These were manipulated to flood web infrastructure with traffic exceeding 71 million requests per second.
- Beacons in Command and Control (C2) architecture, Beacons are small, periodic communication signals sent from a compromised system (also called an implant or agent) to the attacker's command server. Unlike the more visible activities of bots or botnets, beacons operate stealthily, allowing adversaries to maintain persistent access while avoiding detection. These signals typically check in with the C2 server to receive instructions, update system status, or exfiltrate data. The intervals at which beacons communicate known as "beaconing" are often randomized to mimic legitimate network traffic, making them harder to detect through conventional monitoring tools.

  Beacons are a critical part of APT operations and are designed to be lightweight to evade intrusion detection systems (IDS) and firewalls. They can use various protocols, such as HTTP/S, DNS tunnelling, or even social media platforms, to blend in with normal traffic and communicate covertly as illustrated in Figure 2.1. Some of the recent examples for Beacons include:
  - Cobalt Strike Beacons in BlackCat/ALPHV (2024): In recent ransomware campaigns, attackers used customized Cobalt Strike beacons to maintain access to infiltrated networks. These beacons were disguised in HTTPS traffic to bypass network defenses.
  - UNC3944 (Scattered Spider) Campaign (2023): This financially motivated threat group deployed beaconing implants over Azure-based infrastructure. The beaconed traffic used cloud-based servers, complicating attribution and detection.
  - Volt Typhoon APT (2023): This China-linked threat group utilized living-off-the-land techniques combined with beaconing through compromised routers. Their strategy relied on minimal malware use, with stealthy beacons communicating over obscure ports and protocols.

The foundation of Command and Control (C2) infrastructure lies in deploying C2 servers, which are frequently dispersed across various geographical locations and hosted on anonymous or compromised systems to minimize the chances of being discovered as illustrated in Figure 2.2. Adversaries utilize domain generation algorithms (DGAs) to produce a

```
dnscat2> New window created: 1
Session 1 security: ENCRYPTED BUT *NOT* VALIDATED
For added security, please ensure the client displays the same string:

>> Harold Tubule Powers Roving Impish Volume
window -i 1
New window created: 1
history_size (session) => 1000
Session 1 security: ENCRYPTED BUT *NOT* VALIDATED
For added security, please ensure the client displays the same string:

>> Harold Tubule Powers Roving Impish Volume
This is a command session!

That means you can enter a dnscat2 command such as
'ping'! For a full list of clients, try 'help'.

command (WIN-M5HIE8S7FTB) 1> download C:/ImportantSecrets.txt /home/ImportantSecrets.txt
Attempting to download C:/ImportantSecrets.txt to /home/ImportantSecrets.txt
command (WIN-M5HIE8S7FTB) 1> Wrote 7 bytes from C:/ImportantSecrets.txt to /home/ImportantSecrets.txt!
```

Figure 2.1 C2 sever in action.

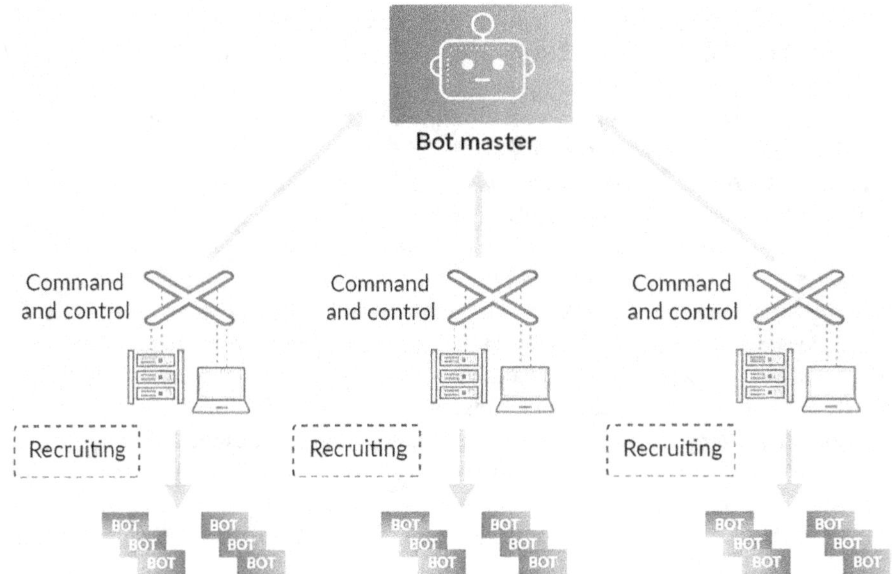

Figure 2.2 C2 architecture.

large number of domain names dynamically. This strategy allows them to bypass blacklists and makes it more challenging for security tools to monitor or block their communication channels.

Types of Architecture for Command and Control Servers are:

- Centralized command and control model: This process operates similarly to a conventional client-server model, where the malware acting as the client periodically contacts a Command and Control (C2) server to receive further instructions. However, in real-world scenarios, the attacker's backend infrastructure is typically more elaborate than a single server. It often incorporates elements such as redirectors, load balancers, and counterintelligence mechanisms designed to identify and evade detection by cybersecurity professionals or law enforcement agencies. To conceal their operations, attackers frequently leverage public cloud platforms, Content Delivery Networks (CDNs), and Internet Relay Chat (IRC) services. Additionally, it is a common tactic for threat actors to hijack legitimate websites and covertly use them as C2 hosts, often without the knowledge or consent of the original site owners.

- P2P C&C model: In this approach, commands are distributed across a peer-to-peer (P2P) structure, where individual bots within the network pass messages to each other rather than relying on a central controller. While some bots may still take on server-like roles, there is no single authoritative node managing the entire network. This decentralized model is more resilient against takedown efforts compared to centralized systems, as there's no single point of failure. However, it can also pose challenges for the attacker when attempting to coordinate or broadcast instructions uniformly across the entire botnet. P2P communication is often employed as a backup strategy when the main command-and-control channel becomes inaccessible.

- Out of band and random: This refers to unconventional methods used by attackers to communicate with compromised systems. Instead of traditional channels, cybercriminals often leverage widely accessible and rarely restricted platforms, such as social media to deliver commands discreetly. For instance, a project known as Twitter was developed to operate a complete command and control system solely through Twitter's direct messaging feature. Similarly, there have been documented cases where adversaries utilized services like Gmail, IRC chatrooms, and Pinterest to transmit instructions to infected machines. Some security researchers have even proposed that a command-and-control network could function without a fixed infrastructure, relying instead on attackers randomly scanning the internet in search of responsive, infected systems. This dynamic and decentralized approach makes detection and disruption significantly more difficult.

The process for Command and Control activities includes the following:

- Initial Compromise, which starts with an entry point, which may involve tactics like deceptive phishing emails, exploiting unpatched system flaws, or delivering malware through compromised files or links. Once executed, the harmful software, commonly known as a "bot" or "agent" is installed on the target system, enabling the attacker to establish remote access and control over the affected device.

- Callback Mechanism initiates after installation as the agent initiates communication with the Command and Control (C2) server, a process commonly known as a "callback." This interaction typically follows a specified protocol and leverages commonly used network services such as HTTP, HTTPS, DNS, or ICMP, allowing the connection to blend in with regular traffic patterns.

- Command and Control Channel (C2) channel functions as the communication pathway between an infected system (bot) and its controlling C2 server. This channel enables the attacker to deliver commands, receive responses, and extract sensitive information from the compromised host. To avoid being identified by security tools, C2 communications are frequently disguised through methods such as encryption or data encoding.

- Command Execution has the C2 servers in a pivotal role directing infected systems to carry out harmful operations. These instructions may involve deploying new attacks, downloading supplementary malware, or gathering intelligence within the targeted network. The nature of the commands is often customized to align with the attacker's specific goals and intentions.

- Evasion Techniques involve the malicious actors deploying a range of stealth strategies to bypass modern security defenses. These tactics may involve rapidly switching domains, encrypting communications, or disguising the C2 traffic within trusted platforms to evade scrutiny. One commonly used method is the implementation of DGAs, which create numerous unpredictable domain names on the fly, complicating efforts to identify, monitor, or disrupt the attacker's C2 infrastructure.
- Persistence Mechanisms enable the attackers to maintain a foothold within infected systems by deploying persistence techniques that keep malware operational and concealed. These techniques often involve modifying system components such as registry keys, configuring scheduled tasks, or installing background services to ensure the malware is not easily detected or removed.
- Remote access and control empower cyber attackers to infiltrate and operate compromised devices from a distance. Once access is established, they can perform a range of intrusive actions such as capturing screen images, logging keystrokes, and even activating the device's microphone or camera to conduct covert audio and video monitoring.
- Multistage Attacks are sophisticated cyberattacks typically unfold in multiple stages, each serving a specific function. In many cases, the attack begins with a lightweight component, commonly known as a dropper or downloader that initiates communication with the attacker's Command and Control (C2) server to retrieve further malicious payloads. This modular strategy enables threat actors to launch campaigns that are both broad in reach and precise in execution. The initial dropper may compromise numerous systems, but only high-value targets receive tailored secondary malware designed for a more significant impact. This approach not only enhances operational flexibility but also supports a decentralized and scalable ecosystem of cybercrime activities.
- Data Exfiltration is the use of C2 servers in a two-way communication, enabling attackers not only to issue commands to compromised systems but also to receive extracted data from them. This exfiltrated information may range from login credentials and confidential files to personally identifiable or financially sensitive records, depending on the nature of the targeted organization. In many cases, particularly with ransomware groups, data theft serves a dual purpose: even if a victim restores their systems from backups, attackers may still use the threat of leaking stolen and often damaging, information to increase pressure and demand payment. Methods used to exfiltrate data differ widely and can include uploading files to external servers, transmitting content through email, or utilizing hidden communication channels that mask the transfer from standard network monitoring tools.

Adversaries are constantly evolving their command and control (C2) methods and infrastructure to evade detection and bypass modern security controls. This dynamic environment necessitates cybersecurity teams and organizations remain proactive, leveraging sophisticated monitoring and defense techniques to uncover and neutralize C2-related threats. Given the increasing frequency and sophistication of cyberattacks, recognizing and responding to C2 operations has become a critical component of effective cyber defense. Timely detection and disruption of C2 channels are essential for protecting vital systems and sensitive information, positioning C2 mitigation as a top priority in today's cybersecurity efforts.

2.4 TACTICS, TECHNIQUES, AND PROCEDURES (TTP)

TTPs represent identifiable system patterns or attacker behaviors that security professionals recognize through observation. These behaviors often reveal attempts by unauthorized actors to perform prohibited actions – such as infiltrating a network, modifying its structure, deploying malicious code or scripts, accessing protected resources, or transferring data to unauthorized external destinations. TTPs typically align with recognizable behavioral models that suggest ongoing or imminent security threats. When analyzed effectively, these indicators become valuable for cybersecurity teams, including CTI analysts and SOC staff, enabling proactive identification and mitigation of threats. A widely adopted framework that catalogs real-world TTPs is the MITRE ATT&CK framework, which serves as a detailed knowledge base of adversary tactics and techniques observed in actual cyber incidents.

2.4.1 Tactics

These are broad overview of how a threat actor operates and strategizes throughout various phases of an attack, as outlined in the Cyber Kill Chain model. The tactics represent the patterns of activity and techniques used by the attacker to accomplish a defined malicious goal. The stages include:

- Reconnaissance and scan for targets.
- Bypass controls for exploitation.
- Acting on the objectives.

For instance, when threat actors exhibit recognizable behaviors typical of DDoS attacks – such as overwhelming servers or networks with high volumes of traffic – it becomes possible to anticipate subsequent phases. These may involve evading perimeter defenses like firewalls or IDS and probing for vulnerable entry points within the internal office network as part of their infiltration strategy.

2.4.2 Techniques

Threat actors execute a series of actions designed to initiate or escalate cybersecurity incidents. These actions represent generalized procedures and transitional approaches that outline how specific tactical objectives may be achieved. For instance, they might employ social engineering techniques like phishing to deceive users into revealing their login credentials, deploy malicious software onto local systems, compromise vulnerable endpoints, and leverage stolen credentials to gain unauthorized access to critical databases so that adversaries can:

- Gain unauthorized access to a network by evading perimeter defenses such as firewalls and IDS.
- Set up C2 infrastructure, enabling remote management of compromised systems.
- Identify vulnerable systems within the network and navigate laterally between them while minimizing detection.
- Retrieve and execute malicious scripts or binary files to propagate the infection across multiple nodes and endpoints within the infrastructure.
- Maintain persistent and covert control over critical network components, allowing adversaries to alter systems without being noticed.
- Extract sensitive information from the environment, often transferring it to external servers without alerting monitoring mechanisms.

2.4.3 Procedures

These represent a clearly outlined series of steps or actions that illustrate how a particular technique is employed to carry out an attack tactic. Each procedure provides a comprehensive breakdown of specific, customized operations that allow a threat actor to effectively reach their objectives. For instance, a harmful script might be deployed to exploit weaknesses in software applications, enabling automated extraction of sensitive data. Once executed, the script may self-decrypt and utilize system services and operating system utilities to extend its functionality. This often results in the attacker gaining direct, interactive access to the compromised system, effectively controlling it remotely.

2.5 THREAT INTELLIGENCE LIFECYCLE

The Threat Intelligence Lifecycle as illustrated in Figure 2.3 refers to a systematic six-phase approach aimed at gathering, refining, evaluating, and distributing cybersecurity information. Its purpose is to convert unstructured data into meaningful, actionable intelligence. This framework supports ongoing adaptation and learning in response to the ever-changing cyber threat landscape.

2.5.1 Requirements: Scope your threat intelligence

This phase serves as the foundation for any intelligence initiative, focusing on clearly defining its purpose and aligning it with organizational risk and business goals. During this stage, it is essential to determine the specific type of threat intelligence to be gathered and ensure its relevance to the organization's strategic needs. This process requires close collaboration between the CTI team, potentially the Red Team and key stakeholders across departments or leadership levels. For example, if the goal is to monitor IABs known to target the healthcare

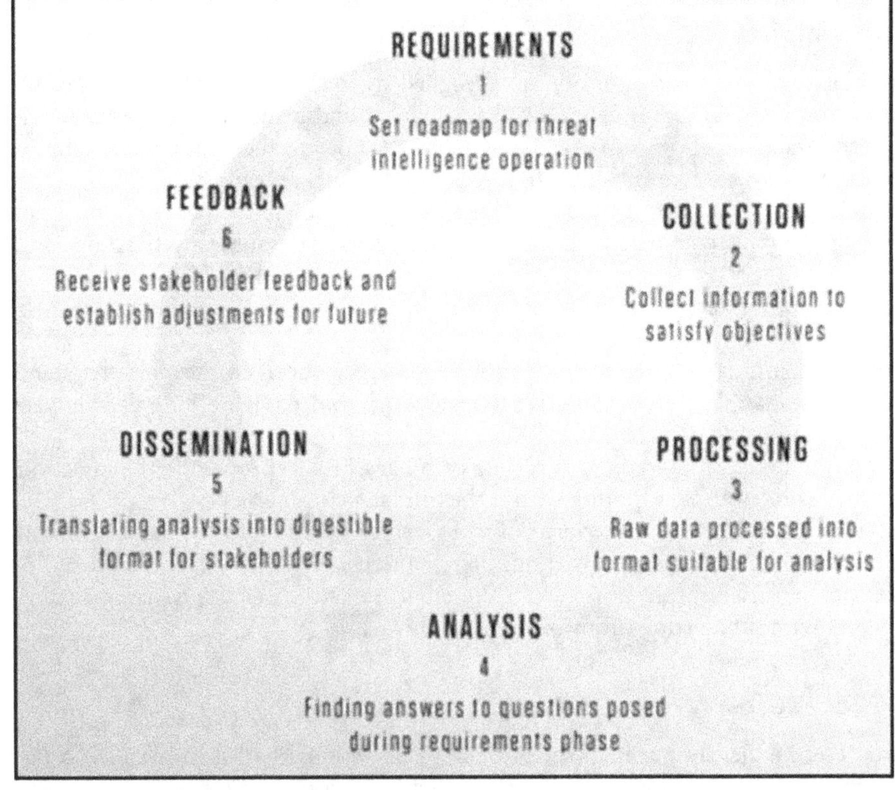

Figure 2.3 Threat Intel lifecycle.

sector, the Requirement phase would focus on formulating a plan to collect intelligence specifically on these actors. Key activities include identifying the IABs involved, cataloguing their known aliases or personas, gathering contextual data on the healthcare organizations they target, and analyzing their techniques, tactics, and procedures (TTPs). This intelligence helps build a threat profile that supports risk mitigation strategies tailored to these threats.

2.5.2 Collection: Gather raw threat intelligence data

During the Collection stage of the threat intelligence process, the primary objective is to identify relevant sources and begin acquiring raw data. If the organization utilizes a dedicated threat intelligence platform, tool, or third-party service, this information can be automatically sourced and centralized. In the absence of such infrastructure, however, the team may need to manually gather data from a range of open and closed sources – including threat intelligence blogs, underground forums, and social platforms like Twitter. In the context of a theoretical investigation into IABs, analysts would focus on dark web forums known for hosting IAB activity. These platforms are commonly used by brokers to auction unauthorized access to corporate networks. A threat intelligence system, if in place, might extract this information automatically in a usable format. Without such a tool, analysts would resort to manual methods, such as navigating TOR-based websites, monitoring discussion threads, analyzing user behavior, and logging potential transactions. The primary goal at this stage is to collect as much unprocessed data as possible concerning IAB operations, laying the groundwork for later stages where the information is assessed, contextualized, and transformed into meaningful threat insights.

2.5.3 Processing: Process the raw threat intelligence data

At this stage of the threat intelligence process, the information gathered is systematically processed to prepare it for in-depth analysis. The team begins by eliminating extraneous or unrelated data that may have been unintentionally captured during collection. The relevant insights are then organized into coherent formats that enable smoother analytical workflows. This often involves categorizing data into logical groupings that support effective cross-referencing and contextual examination later on. Key activities in this phase include compiling structured datasets, such as spreadsheets, that connect isolated data points to establish a broader contextual understanding. These compilations might involve generating timelines, mapping threat actor behavior to specific indicators, and associating incidents with known vulnerabilities or targets. Additionally, IOCs are integrated into systems like SIEMs or SOAR platforms, allowing analysts to correlate them with live network data to detect suspicious activity or breaches in progress. In scenarios focusing on IABs, whether managed by a CTI or red team, analysts may develop visual representations, such as matrices to map connections between observed IAB entities, their TTPs, and the digital platforms where they operate. These visuals aid in recognizing operational patterns, tracking behaviors, and identifying anomalies critical to threat analysis.

2.5.4 Analysis: Interpret the processed data

This stage focuses on examining the refined data to extract valuable and relevant insights. The goal is to develop a clear picture of the threat environment, identifying the potential adversaries, understanding their TTPs, and recognizing the sectors or organizations they are likely to target. The resulting intelligence serves as a foundation for providing practical guidance aimed at minimizing the organization's exposure to threats, particularly those posed by IABs.

2.5.5 Dissemination: Report your threat intelligence

During the dissemination phase, well-structured intelligence reports are developed using the insights gathered throughout the analysis process. These reports are then shared with appropriate stakeholders in a clear and accessible format. They should offer practical, actionable guidance aimed at addressing and reducing the risks posed by the identified threats.

2.5.6 Feedback: Gather feedback from stakeholders

The feedback stage focuses on collecting input from stakeholders who have utilized the delivered intelligence reports. Their insights are crucial for evaluating how useful and actionable the intelligence was, and for pinpointing areas that may need refinement in future efforts. Based on this feedback, modifications can be made to enhance how information is gathered, interpreted, and shared. This stage is not isolated – it feeds directly into redefining requirements for the next intelligence cycle, enabling an ongoing process of improvement and ensuring responsiveness to the constantly changing threat landscape.

2.6 THREAT INTELLIGENCE TYPES

There are four different types of threat intelligence, which are Technical, Operational, Strategic, and Tactical as displayed in Figure 2.4.

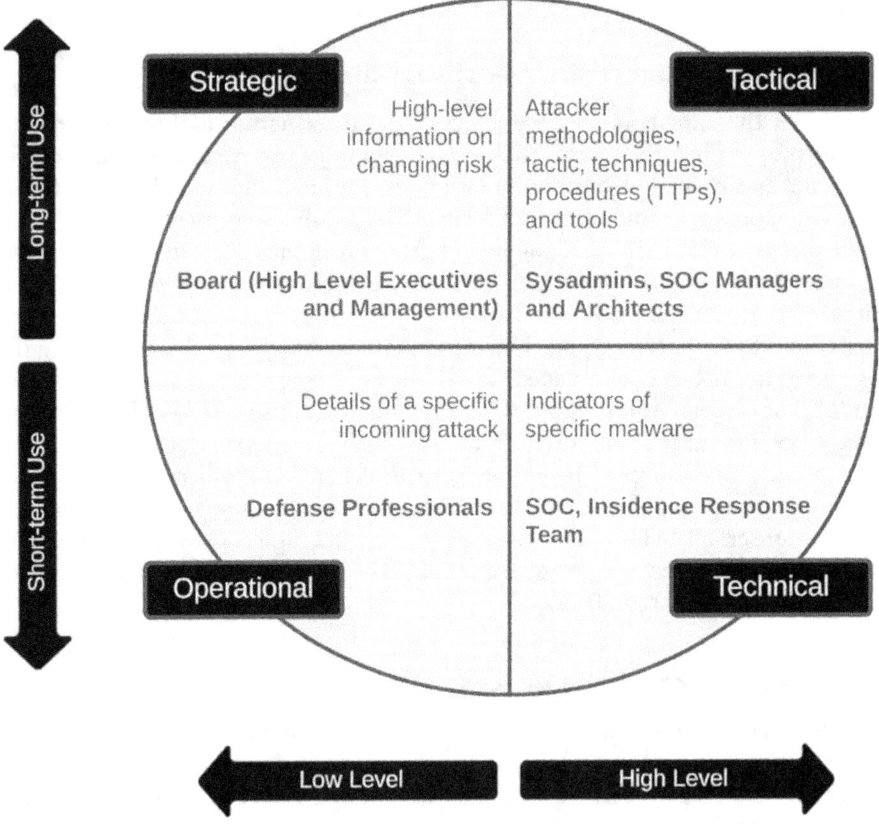

Figure 2.4 Types of threat Intel.

2.6.1 Tactical threat intelligence

Tactical threat intelligence represents a critical facet of CTI, emphasizing the short-term and operational-level activities of malicious actors. This form of intelligence delves into the specific TTPs used by adversaries during cyberattacks. It involves the detailed analysis of elements such as malware behavior, IOCs, suspicious network traffic, and malicious infrastructure like harmful IP addresses and URLs. Moreover, it incorporates forensic data gathered from logs, stolen credentials, and evidence linked to targeted attacks, including those by APTs, ransomware groups, and phishing campaigns.

Designed for a technically proficient audience, including cybersecurity analysts, SOC teams, and threat hunters, tactical intelligence provides these professionals with the contextual knowledge required to detect, analyze, and counter imminent cyber threats. By understanding the granular details of attacker methodologies, defenders can formulate timely and informed responses that disrupt adversarial actions and reinforce security controls. In practical application, tactical CTI plays a vital role in incident response, rapid triage, and strengthening the overall security posture of an organization. It converts raw threat data into actionable insights, facilitating quicker identification of system vulnerabilities and exposure points. This real-time intelligence not only supports immediate defensive measures but also contributes to a more adaptive and proactive approach to cybersecurity. Ultimately, tactical CTI serves as a foundational element in modern cybersecurity strategies, ensuring organizations can swiftly respond to threats and adapt to the continually shifting cyber threat environment.

2.6.2 Technical threat intelligence

Technical CTI delivers precise and actionable insights into cyber threats, primarily focusing on IOCs such as suspicious IP addresses, harmful URLs, and known malware hashes. It provides detailed information about the nature of an attack, including the malware's behavior and the techniques used by threat actors. This intelligence is critical for SOCs and incident response teams as it equips them with the knowledge needed to assess threats, prioritize alerts, and implement appropriate defense mechanisms.

The effectiveness of technical threat intelligence largely depends on how quickly and accurately it is shared, as IOCs can lose relevance over time. When integrated into security infrastructure, this intelligence enhances threat detection capabilities by enabling faster identification of anomalies or malicious behavior. It also supports the identification of harmful traffic patterns and addresses linked to cybercriminal activity, thus strengthening an organization's ability to respond proactively to emerging threats.

2.6.3 Operational threat intelligence

Technical CTI offers highly specific and practical data related to cyber threats, with an emphasis on identifying IOCs such as malicious IP addresses, harmful web links, and recognizable malware signatures. This form of intelligence sheds light on the characteristics of cyberattacks, including how malware operates, and the tactics employed by attackers. For SOCs and incident response teams, such intelligence plays a vital role. It enables them to evaluate potential threats more effectively, prioritize security alerts based on risk level, and deploy the right countermeasures to safeguard systems. By understanding the technical elements of threats, cybersecurity professionals can respond faster and more accurately to evolving risks.

The effectiveness of technical threat intelligence largely depends on how quickly and accurately it is shared, as IOCs can lose relevance over time. When integrated into security infrastructure, this intelligence enhances threat detection capabilities by enabling faster identification of anomalies or malicious behavior. It also supports the identification of harmful traffic patterns and addresses linked to cybercriminal activity, thus strengthening an organization's ability to respond proactively to emerging threats.

2.6.4 Strategic threat intelligence

Strategic threat intelligence plays a pivotal role in shaping an organization's overarching cybersecurity strategy by providing a comprehensive understanding of emerging threats along with their potential financial and operational consequences. This form of intelligence is particularly valuable to senior leaders such as Chief Information Security Officers (CISOs), Chief Executive Officers (CEOs), and other executive-level stakeholders who are tasked with managing complex cyber risk landscapes. By focusing on a risk-based approach, strategic intelligence supports long-term planning and empowers decision-makers to make informed, proactive choices. It aids in identifying priorities such as how to best allocate cybersecurity funding, whether to invest in specific defensive technologies, or how to enhance human resources and training programs aimed at safeguarding critical infrastructure and sensitive data.

In contrast to tactical or technical threat intelligence, which often emphasizes real-time indicators or immediate threats, strategic threat intelligence synthesizes insights from a range of high-level sources. These may include Open-Source Intelligence (OSINT), commercial threat intelligence providers, and sector-specific entities like ISACs. Such broad-scope intelligence equips leadership with a clearer picture of long-term cyber trends and adversary capabilities, which in turn supports policy development, risk management frameworks, and compliance initiatives. Ultimately, strategic threat intelligence enables organizations to transition from reactive to predictive security postures, ensuring that cybersecurity becomes an integral part of business continuity and organizational resilience.

These insights help non-technical executives understand the broader threat landscape, identify patterns in adversary behavior, and prioritize actions that align with business objectives. Even without in-depth technical expertise, leaders can interpret this intelligence to drive organizational resilience, assess cyber risk exposure, and justify investments in cybersecurity infrastructure and policy. Ultimately, strategic threat intelligence serves as a bridge between cybersecurity operations and executive-level decision-making.

2.7 CASE STUDY: SOLARWINDS SUPPLY CHAIN ATTACK

SolarWinds hack (2019) [15] also known as Sunburst or Solorigate, stands as a landmark cyberattack due to its scale and the sophisticated methods employed. The timeline is presented in Figure 2.5. The SolarWinds cyberattack was a sophisticated supply chain breach targeting users of the Orion Platform, including U.S. government agencies and major global corporations. Although the perpetrator remains officially unidentified, the operation is widely attributed to a highly skilled nation-state actor, likely from Russia or Iran. The attackers exploited vulnerabilities in the software update process, allowing them to infiltrate thousands of networks worldwide. This covert access enabled long-term surveillance, data exfiltration, and potential manipulation of critical infrastructure. The incident highlights the far-reaching consequences of supply chain vulnerabilities and the growing threat posed by state-sponsored cyber espionage campaigns on global digital systems.

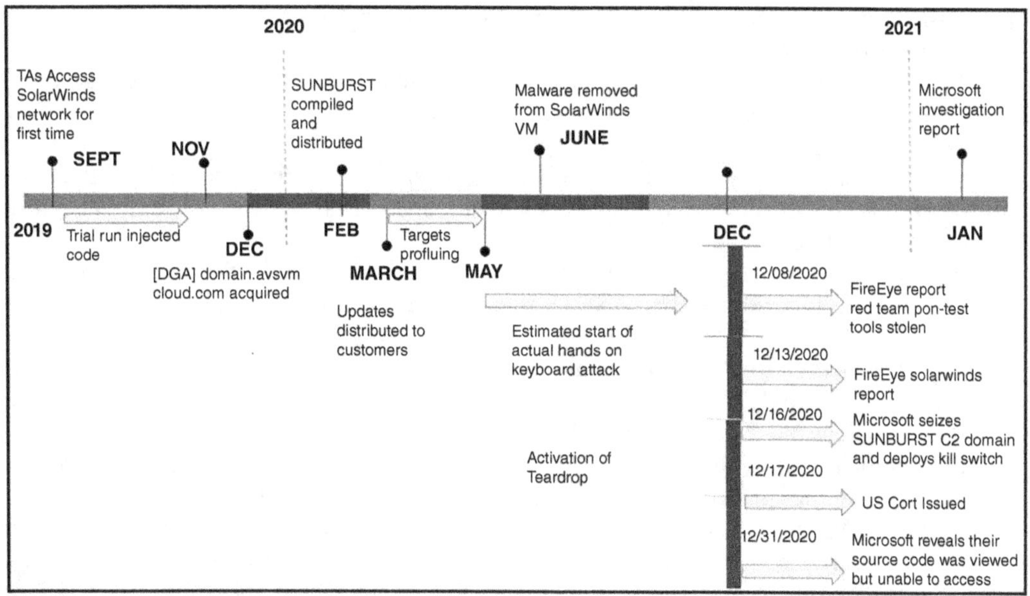

Figure 2.5 SolarWinds attack timeline.

Technical details and steps

1. Compromised Development Environment: Attackers infiltrated SolarWinds software environment. This could have been achieved through various methods, including phishing attacks against developers, exploiting vulnerabilities in their systems, or even physical access.
2. Malicious Code Injection: Once inside, the attackers injected a backdoor (SUNBURST) into a legitimate SolarWinds Orion software component (SolarWinds.Orion.BusinessLayer.dll). This DLL file was digitally signed with a valid SolarWinds certificate, making it appear trustworthy.
3. Software Distribution: The compromised software update containing SUNBURST was then distributed through SolarWinds' legitimate update mechanism. Thousands of SolarWinds Orion customers unknowingly downloaded and installed the malicious update.
4. Backdoor Activation: Upon installation, SUNBURST remained dormant for a period, blending in with regular Orion activity. It then communicated with pre-defined attacker-controlled servers to receive further instructions.
5. Lateral Movement and Espionage: Once activated, SUNBURST allowed attackers to move laterally within victim networks, steal data, and potentially deploy additional malware.

Impact: SolarWinds attack exposed a critical vulnerability in the software supply chain. Organizations using compromised SolarWinds software were potentially exposed to significant risks, including:

- Data Theft: Attackers could steal sensitive information such as trade secrets, customer data, and government secrets.

- Disruption of Operations: Attackers could sabotage critical systems and disrupt normal business operations.
- Escalation of Privileges: Attackers could gain access to highly privileged accounts within a network, granting them extensive control.

While certain domains may have been originally registered before the dates shown, the dates indicated represent when the domains were likely modified or taken over by the threat actors, as illustrated in Table 2.1.

Table 2.2 presents SSL certificates observed in connection with SolarWinds infrastructure. All certificates are issued by Sectigo RSA Domain Validation Secure Server CA.

Lessons Learned: In today's increasingly interconnected digital environment, safeguarding the software supply chain has become a critical component of cybersecurity. As organizations rely more heavily on third-party tools, open-source libraries, and external development teams, the risk of introducing malicious or vulnerable code into enterprise systems has grown substantially. Ensuring the integrity of software throughout its lifecycle – from development and deployment to updates and maintenance – requires robust security controls such as code signing verification and automated vulnerability scanning. These practices help validate the authenticity of code and detect hidden threats before they can cause harm. The infamous SolarWinds breach is a stark illustration of the potential damage when these safeguards are absent. In this incident, attackers injected malicious code into a trusted software update, affecting thousands of organizations globally, including U.S. government agencies and Fortune 500 companies.

Table 2.1 SolarWinds attack domains

Domain	Attacker-controlled date	Registrar
incomeupdate[.]com	08-06-2019	Name Cheap
zupertech[.]com	10-10-2019	Namatilo
avsvmcloud[.]com	12-06-2019	GoDaddy
mobilnweb[.]com	19-12-2019	NameCheap
highdatabase[.]com	26-12-2019	Namesilo
solartrackingsystem[.]net	01-07-2020	Namesilo
webcodez[.]com	15-01-2020	Name Cheap
panhardware[.]com	18-01-2020	Namesilo

Table 2.2 SSL certs from SolarWinds attack infra

Domain	SHA-1	Dates valid
websitetheme[.]com	66576709A115442292838984724FAD485DF143AD	2/3/20–2/2/21
thedoccloud[.]com	49296D5F8A28C3DA2ABE79B82F99A99B40162CE	2/6/20–2/5/21
seobundlekit[.] com	E7F2ECOD868D84A331F2805DA0D989AD068825A1	2/6/20–2/5/21
freescanonline[.] com	8296028C0EE55235A2C8BE8C65E10BF1EA9CES4F	2/11/20–20/10/21
solartrackingsystem[.]net	9189991C10B1DBS1ECAA1E09781608800169E0C	2/12/20–2/11/21
virtualwebdata[.]com	AB93A66C401BE78A4098608D8186A13827DB8E8D	2/13/20–2/13/21
deftsecurity[.]com	12D986A7F4A7D2F80AAF0883EC3231DB3E368480	2/13/20–2/12/21
digitalcollege[.]org	FD8879A2CE7E2CDA26BEC8837D2B9EC235FADE44	3/5/20–3/5/21

Alongside supply chain security MFA is another vital defense mechanism. MFA strengthens identity verification by requiring users to provide multiple forms of authentication – such as a password and a time-sensitive code – before gaining access to systems. Even when attackers successfully steal login credentials through phishing or data leaks, MFA significantly impedes unauthorized access, acting as an effective barrier against intrusions. Moreover, network segmentation is an often underestimated yet powerful strategy for limiting the spread of cyber threats within an organization. By isolating critical systems and sensitive data into separate network zones, companies can contain breaches and prevent lateral movement by attackers. If one segment is compromised, the attacker cannot easily pivot to other parts of the network, thereby minimizing damage.

Finally, routine security audits play a crucial role in proactive defense. These assessments involve evaluating system configurations, reviewing access controls, and scanning for known vulnerabilities. Regular audits help organizations identify weaknesses before they are exploited and ensure compliance with internal policies and industry regulations. Ultimately, the lessons from attacks like SolarWinds underscore the need for a multi-layered security approach. A combination of strong supply chain oversight, identity management, network design, and regular assessments enables organizations to stay resilient in a rapidly evolving threat landscape. By adopting these best practices, businesses can not only reduce their exposure to cyber risks but also strengthen overall trust in their digital infrastructure.

2.8 CONCLUSION

This chapter has provided a thorough exploration of the ever-expanding and evolving cyber threat landscape. From the analysis of prevalent threats like ransomware, phishing, and zero-day exploits, to the profiling of diverse threat actors such as nation-state operatives, cyber-criminals, and insider threats, the chapter highlights the complexity and range of today's digital risks. A detailed discussion on Command and Control (C2) infrastructure illustrated how attackers maintain persistent access and control over compromised systems, enabling operations like data theft, surveillance, and destructive payloads. The explanation of attacker TTPs, along with the Threat Intelligence Lifecycle, emphasized the need for a structured, adaptive approach to identifying and mitigating threats. The inclusion of real-world case studies, like the SolarWinds supply chain attack, underscored the high stakes involved and the need for both technical and strategic resilience. The chapter also emphasized the importance of different intelligence types: tactical, technical, operational, and strategic to provide organizations with a layered defense strategy. In sum, this chapter equips readers with foundational knowledge and practical insights necessary to comprehend, anticipate, and counteract cyber threats in a rapidly shifting digital environment, reaffirming that robust, proactive security practices are no longer optional but essential.

MULTIPLE CHOICE QUESTIONS

1. A global finance company notices unusual login attempts across its hybrid infrastructure. The attempts mimic legitimate user behavior and bypass IP-based blocking. Their SOC observes that the phishing emails look hyper-realistic, even imitating writing style and tone. During investigation, analysts discover video messages sent to executives requesting urgent fund transfers. What type of cyber threat is most likely being used?

    A. Traditional phishing attacks
    B. Deepfake-enabled social engineering
    C. SQL injection
    D. Basic brute-force credential attack

Correct Answer: B

Why correct: Deepfake-enabled fraud aligns with the chapter's example of AI-generated impersonation attacks used to trick executives. Why others are wrong:

- A – Not traditional; these attacks are AI-enhanced.
- C – No database exploitation in the scenario.
- D – The attempts mimic user behavior, not brute force.

2. A technology firm recently adopted Zero Trust Architecture. However, attackers still managed to move laterally from a compromised developer laptop into the cloud environment. Investigation reveals that once authenticated, internal API services still trusted the device by default. Which Zero Trust principle was NOT enforced?

   A. Never trust, always verify
   B. Encrypt data at rest
   C. Principle of least privilege
   D. Continuous authentication and device health checks

Correct Answer: D

Why correct: If initial authentication gave unrestrained access, continuous verification was missing. Why others are wrong:

- A – They *tried* Zero Trust but failed in applying continuous evaluation.
- B – Data encryption irrelevant to lateral movement.
- C – Least privilege matters, but the core issue is lack of ongoing validation.

3. A hospital's network is hit by ransomware. Even after restoring systems from offline backups, attackers threaten to release patient data. Analysts see evidence that gigabytes of information were exfiltrated before encryption. Which ransomware model is being used?

   A. Single encryption model
   B. Fileless malware
   C. Double extortion ransomware
   D. Malvertising attack

Correct Answer: C

Why correct: Data theft + encryption matches the double-extortion model described in the chapter. Why others are wrong:

- A – Single-model does not involve data theft.
- B – Attack used encryption, not memory-only malware.
- D – Not ad-based infection.

4. A telecom SOC uses threat feeds integrated into their SIEM. Detection time drops by 35% because the system correlates login anomalies with known IOCs from global repositories. Analysts can automatically prioritize alerts based on threat severity. What operational improvement is being demonstrated?

   A. Incident postmortem review
   B. Use of threat intelligence in SOC operations
   C. Cloud identity management
   D. Endpoint patch automation

Correct Answer: B

Why correct: Matches chapter's explanation of SOCs integrating CTI feeds to reduce detection time. Why others are wrong:

- A – Not a post-incident review.
- C – Not identity management.
- D – No patching discussion.

5. A mobile operator finds customer metadata exposed. Attack logs show repeated requests to a forgotten microservice endpoint that did not require authentication. Attackers exploited this API to extract sensitive data. Which threat vector is most applicable?

    A. Cloud Security Posture Misconfiguration
    B. Supply chain attack
    C. Injection-based exploit
    D. Cryptojacking

Correct Answer: A

Why correct: Misconfigured cloud APIs reflect the chapter's example of T-Mobile's API abuse case. Why others are wrong:

- B – No third-party compromise.
- C – No malicious script injection.
- D – No crypto mining.

6. An employee receives over 50 MFA push notifications in a single evening. Overwhelmed, they approve one prompt. Attackers then gain access to sensitive resources. What technique was used?

    A. Password spraying
    B. MFA bombing/fatigue attack
    C. MITM interception
    D. Replay attack

Correct Answer: B

Why correct: Matches Uber 2022 breach example in the chapter. Why others are wrong:

- A – Not mass login attempts with one password
- C – No interception.
- D – No reuse of captured packets.

7. A power company finds malware that wipes router firmware across remote sites. Forensics show it resembles the destructive malware used in Ukraine incidents and was delivered via living-off-the-land techniques. Which group's behavior does this MOST resemble?

    A. Lapsus$ teenage thrill-seekers
    B. Sandworm APT
    C. Anonymous hacktivists
    D. LockBit ransomware gang

Correct Answer: B

Why correct: Sandworm is known for destructive malware like AcidRain and WhisperGate. Why others are wrong:

- A – Not destructive malware.
- C – Hacktivists prefer DDoS/defacement.
- D – LockBit focuses on ransomware + extortion.

8. A logistics company's database is erased by a disgruntled employee who resigns the next day. Logs confirm the user accessed administrative commands. What type of cyber threat is this?

   A. Cybercriminals
   B. Nation-state attack
   C. Insider threat – malicious
   D. Hacktivist retaliation

   Correct Answer: C
   Why correct: Matches chapter's insider example, disgruntled employees abusing access. Why others are wrong:
   - A – Actor is internal.
   - B – No geopolitical motive.
   - D – No ideological motive.

9. A company's logs show an unknown user accessed their VPN, then performed basic enumeration. Nothing was encrypted or disrupted. A week later, a ransomware gang breached the same environment using the same account. Which threat actor likely initiated the first intrusion?

   A. Hacktivist
   B. Initial Access Broker
   C. Thrill-seeking hacker
   D. Nation-state espionage actor

   Correct Answer: B
   Why correct: Early intrusion + selling access matches IAB behavior. Why others are wrong:
   - A – No political motive.
   - C – Actions are too structured.
   - D – Ransomware groups typically don't buy from espionage campaigns.

10. An enterprise security team identifies periodic outbound DNS requests to unique, random subdomains. The requests occur at irregular intervals and carry encoded data. What C2 component does this represent?

    A. Dropper
    B. Beacon
    C. Loader
    D. Persistency module

    Correct Answer: B
    Why correct: Beaconing = periodic communication with randomized intervals, as defined. Why others are wrong:
    - A – Droppers install malware.
    - C – Loaders fetch payloads.
    - D – Persistence maintains access.

11. A botnet investigation finds that bots exchange commands among themselves without contacting a central server. Even after authorities take down several nodes, the botnet continues functioning. Which C2 design is this?

    A. Centralized C2
    B. P2P C2
    C. Out-of-band C2
    D. Domain fronting

Correct Answer: B

Why correct: Fully matches the chapter's definition of P2P C2. Why others are wrong:

- A – Would collapse after server takedown.
- C – Would use Gmail/Twitter etc.
- D – Not a communication model.

12. A company experiences malware that installs a tiny first-stage program. This module then contacts a remote C2 server and downloads more complex payloads only on specific high-value systems. What type of attack is this?

    A. Single-stage worm
    B. Multi stage modular attack
    C. Drive-by download
    D. Botnet propagation

    Correct Answer: B

    Why correct: Matches chapter's description: dropper → fetches payload → targets selective systems. Why others are wrong:

    - A – Not single-stage.
    - C – Not browser-based exploit.
    - D – Not mass infection.

13. A SOC notices encrypted outbound traffic from a system at midnight daily. The data volume slowly increases. The source matches a system undergoing investigation for a breach. Which C2 activity does this indicate?

    A. Initial compromise
    B. Persistence mechanism
    C. Data exfiltration
    D. Evasion via polymorphism

    Correct Answer: C

    Why correct: Large outbound transfers over C2 = exfiltration. Why others are wrong:

    - A – Breach already occurred.
    - B – Would show repeated registry changes, not data transfer.
    - D – Not about code mutation.

14. A CTI team gathers IAB data from dark web forums, categorizes access types, builds matrices showing attacker TTPs, and correlates indicators with known vulnerabilities. Which lifecycle stage is this?

    A. Requirements
    B. Processing
    C. Dissemination
    D. Feedback

    Correct Answer: B

    Why correct: Processing = filtering, structuring, organizing raw data (matrices, categories). Why others are wrong:

    - A – Requirements define goals.
    - C – Dissemination shares reports.
    - D – Feedback occurs after reporting.

15. A government agency installs a legitimate software update. Unknown to them, the update contains a digitally signed malicious DLL that remains dormant for weeks before activating C2 communication. Which type of attack is this?

    A. Man-in-the-browser
    B. Supply chain attack
    C. Credential stuffing
    D. DoS attack

Correct Answer: B Why correct: Matches SolarWinds model: compromised update delivery. Why others are wrong:
- A – No browser manipulation.
- C – No bulk password attempts.
- D – No service disruption.

REFERENCES

1. Vasu Jakkal, "Microsoft unveils Microsoft Security Copilot agents and new protections for AI | Microsoft Security Blog," *Microsoft Security Blog*, Mar. 24, 2025. https://www.microsoft.com/en-us/security/blog/2025/03/24/microsoft-unveils-microsoft-security-copilot-agents-and-new-protections-for-ai

2. "8 LOLBins every threat hunter should know," *Crowdstrike.com*, 2025. Accessed Jul. 1, 2025. https://www.crowdstrike.com/en-us/resources/white-papers/8-lolbins-every-threat-hunter-should-know

3. N. Robins-Early, "CEO of world's biggest ad firm targeted by deepfake scam," *The Guardian*, May 10, 2024. https://www.theguardian.com/technology/article/2024/may/10/ceo-wpp-deepfake-scam

4. Palo Alto Networks, "What is a zero trust architecture?," *Paloaltonetworks.com*, 2019. https://www.paloaltonetworks.com/cyberpedia/what-is-a-zero-trust-architecture

5. CISA, "Executive order on improving the nation's cybersecurity | CISA," Cybersecurity and Infrastructure Security Agency CISA, 2021. https://www.cisa.gov/topics/cybersecurity-best-practices/executive-order-improving-nations-cybersecurity

6. "BeyondCorp zero trust enterprise security," *Google Cloud*, 2022. https://cloud.google.com/beyondcorp?hl=en

7. "Understanding zero trust: Why 'trust no one' is the new security paradigm," *Centreforcybersecurity.com*, 2024. https://www.centreforcybersecurity.com/en-sg/post/understanding-zero-trust-why-trust-no-one-is-the-new-security-paradigm

8. D. BondGraham, "Oakland ransomware hackers dumped gigabytes of sensitive city files on the web," *The Oaklandside*, Mar. 6, 2023. https://oaklandside.org/2023/03/06/oakland-ransomware-hackers-leak-sensitive-city-files-data

9. "Ransomware mitigation," Intel 471, 2024. Accessed Jul. 1, 2025. https://intel471.com/solutions/ransomware-mitigation

10. E. Kost, "What caused the uber data breach? | UpGuard," *upguard.com*, Nov. 18, 2024. https://www.upguard.com/blog/what-caused-the-uber-data-breach

11. "Gamaredon Group, Group G0047 | MITRE ATT&CK®," *attack.mitre.org*, 2026. https://attack.mitre.org/groups/G0047

12. "Sandworm Team, ELECTRUM, Telebots, IRON VIKING, BlackEnergy (Group), Quedagh, VOODOO BEAR, Group G0034 | MITRE ATT&CK®," *attack.mitre.org*, 2024. https://attack.mitre.org/groups/G0034

13. CrowdStrike Intelligence Team, "Technical analysis of the WhisperGate malicious bootloader | CrowdStrike," *Crowdstrike.com*, 2024. https://www.crowdstrike.com/en-us/blog/technical-analysis-of-whispergate-malware

14. Juan Andrés Guerrero-Saade, "AcidRain | A modem wiper rains down on Europe," *SentinelOne*, Mar. 31, 2022. https://www.sentinelone.com/labs/acidrain-a-modem-wiper-rains-down-on-europe

15. Fortinet, "SolarWinds supply chain attack," *Fortinet*, 2025. https://www.fortinet.com/resources/cyberglossary/solarwinds-cyber-attack

Chapter 3

Threat hunting

Static and dynamic analysis

3.1 THREAT HUNTING PROCESS

Threat hunting [1] is a proactive cybersecurity approach aimed at detecting and mitigating threats that may have bypassed traditional security defenses. Unlike reactive methods that respond to alerts and known signatures, threat hunting involves actively seeking out suspicious behaviors, anomalies, or patterns within an organization's network that may indicate a hidden or emerging threat. The process begins with the development of a hypothesis. This hypothesis is based on threat intelligence, behavioral patterns, or recent incidents and serves as the starting point for an investigation. For instance, a hunter might hypothesize that attackers are using a specific malware variant to establish persistence on the system. Using this assumption, the threat hunter selects appropriate data sources such as endpoint logs, network traffic, or system event logs to validate the theory.

The next stage involves data collection and enrichment. Threat hunters typically work with a vast range of telemetry data obtained from security information and event management (SIEM) systems, endpoint detection and response (EDR) tools, and log analytics platforms. This raw data is processed, filtered, and enriched with contextual information, such as user identity, device details, geolocation, and time-based attributes, to uncover unusual patterns. Following this, the data is analyzed to identify Indicators of Compromise (IoCs) and Indicators of Attack (IoAs). Advanced analytics, including behavioral analysis, machine learning models, and correlation engines, are often applied to detect deviations from normal user or system behavior. Once anomalies are identified, threat hunters begin the investigation phase. Here, the goal is to trace the origin of the threat, understand its methodology, and determine the potential impact. This often involves pivoting across multiple datasets, examining process trees, registry modifications, unusual network connections, or privilege escalations. The investigation seeks to answer critical questions such as how the attacker gained access, what systems were affected, and whether any data was exfiltrated or modified. Once a threat is confirmed, it is documented in detail and handed off to the incident response team for containment, eradication, and recovery procedures.

The final phase of the threat hunting process is refinement and feedback. All findings are analyzed to improve future hunting operations. This could include updating detection rules, enhancing SIEM dashboards, tuning alert thresholds, or refining machine learning models. Additionally, the lessons learned are often incorporated into security awareness programs, employee training, and organizational policies. Threat hunting is a continuous cycle rather than a one-time event. As threats evolve and attackers become more sophisticated, the hunt must adapt accordingly, leveraging both human intuition and advanced technology. Threat hunting is a strategic blend of hypothesis-driven inquiry, data analysis, and investigative techniques aimed at uncovering threats that may otherwise remain hidden. It enhances an organization's security posture by going beyond traditional monitoring and enabling a more

DOI: 10.1201/9781003730583-3

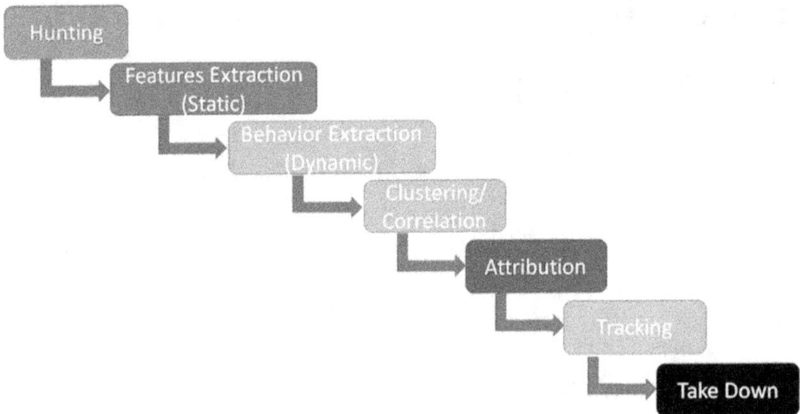

Figure 3.1 Threat hunting process flow.

resilient, adaptive defense mechanism. With a skilled team and the right tools, organizations can significantly reduce dwell time, detect advanced persistent threats earlier, and minimize the risk of costly breaches.

Figure 3.1 illustrates the steps during a Threat Hunting process:

1. Hunting: before starting to do anything, you need to have malware samples to understand what it is doing. You need to have skills to find those on the Internet/Github.
2. Feature Extraction: once you have the hunting sample, you need to find the static features.
3. Behavior Extraction: next is the behavior of that sample, which is usually dynamic – downloads a script from Internet, to steal credentials or executes the script to open a port, that connects to an IP, that IP sends a scanner, that further checks the OS environment or scans for sensitive files. The downloader brings in the customized pre-requisites which ultimately downloads the malware, encryption may start, and data are sent out.
4. Clustering/Correlation: once these behaviors are found, cluster in groups as per specific malware families and correlate that info to have a better understanding of the attack flow.
5. Attribution: finding who is behind the malicious operations.
6. Tracking: finding the attack, when does he get activated, when does he releases the malware to victims, and when/where does he open a new C2 server.
7. Takedown: once identified, LEAs go about dismantling the C2 setup, domains, and tools.

3.2 HUNTING FOR MALICIOUS SAMPLES

Threat hunting is an active cybersecurity approach that involves proactively searching for signs of malicious activities within an organization's environment, rather than relying solely on automated alerts. One of the most critical components of effective threat hunting is the collection and analysis of malware samples [2]. These samples serve as raw data for understanding the tools, techniques, and procedures (TTPs) used by threat actors. The primary goal is to gather these samples from both internal and external sources, enabling the development of comprehensive threat profiles that help security teams anticipate, detect, and mitigate future attacks more efficiently.

Internal sources of malware samples are especially valuable because they provide context-specific data that reflects real threats targeting the organization. These sources include network traffic logs, compromised endpoints, and SIEM reports. For instance, packet captures (PCAPs) from the network can reveal suspicious communication with known command-and-control (C2) servers. Endpoints that show signs of compromise, such as unknown executable files, registry changes, or unusual process activity, often host actual malware binaries that can be extracted and analyzed. SIEM platforms aggregate logs from various assets across the enterprise, often revealing IOCs like unusual logon patterns, privilege escalation attempts, or data exfiltration, which may be tied to specific malware behaviors.

Equally important are external sources, which offer a broader view of the threat landscape and allow threat hunters to correlate internal findings with known threat actor activities. Blogs maintained by cybersecurity researchers, public threat feeds, and technical threat intelligence reports from vendors are rich sources of malware hashes, YARA rules, and behavioral analysis. Public databases like VirusTotal, MalwareBazaar, and Hybrid Analysis offer samples and sandbox results that detail how malware behaves in controlled environments. Forums, dark web platforms, and underground communities, although harder to access, can also be valuable for discovering zero-day malware variants or learning about the latest tools shared among cybercriminals. These sources collectively help in mapping malware to specific threat actors, often based on reused code, similar infrastructure, or identical evasion techniques.

Once collected, malware samples undergo static and dynamic analysis. Static analysis involves examining the binary without executing it, identifying strings, metadata, and embedded resources. Dynamic analysis, on the other hand, involves running the malware in a controlled sandbox to observe its behavior, such as API calls, file system changes, and network communication. Both methods provide key insights into the malware's capabilities and the threat actor's intent. By continuously gathering and analyzing these samples, organizations can build threat actor profiles that include preferred malware families, attack vectors, geographic targeting patterns, and operational timelines.

The most effective way to carry on the collection process is to use a collection management framework (CMF) as presented in Table 3.1. Using CMF allows you to identify data sources

Table 3.1 Collection management framework

Source/type	URL	IP address	WhoIs	First seen	Hash (SHA256)
MalwareBazaar	https://bazaar.abuse.ch/sample/	185.183.96.57	abuse.ch/ Switzerland	15-06-2025	a1b2c3d4e5f6g7890h1i2j3k4l5m6n7o8p9q0r1s2t3u4v5w6x7y8z9a0b1c2
Internal Compromised Host	N/A	10.0.0.25	Internal Asset	28-06-2025	d3e4f5a6b7c8d9e0f1a2b3c4d5e6f7a8b9c0d1e2f3g4h5i6j7k8l9m0n1o2
Threat Intelligence Feed	https://ti.vendor.com/feed/1234	162.125.19.5	Vendor Ltd/ USA	30-06-2025	f1e2d3c4b5a697887766554433221 1aabbccd deeff001122334455667788
Dark Web Forum Leak	hidden.onion/forum/files/malx	192.168.1.35 (Tor)	Hidden Service (Unknown)	20-06-2025	1234567890abcdef1234567890abcdef1234567890abcdef1234567890abcd
Public Threat Report	https://blog.cyberfirm.com/mal/	104.26.10.123	Cloudflare/ USA	18-06-2025	abcdefabcdefabcdefabcdefabcdefabcdefabcdefabcdefabcdefabcdef

and easily track the type of information you are gathering for each. It can also be of use to rate the data that's been obtained from the source, including how long that data have been stored, and to track how trustworthy and complete the source is. It is advised that you use the CMF to track not only the external sources, but also the internal ones.

Collecting malware samples from both internal and external sources forms the bedrock of modern threat hunting. It empowers cybersecurity teams to move beyond reactive defense, enabling them to identify adversary behavior proactively and attribute activity to known or emerging threat actors. Over time, this data-driven approach enhances an organization's resilience by enabling faster detection, more accurate attribution, and informed decision-making during incident response.

3.2.1 Virus total

VirusTotal [3] stands as one of the most widely trusted and utilized tools in the cybersecurity community for detecting, analyzing, and researching potential threats. At its core, VirusTotal functions as a centralized hub where security analysts, incident responders, and researchers can submit suspicious files, URLs, IP addresses, or even cryptographic hashes. Once submitted, these items are subjected to simultaneous analysis by multiple antivirus engines and security tools. This multi-engine scanning process provides a consolidated and comprehensive verdict on the potential maliciousness of the submitted item, thereby enabling quick threat assessments that go far beyond traditional signature-based scanning methods.

The strength of VirusTotal lies not just in its ability to detect malware, but also in its role as a robust threat intelligence platform. Each submission yields detailed metadata about the file or URL, such as the file's name, type, size, and hash, along with behavioral information that may include execution patterns, command-and-control communication, registry modifications, and system file alterations. This wealth of information enables analysts to understand not just whether a file is malicious, but also the nature and severity of its behavior. It becomes a valuable tool for gauging the potential impact of a threat and for formulating an appropriate containment or mitigation strategy.

One of the most valuable components of VirusTotal's intelligence capabilities is its integration with behavioral analysis and dynamic sandbox environments. For executable files, VirusTotal can simulate a runtime environment in which the file's behavior is observed in real-time. This provides insights into how the malware interacts with the system once executed, offering visibility into things such as process injection, file system manipulation, or attempts to contact external servers. Such dynamic insights are crucial for understanding polymorphic malware or threats that evade traditional static scanning techniques.

Moreover, VirusTotal is not limited to offering static intelligence. It also empowers cybersecurity professionals to craft and utilize YARA rules. YARA, short for "Yet Another Recursive Acronym," is a tool designed to help identify and classify malware samples based on textual or binary patterns. These rules can be tailored to match specific characteristics of known threats or new IOCs. VirusTotal allows users to upload and apply these custom YARA rules to its vast repository of files, effectively enabling users to detect specific malware families, variants, or even targeted attacks. Once configured, these rules can trigger automatic notifications whenever new submissions match the predefined patterns, thereby enhancing proactive threat detection.

Beyond the creation and application of YARA rules, VirusTotal also provides a powerful retro-hunting feature. Retro-hunting refers to the ability to apply newly created YARA rules to historical data stored within VirusTotal's archives. This capability allows analysts to scan through millions of previously submitted files, including those that may not have been flagged as malicious at the time of submission. In doing so, security teams can uncover older malware samples or campaigns that had evaded detection, thus enabling retrospective analysis and improved understanding of past incidents. This historical perspective is especially useful in attributing attacks, identifying recurring patterns, and fortifying defenses against previously missed threats.

VirusTotal's advanced hunting capabilities further extend its utility. The platform supports complex queries that allow analysts to search across its massive dataset based on numerous criteria. Searches can be performed using file hashes (MD5, SHA-1, SHA-256), file names, domains, IP addresses, file types, and submission metadata. This enables security teams to uncover related threats, map out the infrastructure used by adversaries, and identify emerging malware trends. The ability to filter data with such precision ensures that analysts can zero in on exactly the information they need, making the threat-hunting process both efficient and highly targeted.

Incorporating VirusTotal into the daily workflow of threat analysts significantly enhances visibility into the evolving threat landscape. For instance, if a suspicious IP address is observed communicating with an internal endpoint, VirusTotal can be used to check the IP's reputation and history of malicious activity. Similarly, URLs received in phishing emails can be quickly verified for malicious behavior, giving security teams immediate feedback and the context necessary to take action. This real-time verification capability is vital in minimizing dwell time and limiting the scope of potential breaches.

Additionally, VirusTotal acts as a collaborative ecosystem where researchers and organizations contribute findings to a shared knowledge base. Public submissions and detection results help enrich the platform's intelligence, which in turn benefits the global security community. This shared intelligence model encourages transparency, facilitates collaboration, and fosters rapid collective response to emerging threats. Users can view community-sourced comments and analyses that offer deeper insights or suggest possible links to known malware campaigns, threat actors, or tactics, techniques, and procedures (TTPs).

VirusTotal Graph feature is another key asset, offering visual representations of relationships between different malware samples, URLs, domains, and IP addresses. It helps analysts visualize how seemingly unrelated artifacts may be part of a broader campaign. By examining these relationships, one can often uncover infrastructure reuse by threat actors or trace the lineage of evolving malware strains. These visual insights not only make complex data more digestible but also aid in storytelling and reporting to non-technical stakeholders. The use of VirusTotal does not end with reactive analysis. The tool can also play a proactive role in cybersecurity strategy. By leveraging its API, security operations centers (SOCs) and SIEM systems can automate the enrichment of alerts with VirusTotal intelligence. This means that security alerts generated within the organization can be automatically supplemented with contextual threat information from VirusTotal, thereby enhancing the quality of alerts and accelerating triage processes.

Link: https://www.virustotal.com/gui/home/upload

3.2.2 Underground hacking forums

Underground forums [4] represent a unique and often underexplored domain for extracting rich and actionable threat intelligence. Unlike indexed websites that appear through conventional search engines like Google, these forums reside in the deep and dark web, accessible only through specific browsers or with community credentials. Within these digital enclaves, hackers and cybercriminals engage in candid discussions that often reveal crucial insights into their operations, including the disclosure of software vulnerabilities, attack techniques, malware development, and the sale or exchange of nefarious digital tools. The open nature of these conversations, sometimes conducted in fragmented slang, code words, or encrypted channels, offers a lens into the evolving threat landscape that traditional IOC may fail to reveal in real time.

Cybersecurity professionals and threat intelligence analysts are increasingly leveraging the content of these forums to understand attacker motivations, emerging TTPs, and even specific tools or malware families currently in circulation. These insights are invaluable for pre-emptive security planning and the fine-tuning of detection mechanisms. For instance, when a hacker discusses an exploit for an unpatched zero-day vulnerability, analysts monitoring the forum may catch wind of the conversation and take measures to mitigate the threat before it becomes widespread. Furthermore, attackers sometimes upload actual malware samples within these threads, often to showcase the effectiveness of their code to potential buyers or collaborators. Such uploads, while dangerous, present a rare opportunity for researchers to obtain raw threat artifacts for sandbox analysis.

In a controlled virtual environment, such as a sandbox, security researchers can dissect malware behavior without endangering live systems. This reverse engineering process allows professionals to create YARA rules, update antivirus definitions, or develop behavioral detection logic. The proactive identification and examination of these digital threats can significantly reduce response times when similar samples eventually emerge in the wild. Early access to malware variants can give cybersecurity teams the edge they need to create signatures and enhance firewall or intrusion detection system (IDS) configurations well before the malware is deployed in large-scale campaigns.

However, accessing and engaging with underground hacking forums is fraught with serious challenges and potential repercussions. These forums are not merely niche message boards; they are highly guarded, often requiring vetted invitations, the use of anonymous browsers such as Tor, and a credible alias backed by a synthetic digital identity. This fictitious identity, often referred to as a sock puppet, must be convincing enough to avoid suspicion from seasoned cybercriminals who are adept at identifying law enforcement infiltrators. These fake personas are not casually created; rather, they are meticulously crafted with fabricated work histories, digital footprints, and believable behavior patterns that blend into the criminal ecosystem. Intelligence agencies like the FBI and Interpol, as well as advanced threat hunting groups, have documented and sometimes deployed such synthetic IDs to infiltrate these communities.

Legality is one of the foremost concerns when exploring underground forums. Many of the discussions and transactions within these spaces pertain to explicitly illegal activities, including the trafficking of stolen data, ransomware-as-a-service (RaaS), botnet leasing, and targeted attack planning. Merely being present in these forums – or worse, downloading malicious samples – can expose researchers or analysts to legal consequences, depending on jurisdiction. Such actions might be construed as aiding, abetting, or facilitating cybercrime, especially if the researcher cannot demonstrate intent for legitimate investigative purposes under proper authorization.

Another significant hazard associated with underground forum access is the prevalence of live malware. Unlike public security blogs or GitHub repositories, where malicious code is often sanitized, these forums may host fully functional exploits, loaders, remote access trojans (RATs), or ransomware payloads. Downloading such content without a secure, air-gapped environment and specialized protocols could lead to accidental infection. Some malware types are programmed to auto-execute, exfiltrate data, or install backdoors, making even passive browsing a potential attack vector.

In addition to these risks, the reliability of information on underground forums must always be questioned. Not all forum members are what they claim to be. Some posts are designed to mislead competitors, confuse security researchers, or inflate the value of a tool or service for commercial gain. Deliberate misinformation campaigns can also sow distrust among analysts who rely on these conversations for actionable insights. False flag operations, staged breaches, or exaggerated threat claims are all strategies used to manipulate perception and obscure the real intention of threat actors.

Given these complexities, any organization or analyst engaging with underground forums must adopt a robust operational security (OpSec) framework. This includes the use of isolated virtual machines, non-attributable internet access, encrypted communication channels, and strict access protocols. Legal and ethical boundaries must also be clearly defined and adhered to, typically with guidance from legal counsel or under formal threat intelligence operations sanctioned by institutional frameworks.

Despite these inherent dangers, underground forums remain one of the most revealing sources of early-stage threat intelligence. They serve as the virtual marketplace and brainstorming venue for cybercriminals who are actively shaping the threat landscape. For defenders, tapping into this environment, ethically and securely provides a unique opportunity to stay ahead of attackers by understanding their language, identifying their tools, and anticipating their next move. When handled correctly, this intelligence can translate into better situational awareness, faster incident response, and more resilient cybersecurity infrastructure.

3.2.3 Deep web/invisible or hidden sites

Some online content, while perfectly legal and widely used, is not entirely accessible through standard search engines like Google, Bing, or Yahoo. This type of material exists in what is often referred to as the "deep web." Unlike publicly indexed web pages, these resources are not discoverable by traditional web crawlers due to various technical and access-related barriers. For example, many academic journal repositories such as JSTOR or IEEE Xplore require institutional logins or paid subscriptions to access their contents, keeping them out of open search engine results.

Additionally, platforms like Gmail, Facebook, LinkedIn, and online banking websites host personal and sensitive data behind login credentials, multifactor authentication (MFA), and encrypted sessions. These security measures intentionally prevent indexing by search engines, safeguarding user privacy. For instance, your personal inbox on Gmail or messages in your Facebook account are part of the deep web because they are not publicly accessible or searchable. Even image files, directories, or documents stored on secure servers remain hidden unless specific permissions are granted. This protected layer of the internet is essential for user security and confidentiality, ensuring that only authorized individuals can access the content, rather than making it universally searchable or openly browsable.

3.2.4 Incident response engagements

Security Operations Center (SOC) teams play a pivotal role in identifying and mitigating cyber threats. One of their proactive strategies involves leveraging various online forums and intelligence-sharing platforms to gather insights about suspicious or malicious artifacts. Rather than relying solely on internal logs or antivirus alerts, SOC analysts often consult threat intelligence communities such as VirusTotal, Hybrid Analysis, Any.run, or forums like Reddit's r/netsec or specialized underground discussions. These platforms provide real-time analysis, behavioral reports, and community-driven feedback on malware samples, helping SOC teams determine if a sample is newly emerging or part of a known campaign.

For example, if a SOC analyst discovers a suspicious executable on a corporate endpoint, they might upload its hash to VirusTotal. If the file has been analyzed previously, the platform will return a detection ratio, showing how many anti-virus engines flag it as malicious. Similarly, uploading the file to Any.run can simulate its behavior in a sandbox environment, revealing actions such as registry modifications, C2 communication attempts, or data exfiltration. By correlating this external intelligence with internal telemetry, SOC teams can more confidently classify threats and take informed action. This approach enhances detection accuracy and shortens response time, especially in cases of targeted attacks or zero-day threats.

3.2.5 Honeypots

Honeypots [5] are a sophisticated and strategic tool used in cybersecurity to serve as decoys, designed to emulate genuine systems such as web servers, databases, applications, or even full-scale enterprise networks. The fundamental concept behind a honeypot is deception: it deliberately mimics a vulnerable environment to attract cybercriminals and malicious actors. Although they appear to be authentic and potentially valuable to attackers, honeypots contain no real operational data. Instead, they are intentionally filled with fabricated or non-critical information, allowing cybersecurity teams to observe, monitor, and analyze unauthorized access attempts in a controlled and secure setting. These systems are deployed with the explicit intention of being discovered and targeted. From a technical standpoint, they are configured with deliberately weak or exposed ports, insecure services, or outdated software to present an inviting attack surface. This calculated vulnerability encourages attackers to engage, thereby triggering the honeypot's surveillance and data collection mechanisms. Once an intruder begins interacting with the honeypot, all activities are meticulously logged, capturing everything from the attacker's IP address to the tools and commands they use. This creates a treasure trove of threat intelligence data that organizations can use to strengthen their defenses.

One of the most significant benefits of deploying honeypots is the ability to gather real-time intelligence about adversarial behavior. By studying how attackers interact with the fake environment, security professionals can gain insights into the methodologies, tactics, and tools commonly employed in the wild. For instance, if a honeypot records multiple attempts to exploit a specific application vulnerability, it signals that this flaw might be a favored vector among threat actors. Security teams can then prioritize patching this vulnerability across actual production systems, thereby reducing the organization's attack surface. Moreover, understanding the sequence of steps taken by the attacker, from reconnaissance to exploitation, helps analysts build more robust incident response strategies and improve threat detection mechanisms.

In addition to intelligence gathering, honeypots can uncover latent weaknesses within an organization's existing security infrastructure. For example, suppose a honeypot designed to simulate an employee login portal captures numerous credential stuffing attempts using valid-looking usernames and passwords. This would indicate that user credentials have potentially been compromised or leaked elsewhere. It also reveals a gap in current protection mechanisms, perhaps the absence of multifactor authentication or insufficient rate-limiting on login attempts. With this knowledge, the organization can not only address the immediate risk but also reinforce system-wide policies to prevent similar intrusions on real systems.

Honeypots also play an instrumental role in acting as a decoy or distraction. In many sophisticated attacks, time and focus are critical factors for adversaries. A well-placed honeypot can divert attackers away from valuable assets such as financial records, customer data, or proprietary business logic. Since the honeypot mimics the look and feel of actual systems, attackers may unknowingly spend significant time and resources engaging with it – giving cybersecurity teams more time to detect, investigate, and respond to the intrusion. For example, in a corporate environment where sensitive documents are stored on specific servers, a honeypot simulating a similar environment could mislead attackers into thinking they've found a lucrative target. While the attacker remains occupied, the organization's monitoring tools can alert defenders and initiate containment protocols.

Furthermore, honeypots provide a sandbox-like environment for security researchers and analysts to study emerging threats without endangering real systems. When new malware strains or attack techniques appear, deploying a honeypot can enable the safe capture and analysis of these threats in action. Analysts can then reverse engineer the payloads, identify command-and-control communication channels, and develop detection signatures for use in antivirus or IDS. This proactive capability gives organizations an edge in responding to zero-day exploits or novel cyberattack strategies before they become widespread.

There are several categories of honeypots, each tailored to different threat scenarios and research goals. For example, a low-interaction honeypot only emulates a few services or ports and is relatively simple to deploy and maintain. It provides limited insights but is useful for identifying broad scanning or opportunistic attacks. On the other hand, a high-interaction honeypot closely replicates a real system and allows attackers to fully engage with the environment, including executing code, installing malware, or navigating file structures. While high-interaction honeypots are more complex and resource-intensive, they yield deeper intelligence and are ideal for studying sophisticated adversaries. Another notable variation is the client-side honeypot, which is designed to proactively interact with malicious servers rather than waiting for an inbound attack. Figure 3.2 presents the architecture for Honeypots. These honeypots simulate web browsers, email clients, or other user-facing systems and can be used to detect drive-by downloads, phishing campaigns, or browser-based exploits. For example, a client honeypot could be configured to visit suspicious URLs harvested from phishing emails, allowing security researchers to analyze any malicious payloads or scripts that attempt to compromise the client.

In practical terms, many organizations integrate honeypots as part of a broader threat detection and intelligence strategy. Consider a financial institution that deploys a honeypot

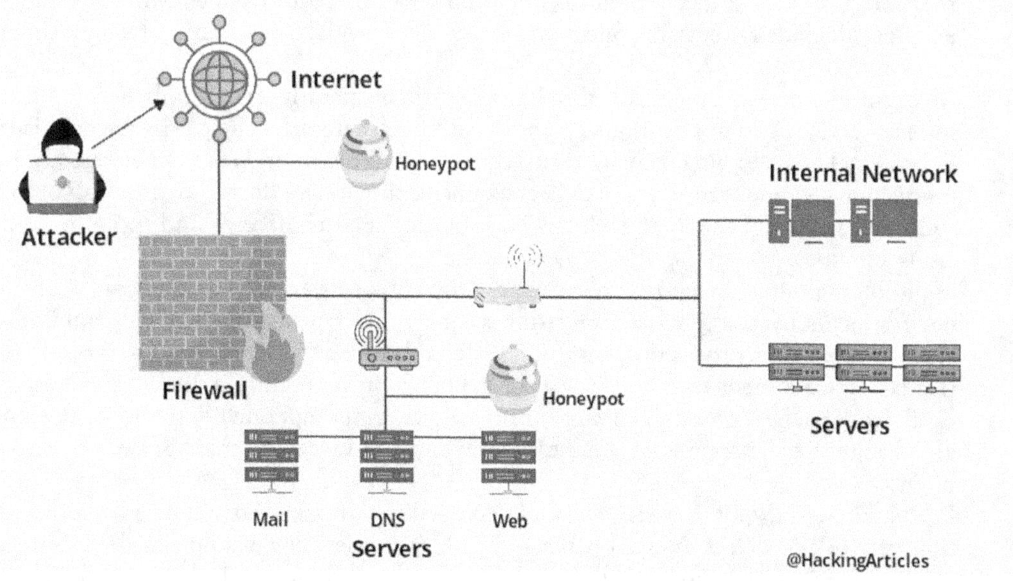

Figure 3.2 Honeypot.

mimicking an online banking interface. If a threat actor attempts to log in using stolen credentials, the honeypot can detect and log this activity, even if the attacker never reaches the real system. Additionally, if the attacker uploads a malicious payload, the security team can isolate and examine it without any risk to customer data or critical systems. This proactive layer of deception allows the institution to stay ahead of attackers by constantly adapting to evolving threat vectors.

Despite their advantages, honeypots must be deployed carefully to avoid unintended consequences. Poorly configured honeypots might be used by attackers as launching pads for attacks against other systems, especially if outbound connections are not properly restricted. Similarly, if attackers realize they are interacting with a decoy, they may alter their tactics to avoid detection or use the honeypot as a smokescreen for attacking real assets. Therefore, successful honeypot deployment requires proper segmentation, containment, and monitoring practices to ensure the system remains a net benefit to the organization's security posture. The kind of data that honeypots generally capture:

- Keystrokes entered by the attacker.
- IP address of the attacker.
- Usernames & privileges used by attackers.
- Type of data accessed, deleted, or altered.

Honeypots can be deployed in various environments and categorized into the following types based on their level of fidelity or deception:

- Low-interaction Honeypots are simple setups that simulate only a limited range of services, such as HTTP, FTP, or DNS, to mimic real systems without offering full functionality. These honeypots are easy to deploy and maintain, making them ideal for environments with limited resources. While they don't capture highly detailed attacker behavior, they are effective in identifying scanning and probing activities across TCP, UDP, and ICMP protocols. By deploying decoy files, fake databases, or dummy data, they lure attackers and help monitor potential intrusion patterns in real-time. Common examples include Honeytrap, Specter, and KFsensor, widely used for lightweight threat detection.
- Medium-interaction Honeypot simulates real-time operating environments, replicating the services and applications of an actual target network. Their primary goal is to delay attackers, allowing security teams more time to detect and respond effectively. By mimicking genuine systems, they collect extensive threat data during an attack. Notable examples include Cowrie and HoneyPy, both designed to deceive and monitor malicious activities.
- High-interaction Honeypots are advanced honeypot systems that replicate realistic environments by using actual operating systems and real application vulnerabilities, closely mimicking production setups. This enables security teams to observe sophisticated attacker behavior. For instance, a honeypot simulating a Linux server with outdated Apache can attract real-world exploits. Although such systems yield valuable insights, their complexity makes deployment and ongoing management resource intensive.
- Production Honeypots are strategically deployed within an organization's live production network to detect internal threats or vulnerabilities. For example, a decoy server may expose hidden malware or unauthorized access attempts. However, maintaining these traps requires significant expertise and constant monitoring.

- Research Honeypots are high-interaction honeypots specifically designed for research purposes, often deployed within government or military networks. Their goal is to study attacker behavior in depth. For example, a military server may simulate sensitive data to attract sophisticated intrusions.
- Malware Honeypots are decoy systems designed to lure and engage malicious software or attackers. These traps allow the malware to execute its behavior in a controlled environment, helping analysts observe attack patterns. For example, a fake database server may attract SQL injection attempts to study exploit methods safely.
- Email Honeypots decoy accounts set up to lure cyber attackers. These fake addresses receive emails from malicious sources, which are then analyzed to identify phishing patterns. For instance, if a spammer sends a phishing link to the honeypot, security teams can study it to improve threat detection systems.
- Database Honeypots are intentionally crafted to resemble vulnerable databases, often named to attract malicious actors. For example, a database named "credit_card_records" may invite SQL injection attempts. These traps help security teams analyze attacker behavior and uncover exploitation techniques, enabling better defenses against threats targeting actual sensitive data repositories.
- Spider Honeypots are strategically deployed to attract and detect web crawlers or spiders that attempt to extract sensitive data from web applications. For instance, a hidden link may lure malicious bots, revealing unauthorized scraping attempts without endangering real assets.
- Spam Honeypots simulate fake email servers to lure spammers into targeting insecure email components. By interacting with these traps, spammers unknowingly reveal their methods. For example, forged login pages or dummy inboxes record spam-sending behaviors for further analysis.
- Honeynets refers to a group of interconnected honeypots placed in a secure, isolated virtual environment to monitor attacker behavior. For instance, fake servers mimicking real systems can lure intruders, helping researchers study malware patterns and intrusion techniques safely.

Honeypots can be deployed on physical or virtual machines positioned either within isolated network segments like a DMZ or exposed to the public internet. In more advanced setups, multiple honeypots form a honeynet as displayed in Figure 3.3 as a coordinated network that simulates realistic, complex environments to attract and study attackers. These systems are instrumental in collecting comprehensive intelligence, including network packets, system logs, and attempts to access files. Security professionals analyze this rich data to uncover attacker behaviors, techniques, and patterns. Such insights play a crucial role in threat detection, improving defense mechanisms, and proactively identifying vulnerabilities before real systems are compromised.

Some critical terms in Honeypot:

- Intranet: This represents your organization's internal network hosted web portals.
- Honeypot: This is the decoy system designed to mimic a vulnerable target.
- DMZ (Demilitarized Zone): This is a network segment that sits between the internal network and the public internet. The honeypot is often placed in the DMZ to provide a degree of isolation from the internal network.
- Firewall: This device controls traffic flow between the different network segments. It can be configured to direct suspicious traffic toward the honeypot.
- Public Web Server: This represents a publicly accessible web server that might be a target for attackers.

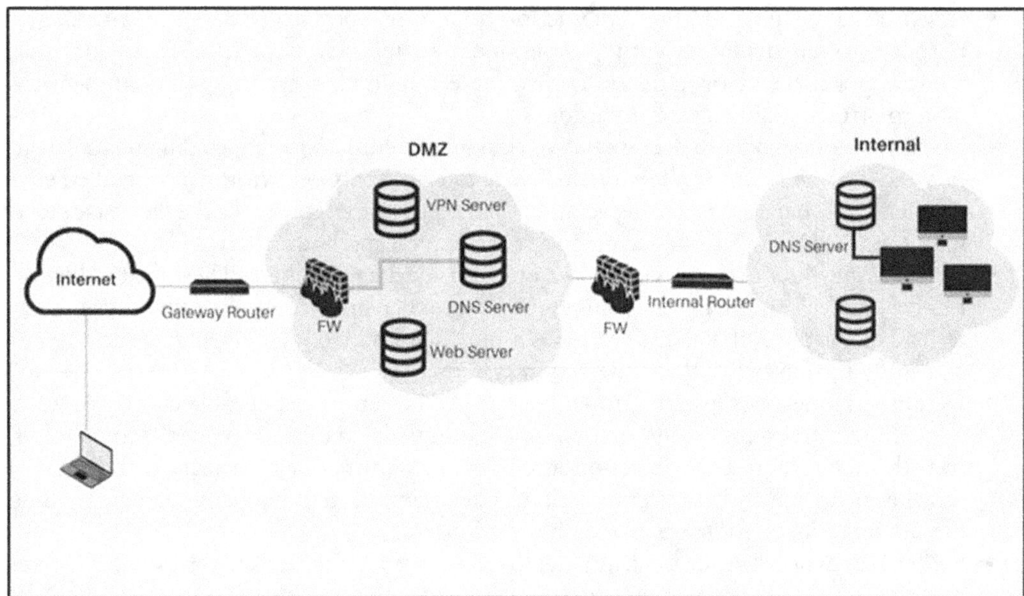

Figure 3.3 Honeypot-DMZ-LAN.

3.3 FEATURE EXTRACTION (STATIC)

Static extraction [6] phase of malware analysis, the goal is to extract and recognize distinguishing static characteristics from collected malicious binaries. These static features, which remain unchanged during execution, serve as valuable indicators to classify malware into specific families or threat actor groups. Such categorization is essential for building a foundational knowledge base about various malicious entities, allowing cybersecurity analysts to map out behaviors and relationships between different malware strains. One of the critical attributes examined is the timestamp, which reflects the date and time when the binary was originally compiled. This information can offer insights into the development timeline or reveal attempts to manipulate creation dates to avoid detection. Another important feature is the digital certificate associated with the binary. Malicious actors may use self-signed certificates, exploit stolen certificates from legitimate organizations, or rely on expired ones to lend their binaries an appearance of legitimacy and bypass security controls. Additionally, the user identity responsible for compiling or creating the binary, when available, provides further attribution clues that can link samples to specific campaigns or attackers. By analyzing these static indicators, analysts can systematically group related malware samples and improve threat detection, attribution, and the development of targeted defensive measures.

3.3.1 Import table hash (imphash)

Hash functions are unique digital fingerprint assigned to a file, enabling systems to precisely identify its contents. When even a single bit within a file is altered, the resulting hash value drastically changes, making it an effective tool for detecting file modifications. This property is extensively utilized in file integrity verification. Antivirus and anti-malware software, for instance, rely on vast databases of hash values representing both trusted and known malicious files. By comparing a file's current hash against this database, these applications can quickly determine whether a file is safe or potentially harmful. Importantly, hashing is a one-way process – it's computationally infeasible to reverse-engineer a file's original content from its hash, reinforcing its utility in secure verification rather than content reconstruction.

Dynamic Link Libraries (DLLs) are essential building blocks in the Windows operating system. They contain shared sets of functions, variables, and resources that multiple programs can access concurrently to perform system-level operations. These libraries ensure code reusability and efficient memory usage across the OS and applications. However, as Windows is routinely updated and users frequently install new applications, the system files and related components are often modified. Despite this, the functions imported by programs must remain consistent or be properly signed by a trusted vendor like Microsoft to maintain reliability and trust.

To track the usage of DLLs and detect possible malicious modifications, a technique called *imphash* (import hash) is used. It generates a hash value based on the imported functions listed in a program's import table. This helps in identifying files that may not be identical but share similar behavior by referencing the same set of APIs or DLLs. Security researchers and tools use imphash to detect malware that mimics legitimate system behavior, thus aiding in uncovering disguised or repackaged threats based on DLL usage patterns.

3.3.2 Strings

In programming, particularly in Python and many other modern languages, strings serve as one of the most essential and versatile data types. A string is essentially a sequence of characters, often used to represent textual data, structured information, or even embedded code fragments. These sequences are enclosed within quotation marks, either single (') or double ("). For example, in Python, a string can be defined as my_string = "This is a string". This simple declaration highlights how intuitive it is to work with strings in Python, making them a foundational concept for beginners and experts alike.

One of the key characteristics of strings in Python is their immutability. Once a string has been created, its contents, each character within it, cannot be altered. This means that any operation that seems to change a string actually creates a new one. While this might appear limiting at first, immutability ensures safer and more predictable code by preventing unintended side effects. Python offers a wide array of operations that can be performed on strings. Slicing allows developers to extract specific portions or substrings using index ranges. Concatenation is the process of joining two or more strings together, which is often used to build dynamic text. String formatting provides a way to insert variables or expressions directly into a string, which is useful for generating messages or displaying data. Additionally, escape sequences like \n for a newline or \" for a quotation mark enable the inclusion of special characters that would otherwise disrupt the syntax. Lastly, multiline strings, defined using triple quotes ("' or """), allow for the creation of strings that span several lines, which is ideal for large blocks of text or documentation. Overall, understanding strings and their properties is critical for effective programming.

One of the primary use cases of strings involves user input. Login forms, search bars, and other web-based fields receive input in the form of strings. If this input is directly processed without validation, it can open doors to injection-based attacks. SQL Injection and Cross-Site Scripting (XSS) are two common examples where malicious strings inserted by users manipulate the intended behavior of an application, often leading to data breaches or unauthorized access. In the context of network communication, strings also traverse data packets that may include credentials, session tokens, or URLs. These strings can be intercepted, modified, or spoofed in attacks such as Man-in-the-Middle (MitM), highlighting the need for encryption and secure communication protocols.

Strings are often embedded in malware or malicious scripts to exploit vulnerabilities in software systems. Attackers might use obfuscated strings to hide harmful payloads, making it difficult for conventional security tools to detect them. Analysts also use strings to trace suspicious binaries, searching for file paths, author usernames, or specific API calls within the code. Overall, the way strings are managed and monitored greatly impacts the security posture of any digital environment, underscoring their importance in both offensive and defensive cybersecurity operations.

3.4 HANDS-ON EXERCISE: IP PIVOTING

Pivoting is a technique used to analyze and explore data gathered from various sources to uncover connections between different elements. It is essentially following a trail of breadcrumbs to unearth a bigger picture.

1. Security analysts might start with a single indicator of compromise (IOC) like a suspicious IP address.
2. They then use this IP address to pivot through threat intelligence tool portals and databases.
3. This process helps them identify other malicious IPs, URLs, domains, geolocation, or even entire campaigns that might be linked to the initial IOC.

By pivoting on IPs and other IOCs, analysts can gain valuable insights such as:

- Scope of a cyber attack
- Attacker's infrastructure – Other IPs used, Geolocation, Apps involved, Versions.
- TTPs used by the attacker.
- Potential future attacks

Select any IP from https://github.com/stamparm/ipsum (Example: Malicious IP → 91.229.79.138)

Step 1:   Open DomainTools from https://whois.domaintools.com/ as shown in Figure 3.4.

Figure 3.4 DomainTools portal.

Step 2:   Enter the IP address to find information about the IP address as illustrated in Figure 3.5.

Step 3:   Figure 3.6 reveals the organization details like the Domain Creator and Administrator.

Step 4:   Search and confirm the Geolocation from www.ip2location.com as shown in Figure 3.7.

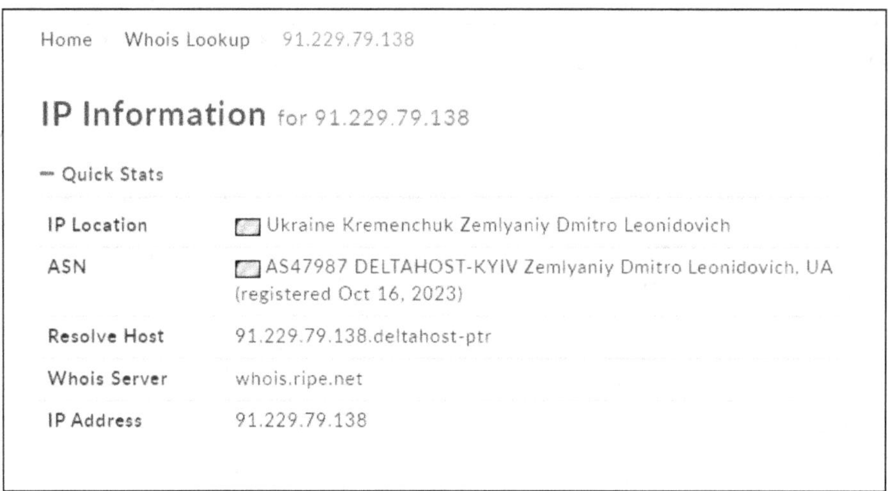

Figure 3.5 WhoIs lookup for IP address.

```
organisation:   ORG-FZDL2-RIPE
org-name:       Zemlyaniy Dmitro Leonidovich    person:    Zemlyaniy Dmitro Leonidovich
country:        UA                               address:   Ukraine, Kyiv
org-type:       LIR                              phone:     +380442470862
address:        Liskivska 37, 36                 nic-hdl:   ZDL2-RIPE
address:        02167                            e-mail:    info@deltahost.com.ua
address:        Kyiv
address:        UKRAINE                          mnt-by:    DELTAHOST-MNT
phone:          +380442470862                    created:   2009-05-02T11:46:55Z
e-mail:         info@deltahost.com.ua
```

Figure 3.6 Organization & domain administrator.

Permalink	https://www.ip2location.com/91.229.79.138
IP Address	91.229.79.138
Country	Ukraine [UA]
Region	Kyiv
City	Kiev
Coordinates of City	50.454660, 30.523800 (50°27'17"N 30°31'26"E)

Figure 3.7 Geolocation information.

Step 5:   Validate and view the location using the latitude and longitude from https://maps.google.com, as shown in Figure 3.8.

Step 6:   Figure 3.9 displays the range of IP addresses involved, here if one IP is blocked by IT network team/security, other takes over.

Step 7:   Use VirusTotal to find malicious info from this IP as shown in Figure 3.10.

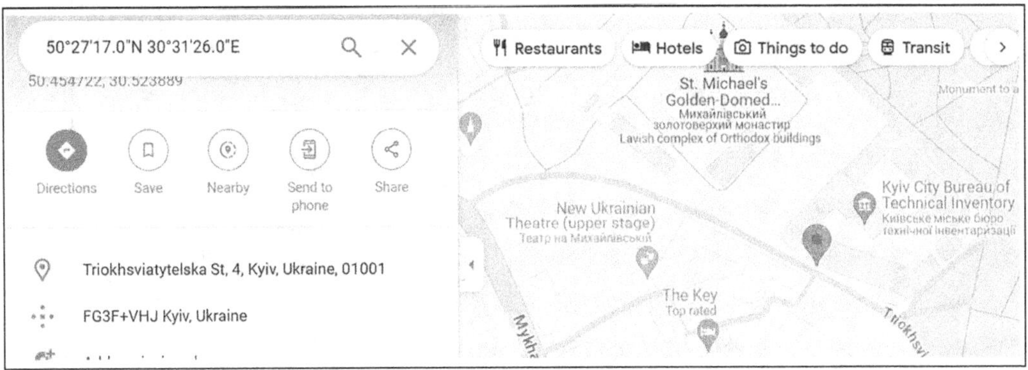

Figure 3.8 Google Maps.

```
% Abuse contact for '91.229.76.0 - 91.229.79.255'

inetnum:        91.229.76.0 - 91.229.79.255
netname:        DELTAHOST-NET2
```

Figure 3.9 IP address range found.

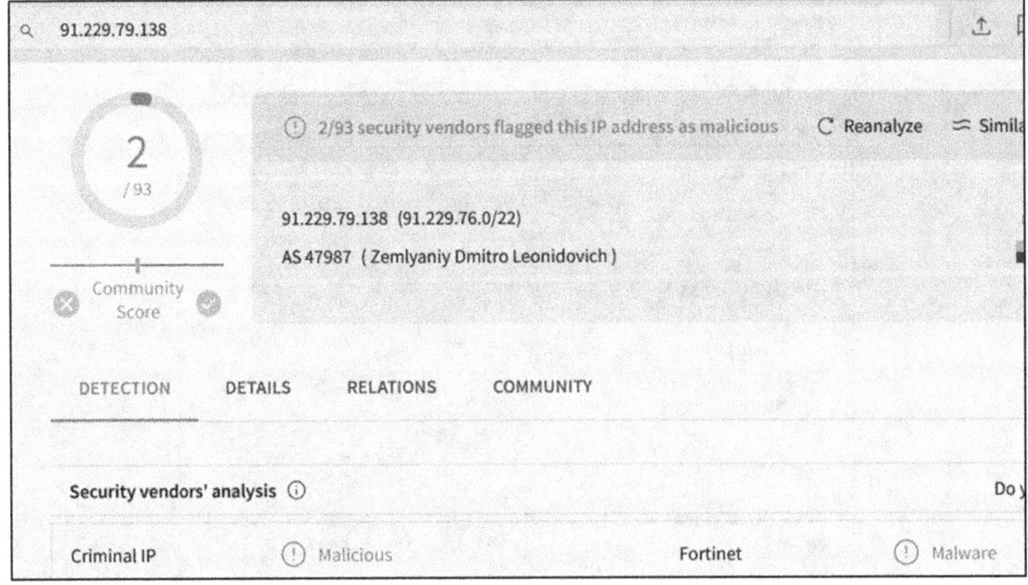

Figure 3.10 Use VirusTotal to validate a malicious IP address.

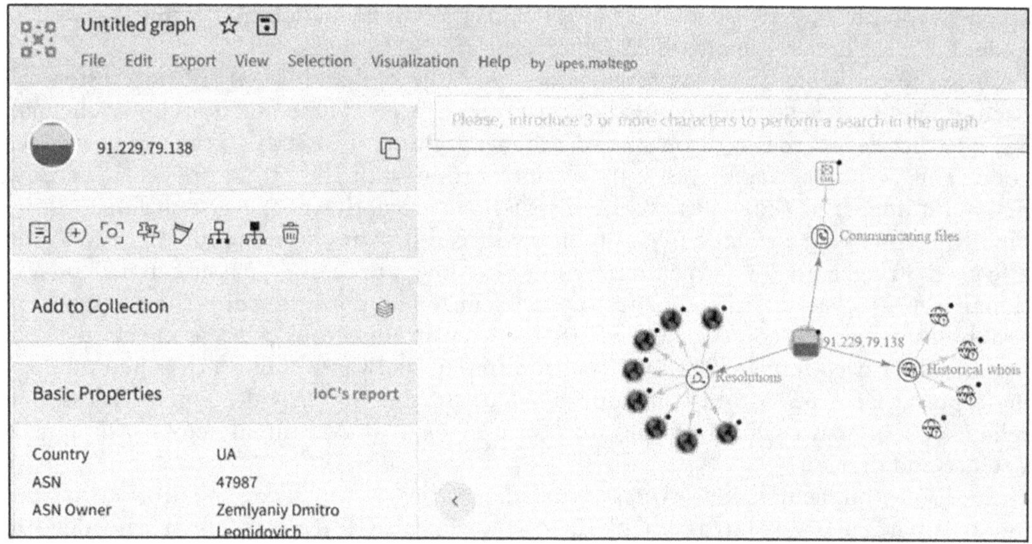

Figure 3.11 VirusTotal graph.

Step 8:   Use the VirusTotal Graph to view IP activities as shown in Figure 3.11.

3.5 BEHAVIOR EXTRACTION (DYNAMIC)

The goal for Behavior Extraction is to identify unique Dynamic features in Binaries that can help classify them into specific malicious groups. This is dynamic, which means it works while running to extract the features using online Cukoo Sandbox. Understanding the evolving tactics employed by malicious software requires a deep dive into behavioral indicators that signify compromise. In recent cybersecurity workflows, hands-on analysis remains a critical method for dissecting and recognizing these behaviors. Among the many observable patterns, three categories stand out for their frequent use in malware operations: process injection mechanisms, unauthorized input surveillance, and DNS-based reconnaissance. Each of these techniques offers a distinct footprint in system activity and identifying them can significantly bolster defensive strategies.

One of the most telling indicators of malicious activity within an operating system is the manipulation of legitimate processes to execute unauthorized code. This phenomenon is often encapsulated within a class of malware known as process infectors. To effectively identify such behavior, cybersecurity professionals commonly employ isolated execution environments, often referred to as sandboxes. These environments simulate operating system functionality in a secure, detached space, allowing malicious binaries to run without impacting actual systems. By doing so, analysts can observe the behavior of the program, particularly how it interacts with system-level APIs that facilitate communication between the malware and the operating system.

A prominent technique observed during sandbox analysis is the unauthorized use of memory manipulation functions. For instance, the API often misused for this purpose is capable of writing code into the address space of another process. By injecting its payload into a benign system process, the malware camouflages its operations, making it harder for traditional antivirus tools to detect. The attacker uses this method to gain a foothold within the system under the guise of a legitimate process.

Once the malicious code has been successfully injected, additional APIs are often utilized to modify the execution context of the target process. These functions allow the malware to dictate where execution should resume, pointing it directly to the newly injected code. This technique facilitates seamless integration with the target application's flow, making it appear as though the rogue instructions are native to the system's operations. Finally, by invoking a resume function on the thread that has been modified, the malware effectively triggers its own execution within the foreign process, bypassing many conventional security checks. This sequence (memory injection, context redirection, and thread resumption) forms a core behavioral pattern seen in numerous process injection cases. Despite the varied implementations across different malware families, this methodology underpins a large portion of contemporary fileless attacks. Its stealth, effectiveness, and reliance on standard system utilities make it a favorite among threat actors seeking persistence and evasion.

Another prominent tactic leveraged by adversaries is the silent monitoring of user inputs – particularly keystrokes and cursor movements. Keyloggers, often embedded in broader threat packages such as ransomware or RATs, serve the purpose of capturing sensitive information without user awareness. These threats are frequently disseminated under the guise of legitimate-looking software, often bundled with freeware and shareware applications. Once installed, they operate silently in the background, harvesting credentials, personal data, or even corporate secrets. Technically, keyloggers exploit specific functionalities within the operating system that allow for event hooking. Hooking is a legitimate mechanism used in software development and accessibility services to intercept system events like keyboard and mouse inputs. However, in malicious contexts, these same mechanisms are used to spy on users. Each hook is associated with an identifier that defines the type of input it monitors.

For instance, one identifier corresponds to keyboard events. When malware registers this type of hook, it gains access to every keystroke made on the system. This includes passwords, search queries, and any other input, regardless of where it is entered. Another identifier is dedicated to mouse movements and clicks, enabling the malware to map user behavior on the graphical interface. Combined, these hooks provide a comprehensive view of a user's digital activity, often without triggering any visible sign of intrusion. The stealth and persistence of keyloggers make them particularly dangerous. Unlike other malware that might disrupt operations or display ransom messages, keyloggers typically function without any user-facing indicators. Their objective is long-term espionage rather than immediate disruption. By collecting and exfiltrating data over time, they contribute to broader goals such as identity theft, credential stuffing, or insider threats. As a result, their presence often remains undetected until significant damage has occurred.

3.5.1 Hands-on exercise: Analyze LB3.exe

Sandbox Link: https://cuckoo.cert.ee/
Malware Samples: https://github.com/fabrimagic72/malware-samples

Step 1:   Figure 3.12 displays the location to download a malware sample (ZIP) on a
          Virtual Machine.

Step 2: Do not unzip, just upload the sample to Cukoo Cert and click analyze as shown in Figure 3.13.

Step 3: To learn about other malicious files, Click RECENT as illustrated in Figure 3.14.

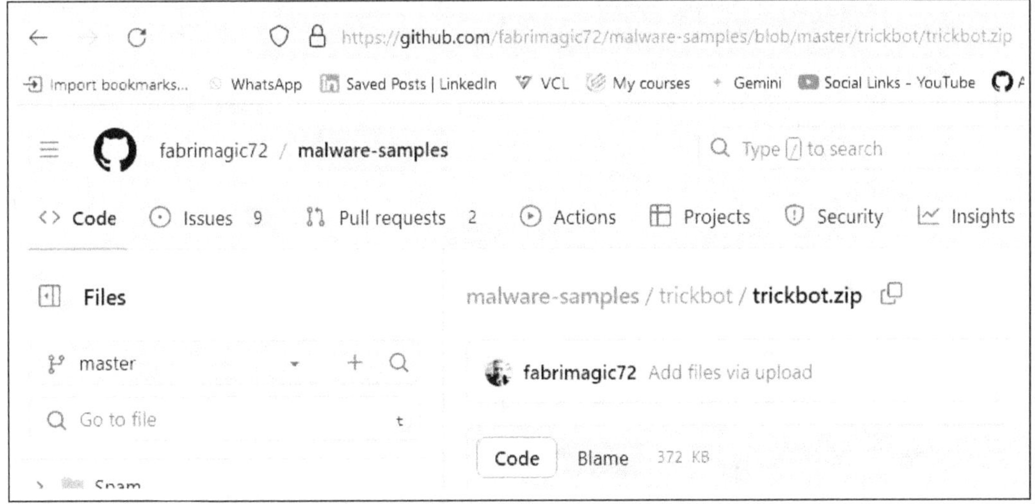

Figure 3.12 Download malware sample.

Figure 3.13 Upload malware to Cukoo Cert.

Figure 3.14 View information about other malicious files.

Step 4:   Check the hash details for the executable file 'LB3.exe' as shown in Figure 3.15.

Step 5:   Submit the hashes to VirusTotal as shown in Figure 3.16.

Step 6:   Figure 3.17 confirms this hash as malicious since 64 AV Labs in VirusTotal mark it as RED.

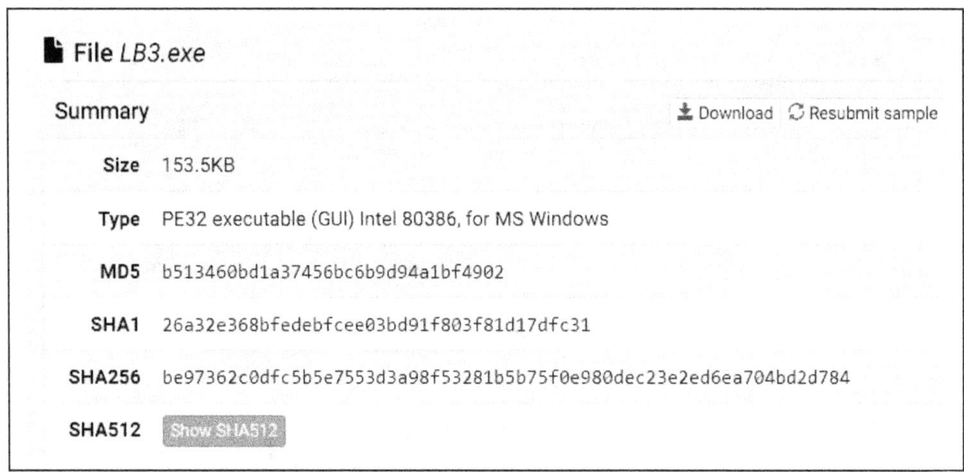

Figure 3.15 Details for executable.

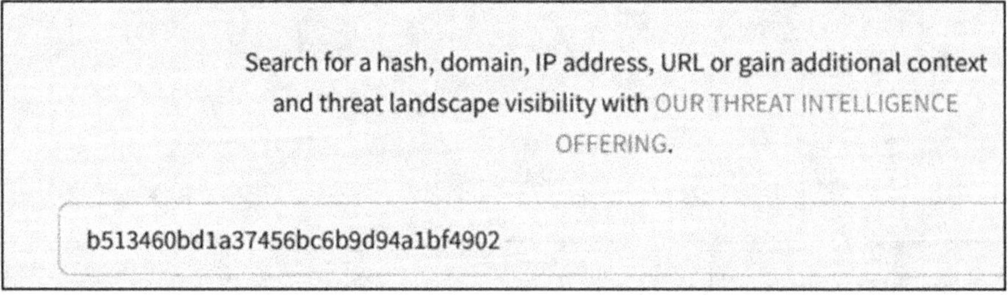

Figure 3.16 Submit hashes to VirusTotal.

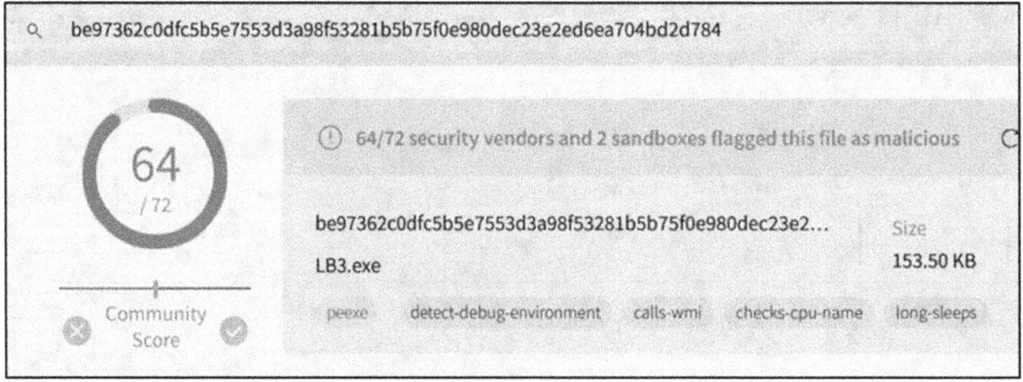

Figure 3.17 Security vendors confirm hash as malicious.

Step 7:   Figure 3.18 displays the details found on VirusTotal for the hash.
Step 8:   Figure 3.19 displays the malicious DLLs downloaded by the malicious executable to replace them in user OS location in C:\Windows\Systems32 folder.
Step 9:   Groove:PathMutex found keyword from initial analysis. Google for these IoCs confirms URLs about VirusTotal mentions are found regarding this malware. Figure 3.20 displays the VirusTotal result for this Hash string.

Imphash	914685b69f2ac2ff61b6b0f1883a054d
SSDEEP	3072:TqJogYkcSNm9V7DVnRobzucXlABZ7bMDztv11nIxT:Tq2kc4m9tDVnRMn1mMDztvY
TLSH	T10CE36C11F15ED073C87718F22726A17DB3EA4D2C1AA57847EAE80F88BCA49232F4555F
File type	Win32 EXE executable windows win32 pe peexe
Magic	PE32 executable (GUI) Intel 80386, for MS Windows
TrID	Win32 Dynamic Link Library (generic) (25%) Win16 NE executable (generic) (19.1%) Win32 Executable
Magika	CT_PEBIN
File size	153.50 KB (157184 bytes)

Figure 3.18 Hash details found on VirusTotal.

Figure 3.19 Malicious DLLs imported into user systems.

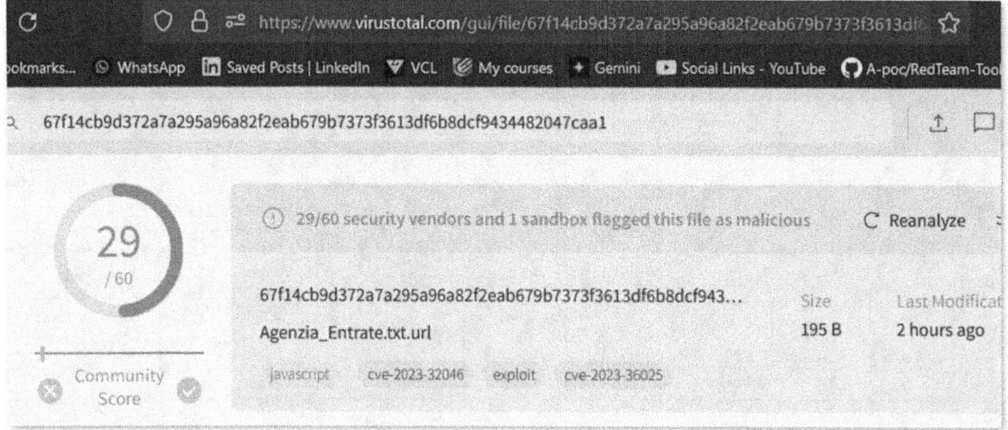

Figure 3.20 VirusTotal results for malicious hash.

Step 10: Figure 3.21 displays the details from the Hash as the file type confirms the file as a Javascript.

Step 11: Figure 3.22 displays the VirusTotal Graph feature, which reveals details about this JavaScript file as well as the contacted five domains, two IP addresses and four URLs, which raises a RED flag.

Step 12: Figure 3.23 reveals each of the contacted Domains, URLs and IP Addresses which can be used for further investigation.

File type	JavaScript source javascript js
Magic	MS Windows 95 Internet shortcut text (URL=<file://109.248.11.162/Agenzia/server.exe>),
TrID	file seems to be plain text/ASCII (0%)
File size	195 B (195 bytes)

Figure 3.21 File reveals JavaScript.

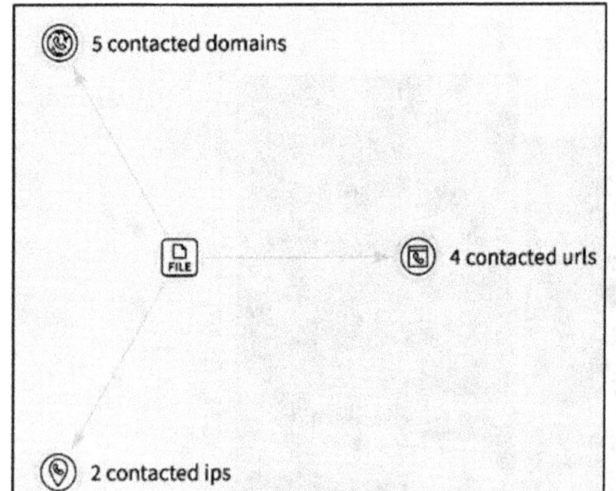

Figure 3.22 Domains, IP and URLs contacted revealed.

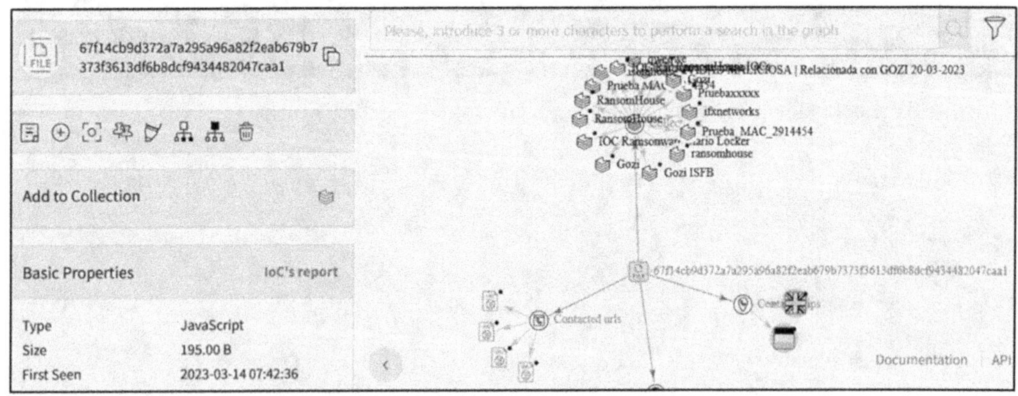

Figure 3.23 Details of contacted artefacts.

While the internal behaviors of malware, such as process injection and keylogging, are critical for endpoint detection, network-level behaviors offer equally valuable intelligence. One particularly powerful tool in the cyber threat intelligence (CTI) arsenal is passive DNS (PDNS). Unlike traditional DNS queries, which resolve domain names into IP addresses in real-time, PDNS focuses on capturing and analyzing DNS traffic as it occurs across the internet. This approach aggregates data from multiple vantage points, including sensors deployed at internet exchange points and recursive resolvers. What makes PDNS invaluable is its ability to reconstruct the historical relationships between domains and IP addresses. By maintaining a record of these associations over time, analysts can trace the evolution of a domain's hosting infrastructure. This is particularly useful when investigating command-and-control (C2) servers used by malware. Adversaries frequently rotate their infrastructure to evade detection, using dynamic DNS services or frequently registering new domains. PDNS enables analysts to follow these changes, uncovering previously unknown IOCs and mapping out the adversary's infrastructure.

Moreover, PDNS data supports proactive detection. By correlating observed DNS queries on a local network with known malicious domain histories, defenders can flag suspicious activity even before a full compromise has occurred. This shifts the detection model from reactive to predictive, aligning with modern CTI practices aimed at anticipation and prevention. Another advantage of PDNS is its non-intrusive nature. Because it relies on observed traffic rather than active queries, it avoids alerting the adversary. This stealthy aspect makes it particularly suitable for large-scale monitoring and retrospective analysis. Furthermore, the use of PDNS has expanded beyond simple threat attribution. In some cases, it contributes to threat actor profiling, campaign clustering, and tracking the spread of malware families across geographic regions.

Some of the features revealed by PSDNS are:

- Uncover Hidden Relationships: PDNS excels at revealing connections between domains and IPs that traditional methods might miss. This is because malicious actors often try to hide their infrastructure by frequently changing IP addresses. PDNS data can show this history, helping identify potential threats.
- Threat Hunting: Security analysts use PDNS to proactively search for suspicious activity. By looking for anomalies in DNS data, like rapid changes in IP addresses or new domains linked to known malicious IPs, they can identify potential threats before they cause harm.
- Investigation and Forensics: In an incident response scenario, PDNS data can be crucial for piecing together the timeline of an attack. By examining historical DNS records, investigators can see how domains and IPs were used and identify other compromised systems.
- Improved Threat Intelligence Feeds: PDNS data can be integrated with other threat intelligence feeds to provide a more comprehensive picture of the threat landscape. This allows security teams to prioritize threats and make informed decisions about how to protect their systems.

Passive DNS can help answer:

- Where did this domain point in the past?
- What domain names are hosted by a nameserver?
- What domain names point into a given IP network?
- What sub-domains exist under a certain domain name?

3.5.2 Hands-on exercise: PassiveDNS

Step 1:   Open https://DnsDumper.com and enter a domain name to investigate, as shown in Figure 3.24.

Step 2:   To discover the Surface Infrastructure of a domain, use https://SecurityTrials.com as presented in Figure 3.25.

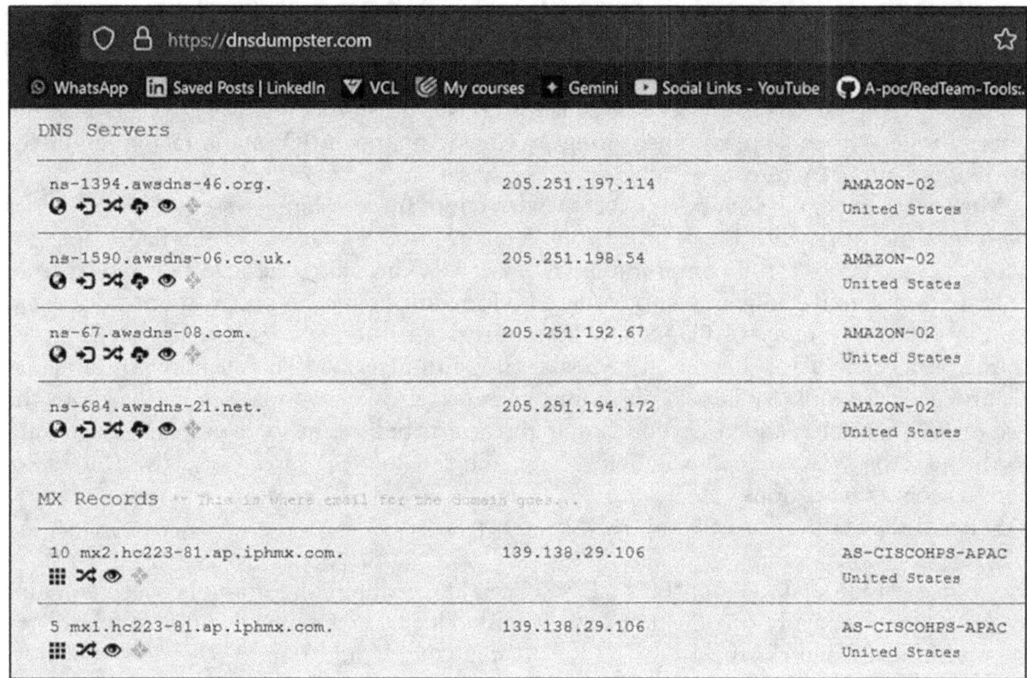

Figure 3.24 DNSDumper investigate a domain.

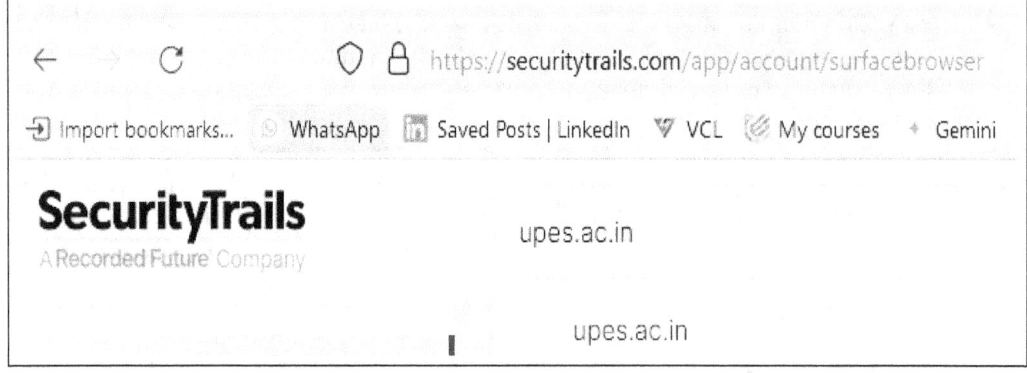

Figure 3.25 SecurityTrials domain check.

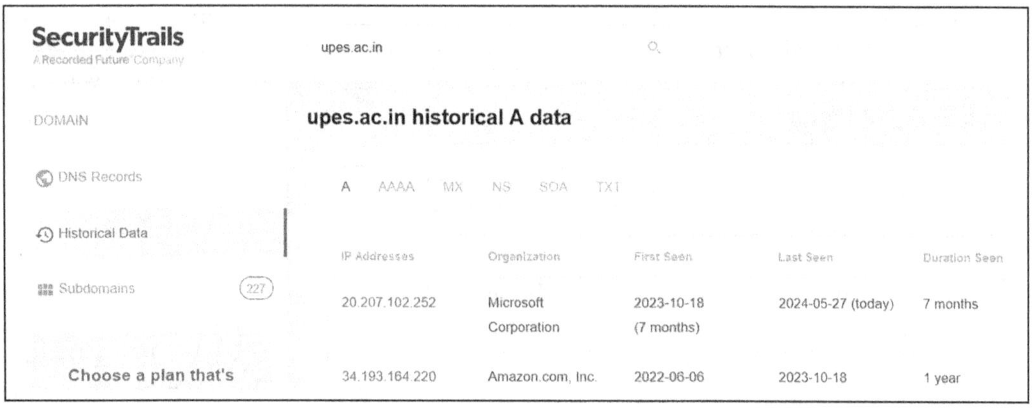

The following is a reproduction of a SecurityTrails portal screen:

	IP Addresses	Organization	First Seen	Last Seen	Duration Seen
	20.207.102.252	Microsoft Corporation	2023-10-18 (7 months)	2024-05-27 (today)	7 months
	34.193.164.220	Amazon.com, Inc.	2022-06-06	2023-10-18	1 year

SecurityTrails — A Recorded Future Company — upes.ac.in

DOMAIN — **upes.ac.in historical A data**

DNS Records — A AAAA MX NS SOA TXT

Historical Data

Subdomains (227)

Choose a plan that's

Figure 3.26 Domain historical information.

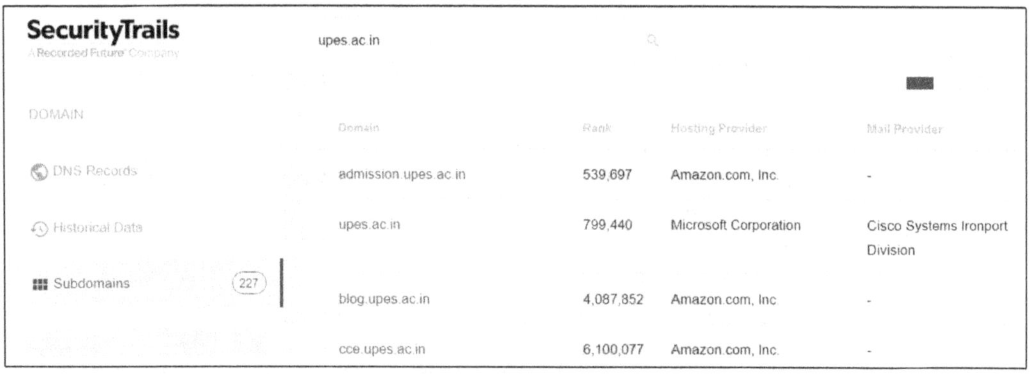

The following is a reproduction of a SecurityTrails portal screen:

Domain	Rank	Hosting Provider	Mail Provider
admission.upes.ac.in	539,697	Amazon.com, Inc.	-
upes.ac.in	799,440	Microsoft Corporation	Cisco Systems Ironport Division
blog.upes.ac.in	4,087,852	Amazon.com, Inc	-
cce.upes.ac.in	6,100,077	Amazon.com, Inc.	-

SecurityTrails — A Recorded Future Company — upes.ac.in

DOMAIN

DNS Records

Historical Data

Subdomains (227)

Figure 3.27 Submains discovered.

Step 3: This portal reveals the Historical Data as illustrated in Figure 3.26.

Step 4: SecurityTrials can also reveal the Sub-domains for a website, as presented in Figure 3.27.

3.6 CONCLUSION

This chapter presents the view of how static and dynamic analysis techniques form the backbone of modern threat hunting practices. Through the integration of these methods, cybersecurity professionals can proactively detect, classify, and understand malicious activity beyond traditional signature-based detection. Static analysis offers valuable insights into the composition of suspicious files, including metadata, file signatures, and structural elements, aiding in early identification and classification of threats. Dynamic analysis, on the other hand, reveals real-time behaviors such as process injection, system manipulation, and network communications that help expose sophisticated malware and zero-day exploits. The combination of these methods enables analysts to generate complete threat profiles and uncover advanced attacker tactics. Tools like VirusTotal, Cuckoo Sandbox, and the use of YARA rules further enhance the depth of analysis by offering collaborative and automated capabilities. The chapter also emphasized the significance of threat intelligence sources, passive DNS, and sandbox environments to correlate artifacts and behaviors. Ultimately, by combining proactive data collection with behavioral forensics and contextual understanding, this approach empowers defenders to detect threats earlier, respond faster, and mitigate risks more effectively. The future of threat hunting lies in this adaptive, evidence-based methodology that evolves alongside emerging attack vectors.

MULTIPLE CHOICE QUESTIONS

1. A threat hunter observes a spike in outbound traffic to an IP in Eastern Europe. Internal EDR logs show a strange PowerShell script launching at 3 AM from a finance workstation. The hunter develops a hypothesis that the script might be downloading a second-stage payload. To validate the hypothesis, the hunter must collect and pivot across the right data sources. Which source should be prioritized first?

   A. Historical DNS logs
   B. Endpoint process execution logs (EDR)
   C. HR user-access logs
   D. Firewall ACL change logs

   Correct Answer: B
   Reason: EDR process execution logs provide visibility into the PowerShell script's parent process, command-line arguments, and indicators pointing to malware download. Why others are wrong:
   - A gives context but not execution detail.
   - C irrelevant to malware activity.
   - D relates to configuration changes, not threat validation.

2. A malware sample is found on a compromised host. Static analysis reveals an unusual timestamp, a self-signed certificate, and multiple uncommon DLL imports. The analyst wants to cluster this malware with similar samples from a known APT. Which static feature best supports clustering?

   A. File size
   B. imphash
   C. File icon metadata
   D. PE header checksum

   Correct Answer: B
   Reason: imphash groups malware based on imported DLLs/functions, strongly correlating with malware families. Why others are wrong:
   - A varies widely, not a reliable indicator.
   - C is easily changed to evade detection.
   - D often modified or meaningless for clustering.

3. During dynamic analysis in Cuckoo Sandbox, a sample uses WriteProcessMemory(), SetThreadContext(), and ResumeThread() on explorer.exe. The analyst suspects advanced process injection. What is the malware most likely trying to achieve?

   A. Increase CPU usage to crash the system
   B. Hide its execution inside a legitimate process
   C. Create persistence via scheduled tasks
   D. Scan ports on the internal network

Correct Answer: B

Reason: This API sequence is classic process-injection to hide malicious execution under explorer.exe. Why others are wrong:

- A not related to these APIs.
- C persistence uses different API sets.
- D network scanning does not require process injection.

4. A suspicious binary was analyzed, showing usage of SetWindowsHookEx() with WH_KEYBOARD_LL and WH_MOUSE_LL parameters. No encryption or network activity was observed. Which threat behavior is this most indicative of?

   A. Data exfiltration via DNS tunnelling
   B. System-level privilege escalation
   C. Local keylogging and user surveillance
   D. Ransomware encryption routines

Correct Answer: C

Reason: Low-level keyboard/mouse hooks directly indicate keylogger or surveillance malware. Why others are wrong:

- A requires DNS queries.
- B not tied to hook APIs.
- D requires file-modifying behavior.

5. An organization creates a new YARA rule for a malware family abusing a stolen certificate. To determine how long the threat has been active, the analyst retro-hunts the rule on VirusTotal. What does retro-hunting primarily allow?

   A. Executing the malware in a sandbox
   B. Scanning historical samples in VirusTotal's archive
   C. Checking domain reputation via PDNS
   D. Mapping attacker infrastructure using graph view

Correct Answer: B

Reason: Retro-hunt matches YARA rules against older samples in VirusTotal's database. Why others are wrong:

- A dynamic analysis is separate.
- C not related to retro-hunt.
- D uses VirusTotal Graph, not retro-hunt.

6. An analyst infiltrates an underground forum with a sock-puppet identity. Members discuss a new loader malware and upload live payloads. The analyst plans to collect samples. What is the greatest risk?

   A. Misinterpreting attacker slang
   B. Downloader infecting the analyst's machine if not isolated
   C. Not receiving forum upvotes
   D. Missing out on vendor-specific signatures

Correct Answer: B

Reason: Live malware on underground forums can infect analyst systems if isolation (air gapped VM) is not used. Why others are wrong:

- A affects comprehension, not risk.
- C irrelevant.
- D is minor; signatures can be obtained elsewhere.

7. A high-interaction honeypot deployed in the DMZ logs repeated credential stuffing attempts using real employee usernames. Analysts suspect internal credential leakage. What should be the *first* investigation step?

   A. Blocking the attacker's IP ranges immediately
   B. Checking if employee credentials were leaked on dark web forums
   C. Updating firewall NAT rules
   D. Replacing the honeypot with a low-interaction version

   Correct Answer: B
   Reason: Real usernames indicate exposed credentials; dark web leaks must be checked. Why others are wrong:
   - A may block but doesn't address the leakage source.
   - C irrelevant to credential stuffing.
   - D reduces intelligence visibility.

8. A SOC is overwhelmed with threat feeds, internal logs, OSINT, and dark-web intel. They struggle to track source trustworthiness. Which CMF attribute helps prioritize reliable sources?

   A. TTL (time to live)
   B. First Seen timestamp
   C. Source trust rating
   D. MD5 hash of the source URL

   Correct Answer: C
   Reason: CMF includes source trustworthiness, enabling prioritization. Why others are wrong:
   - A unrelated.
   - B helps with age, not trust.
   - D meaningless for Intel reliability.

9. A suspicious sample crashes every time analysts run it in the sandbox. However, static analysis reveals encrypted strings and anti-VM checks. What should the analyst do next?

   A. Ignore the sample due to instability
   B. Use static string deobfuscation and unpacking techniques
   C. Switch to PDNS lookup
   D. Only check the file against blacklist feeds

   Correct Answer: B
   Reason: Anti-VM behavior requires bypassing anti-analysis techniques through static unpacking. Why others are wrong:
   - A is unacceptable in threat hunting.
   - C PDNS does not help with internal behavior.
   - D yields limited intelligence.

10. During an incident, analysts see outbound queries to "abc-update-checker.com". PDNS reveals the domain previously resolved to multiple IPs in China, Russia, and Brazil within hours. What does this most likely indicate?

    A. Normal CDN load balancing
    B. Fast-flux infrastructure used by malware
    C. Benign domain parking
    D. Cloud provider migration

Correct Answer: B

Reason: Rapid rotation of IPs across countries with short TTL strongly indicates fast-flux C2 architecture. Why others are wrong:

- A CDNs rotate within regions, not global random IPs.
- C domain parking uses static parking IPs.
- D migrations are slower and predictable.

11. Dynamic sandbox analysis shows LB3.exe dropping DLLs into C:\Windows\System32 and modifying registry Run keys. VirusTotal shows 64 vendors flag it as malicious. What does this combination of behaviors most strongly indicate?

    A. Harmless system patcher
    B. Trojan with persistence and DLL replacement
    C. Browser plugin installation
    D. Keylogging-only malware

Correct Answer: B

Reason: DLL replacement + Run key modification are classic Trojan persistence methods. Why others are wrong:

- A patchers don't modify system32 DLLs.
- C plugins don't target system DLL paths.
- D keyloggers don't replace DLLs.

12. A malware family uses similar import tables, C2 domain patterns, and certificate misuse across multiple campaigns. Which analysis method best supports attribution?

    A. Clustering based on static features
    B. Checking file size variations
    C. Verifying UI strings
    D. Comparing PE checksum values

Correct Answer: A

Reason: Clustering via imphash, static metadata, and domain similarities directly supports attribution. Why others are wrong:

- B not meaningful.
- C easy to fake.
- D checksum changes on small edits.

13. A malware sample behaves benignly in the sandbox but is reported malicious in the wild. The analyst suspects sandbox evasion. Which evidence supports this suspicion?

    A. The sample logs DNS queries inside the sandbox
    B. The sample checks for common VM artifacts like MAC vendor or processes
    C. The sample uses static API imports only
    D. The sample writes logs in %TEMP%

Correct Answer: B

Reason: Checking VM artifacts is a hallmark of sandbox/VM evasion. Why others are wrong:

- A indicates activity, not evasion.
- C unrelated.
- D normal, not evasion.

14. An analyst sees that a malicious SHA256 hash contacted five unknown domains and two suspicious IPs. VirusTotal Graph shows interconnections with known malware clusters. What advantage does the graph provide?

    A. Identifying encryption algorithms in the malware
    B. Visualizing infrastructure links to expose related campaigns
    C. Verifying if DLL files are digitally signed
    D. Determining CPU architecture of malware

    Correct Answer: B
    Reason: Graph visualizes linked domains, IPs, and artifacts to identify campaign structure. Why others are wrong:
    - A, C, D are unrelated.

15. A poorly configured honeypot in the DMZ allows outbound traffic. An attacker uses it to pivot and launch attacks on external systems. Which security principle was violated?

    A. Principle of least privilege
    B. Honeypot must not allow outbound unrestricted traffic
    C. SIEM correlation rules
    D. Use of encrypted tunnels

    Correct Answer: B
    Reason: Honeypots must never be allowed to act as attack platforms. Outbound traffic must be isolated. Why others are wrong:
    - A partially related but not specific.
    - C not the core reason.
    - D irrelevant.

REFERENCES

1. K. Baker, "What is cyber threat hunting? [proactive guide] | CrowdStrike," *Crowdstrike.com*, Mar. 4, 2025. https://www.crowdstrike.com/en-us/cybersecurity-101/threat-intelligence/threat-hunting
2. K. Baker, "12 types of malware + examples that you should know," *Crowdstrike.com*, 2024. https://www.crowdstrike.com/en-us/cybersecurity-101/malware/types-of-malware
3. VirusTotal, "VirusTotal," *virustotal.com*. https://www.virustotal.com/gui
4. M. Motoyama, D. McCoy, K. Levchenko, S. Savage, and G. M. Voelker, "An analysis of underground forums," *Proceedings of the ACM SIGCOMM Conference on Internet Measurement Conference*, Nov. 2011. https://doi.org/10.1145/2068816.2068824
5. Fortinet, "What is a honeypot? Meaning, types, benefits, and more," *Fortinet*, 2023. https://www.fortinet.com/resources/cyberglossary/what-is-honeypot
6. K. Baker, "Malware analysis: Steps & examples | CrowdStrike," *Crowdstrike.com*, Apr. 17, 2023. https://www.crowdstrike.com/en-us/cybersecurity-101/malware/malware-analysis

Chapter 4

Operationalizing CTI

4.1 CYBER THREAT INTELLIGENCE FEEDS

Cyber Threat Intelligence (CTI) feeds are data streams, automated or curated, that deliver structured threat information such as indicators of compromise (IoCs), tactics, techniques, and procedures (TTPs), and contextual metadata. These feeds are essential for operational defenders, enabling timely detection, investigation, and mitigation of cyber threats. They serve as the backbone for proactive security, facilitating everything from real-time alerting to strategic trend analysis. At their core, CTI feeds translate raw data (IPs, domains, hashes, file signatures, and behavioral patterns) into actionable intelligence tailored to specific security use cases. For example, a security operations center (SOC) might integrate a malicious IP feed to automatically flag network traffic for investigation, while security analysts might use contextual TTP data to anticipate advanced persistent threat (APT) behavior. The ability to filter, prioritize, and operationalize these feeds defines their practical value in modern defense architectures.

In recent years, threat intelligence has evolved considerably. Where early feeds focused narrowly on IoCs, modern CTI feeds now encompass richer context: malware family attribution, kill chain stages, behavioral analytics, campaign tagging, and even geolocation. By enhancing each indicator with such context, organizations can perform triage more effectively, and analysts can rapidly pivot from detection to attribution and remediation. For instance, a hash labelled with its associated campaign and known C2 infrastructure empowers a security analyst to not just detect but understand and disrupt threat operations. Integration is a key success factor. CTI feeds are typically consumed via STIX/TAXII protocols, allowing machine-to-machine exchange and often interact with SIEMs, firewalls, EDR systems, and SOAR platforms. Recent platforms support automated ingestion and cross-mapping across feeds, enabling orchestration: when a malicious domain is spotted in network telemetry, a SOAR playbook can automatically quarantine assets, open a ticket, and contextualize the threat with intelligence from multiple CTI sources.

Threat intelligence feeds fall into two broad categories: open-source and commercial. The former, led by community-driven projects like AlienVault OTX and MISP, offers transparency and cost-effective access. The latter such as commercial platforms with proprietary data and deep attribution benefits from higher-value insights such as vulnerability exploit likelihood, zero-day activity, and advanced campaign attribution. Hybrid models are emerging, blending open observables with paid enrichment to deliver comprehensive coverage. In 2025, we see CTI evolving with technology trends. For instance, Generative AI is increasingly used to enrich raw indicators with contextual write-ups and suggested detections. Behavioral analytics platforms are mining network metadata at scale, generating dynamic feeds that flag

DOI: 10.1201/9781003730583-4

anomalous beaconing or DGA (Domain Generation Algorithm) activity in real time. This shift complements static indicators with behavioral "signals," yielding far fewer false positives and richer insight into emerging threats. Some recent examples illustrate these developments.

- StealthVector APT Campaign (March 2025) – Security researchers published a dataset detailing an espionage operation targeting energy firms in central Europe. The campaign used stealthy DLL sideloading and covert DNS-over-HTTPS channels. A CTI provider converted this into a feed that included IoCs (IPs, hashes), TTPs (DLL sideloading, DNS-over-HTTPS usage), MITRE ATT&CK mappings, and suggested YARA rules. SOCs that subscribed to such feeds were able to detect early-stage infections and isolate systems before data exfiltration could occur.
- CryptoMine Botnet Takedown (June 2024) – An international joint operation between law enforcement and cybersecurity firms led to the takedown of a global cryptomining botnet. The threat intelligence generated from the operation was rapidly shared via commercial CTI services, along with network indicators and associated campaign metadata. Many organizations integrated that intelligence to purge persistent miner infections, protecting infrastructures and reducing power consumption – a clear example of CTI in action at scale.
- Behavioral CTI Feed Example: DNS Anomaly Insights – in late 2024, several Managed Detection and Response (MDR) vendors began offering streaming feeds based on DNS queries indicative of potential ransomware communication. These feeds included context like domain age, registration periods, international DNS resolution patterns, and rate of failed resolutions – all processed via machine learning. Subscription to such feeds equips defenders to catch ransomware preparations before encryption begins.

CTI feeds are also central to public-private collaboration in cybersecurity. Governments such as the U.S. CISA and EU's ENISA publish MITRE-aligned advisory feeds, including TLP-designated data that can be cross-consumed by industries. This ensures that both public and private entities are aligned in their detection strategies. For example, after the 2024 Log4Shell revelations, early detection feeds focused not only on IPs known to be scanning or exploiting victims, but also on full HTTP payload signatures and scanning behavior, a richer feed that better serves detection use.

When evaluating CTI feeds, defenders consider seven key criteria:

- Timeliness – How quickly indicators are shared after discovery.
- Relevancy – Suitability to the organization's geography, industry, and technology stack.
- Accuracy – False positive rates and reputation quality.
- Context – Availability of TTP mapping, attribution, and purpose of indicators like infecting, persistence, and C2.
- Format & Integration – STIX/TAXII, JSON, CSV, API, and compatibility with tooling.
- Enrichment – Integration with vulnerability intelligence, geodata, passive DNS intelligence, and malware classifications.
- Privacy and Licensing – Shareability restrictions or legal requirements like TLP traffic-light restrictions.

4.2 CTI FEED PLATFORMS

Recent advancements also include automated feed summarization: natural language briefs accompany raw CTI to help executives and security managers grasp high-level trends. Some vendors provide per-feed performance metrics, displaying false positive counts, hit-per-feed success rates, and coverage overlaps to help subscription decisions. In practical deployment, CTI feeds are used in layered defense. A firewall can block known malicious IPs; an EDR system can detect suspicious file hashes; SIEM correlation can match beaconing domains against behavioral context. On top of that, human-driven threat hunting can leverage CTI to pivot on initial compromises, explore lateral movement, and hunt hidden persistence. CTI enrichment is also used by red teams to emulate adversaries more precisely during penetration testing and purple team exercises.

Looking forward, CTI feeds are evolving toward two major trends:

- Predictive Intelligence: Platforms are embedding forecasting models to anticipate next steps of adversaries, e.g., predicting likely C2 domain patterns or TTP sequences.
- Industry-focused Sharing Consortiums: Sectors like healthcare, finance, and critical infrastructure are standing up feed-sharing communities with dedicated feeds tailored to sector-specific threats and regulatory needs.

CTI feeds are a vital element of modern cybersecurity, transforming dispersed threat data into defensive advantage. Through richer context, improved speed, and better sector alignment, feeds are helping defenders stay ahead of adversaries in a dynamic cyber battlefield. As intelligence models become more predictive and industries collaborate more closely, CTI feeds will remain a keystone of resilient cyber defense strategies. Numerous open-source threat intelligence feeds provide real-time information on cyber threats, malicious activities, and emerging vulnerabilities, offering valuable resources for security professionals. These feeds aggregate data from various sources, such as malware repositories, network traffic analysis, honeypots, and community-contributed reports to deliver timely insights into the evolving threat landscape. Cybersecurity teams rely on this intelligence to proactively detect IOCs, assess potential attack vectors, and fortify their defenses accordingly. By integrating these feeds into their security operations, organizations can enhance their situational awareness, improve response times, and align their threat detection mechanisms with the latest adversarial tactics. As a result, open-source threat intelligence has become a foundational component of modern cybersecurity practices, enabling informed decision-making and adaptive risk mitigation strategies.

4.2.1 AlienVault open threat exchange

AlienVault Open Threat Exchange (OTX) [1] is a freely accessible threat intelligence platform (TIP) that connects a worldwide network of cybersecurity professionals and researchers. Designed as a collaborative ecosystem, OTX enables participants to contribute, share, and analyze real-time threat data, enhancing the global defense against emerging cyber threats. One of the platform's core strengths lies in its ability to crowdsource IoCs, collecting and distributing over 19 million new IoC records daily, as illustrated in Figure 4.1. This dynamic feed of threat intelligence, known as "pulses," allows users to stay informed about the latest malware signatures, attack vectors, and vulnerable systems. OTX supports a wide range of data formats for seamless integration, including STIX, OpenIoC, MAEC, JSON, and CSV, enabling organizations to automate updates within their security systems effectively. By fostering a collaborative research environment, OTX empowers security teams to make informed decisions quickly, reduce threat response time, and strengthen their defensive posture. Widely recognized as a foundational tool in the cybersecurity landscape, this open-source TIP plays a crucial role in helping organizations bolster their threat detection efforts without bearing the burden of added financial costs. Its strength lies in its collaborative framework, which harnesses input from a global network of contributors. This collective participation ensures the platform remains rich with current and varied threat intelligence, drawn from real-world observations and incidents. By facilitating timely sharing and analysis

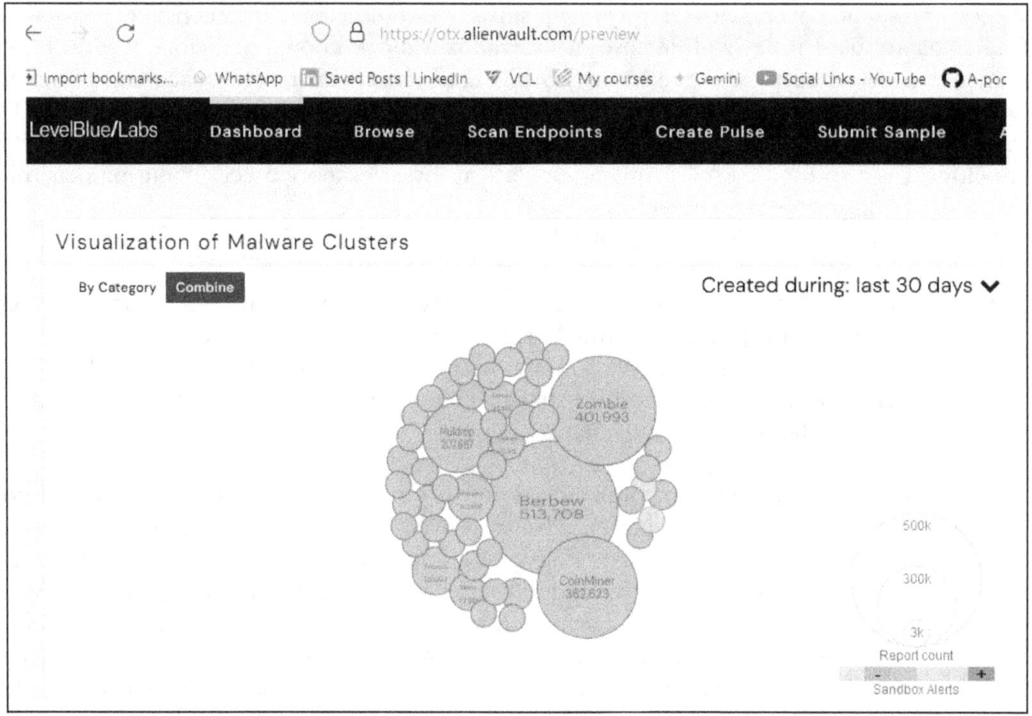

Figure 4.1 AlienVault dashboard.

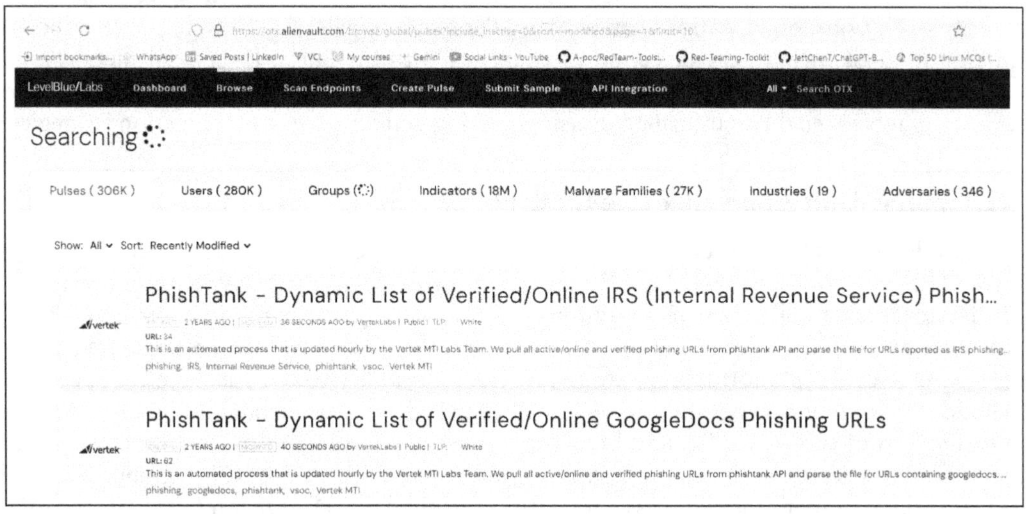

Figure 4.2 AlienVault.

of emerging threats, it empowers security teams to proactively respond to evolving attack vectors and maintain a resilient defense posture.

You can customize your needs by obtaining pre-filtered data and even tailor the feeds based on device types like endpoints or API connections, as shown in Figure 4.2. If any relevant information lies outside your specified feed criteria, it is still made accessible through linked references within the provided data records, ensuring comprehensive coverage.

4.2.2 CTI4SOC

SOCRadar's CTI4SOC [2] is an advanced threat intelligence solution specifically built to enhance the capabilities of SOC teams. This standalone platform streamlines threat detection and response by offering 12 integrated modules tailored for the unique demands of SOC analysts. Unlike conventional threat intelligence tools, CTI4SOC harnesses the power of big data to consolidate critical threat insights from multiple sources into a single, cohesive, and context-rich interface.

Rather than requiring analysts to sift through fragmented data across various platforms, CTI4SOC intelligently filters and organizes threat intelligence. It mimics an analyst's perspective to extract relevant, actionable information and presents it with appropriate context, enabling rapid hypothesis formation and efficient investigation. With direct access to expertly curated threat reports from SOCRadar and other trusted entities, the platform empowers analysts to stay ahead of emerging threats.

One of CTI4SOC's key advantages lies in its ability to track sector-specific threat actors. These adversaries often exhibit unique behavioral traits, motivations, and attack strategies. By understanding the TTPs of such actors, analysts can enhance their threat modeling and improve detection accuracy. The platform also enables users to maintain watchlists for high-priority threat actors, helping SOC teams proactively monitor ongoing malicious activity.

Moreover, CTI4SOC includes a powerful Threat Hunting module, allowing security professionals to search for critical threat indicators such as malware signatures, IP addresses, command-and-control (C2) servers, and malicious domains. Designed for seamless integration, the API-ready architecture ensures that all collected intelligence can be efficiently utilized in real-time defense strategies. In essence, CTI4SOC not only simplifies the threat intelligence process but also equips SOC analysts with the tools necessary to defend against sophisticated cyber threats in a rapidly changing digital landscape.

4.2.3 DOCGuard

DOCGuard [3] is an advanced malware analysis platform designed to seamlessly integrate with Secure Email Gateways (SEGs) and Security Orchestration, Automation, and Response (SOAR) tools. It introduces a novel static analysis approach called structural analysis, which deconstructs malicious files into their structural components. These fragments are then processed through core analytical engines based on their internal file architecture. This enables precise malware identification, extraction of IoCs without false positives, and the detection of sophisticated evasion techniques such as sequence encoding and embedded document encryption. The platform is designed to handle a broad spectrum of file types, ranging from standard office documents and PDFs to web files such as HTML or HTM, as well as shortcut links and scripting formats like JScript. It also accommodates various disk image formats, including IMG, ISO, and VHD files, along with virtual contact files and compressed archive formats such as RAR, ZIP, and 7z. Once a file is analyzed, the structural insights are presented through an intuitive visual dashboard, providing a clear overview of the content. For developers and automated systems, the same analysis can be accessed in JSON format through a dedicated API, enabling seamless integration into existing workflows and enhancing the efficiency of data processing pipelines.

DOCGuard's innovative analysis engine is capable of inspecting files within seconds while maintaining minimal resource consumption. It accurately detects known attack patterns, ensuring high detection reliability. The system supports automated alert validation from diverse sources such as SIEMs, SOAR platforms, PhishMe, and Cofense. With its Docker-based deployment, DOCGuard can be quickly installed and integrated into existing cybersecurity frameworks. Furthermore, its recent collaboration with VirusTotal enhances the community's capabilities in document analysis, providing deeper insights into malicious documents. Through this partnership, users gain a comprehensive view of potential threats, reinforcing DOCGuard's role as a vital component in modern cyber defense strategies. Its powerful, fast, and resource-efficient architecture makes it an essential tool for organizations seeking proactive threat detection and streamlined incident response.

4.2.4 GreyNoise

GreyNoise [4] is a powerful tool designed to support CTI analysts and threat hunters by offering detailed context and clarity around security events. It collects data on internet-wide scanning activity to help distinguish between benign and malicious behaviors, effectively minimizing false positives in threat analysis as presented in Figure 4.3. By monitoring common internet scanners like Shodan and identifying threats such as SSH and Telnet worms, GreyNoise allows security professionals to separate actual threats from harmless background noise that might otherwise be overlooked by traditional SOC workflows. Through its user-friendly interface, API access, and seamless integration with existing security infrastructure, GreyNoise enables faster identification of relevant signals within large volumes of log data. This accelerates decision-making and reduces response times. Integrating GreyNoise with TIPs also enhances data enrichment, helping teams focus only on meaningful indicators.

For threat hunters, GreyNoise offers a practical advantage in identifying unusual patterns in TTPs. It also supports deeper investigation of IoCs, providing insights that reveal attacker infrastructure and campaign strategies. Overall, GreyNoise equips cybersecurity teams with a smarter approach to threat hunting by filtering out internet noise and spotlighting real threats.

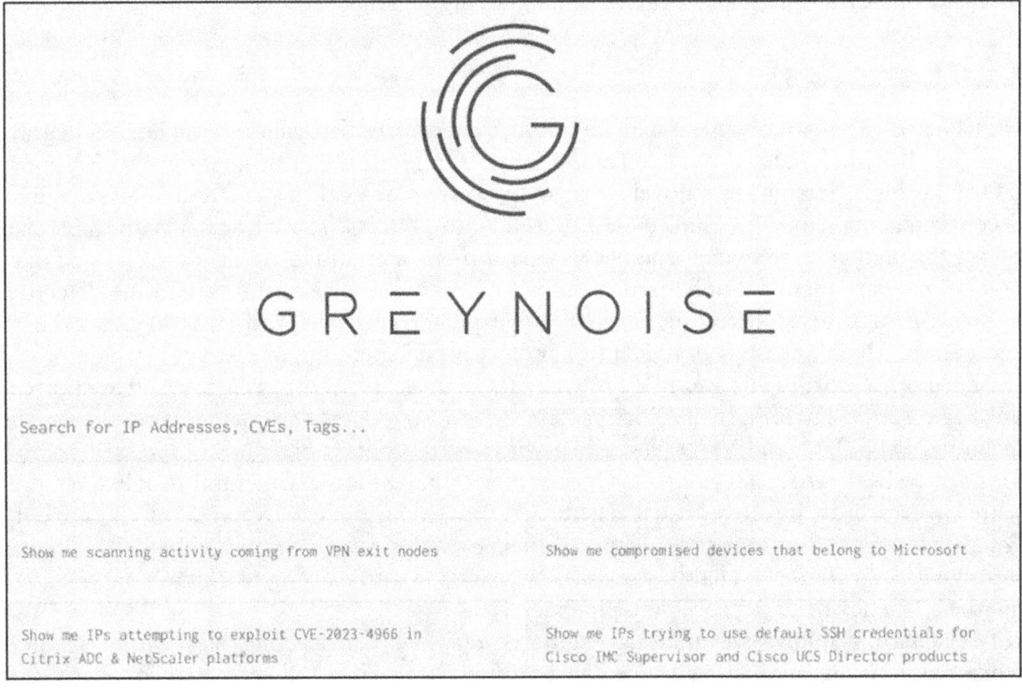

Figure 4.3 GreyNoise.

4.2.5 Intezer

Intezer [5] is a cybersecurity platform that emulates the expertise of a seasoned security analyst and reverse engineer to analyze and respond to security alerts, as displayed in Figure 4.4. Its core strength lies in a proprietary code analysis engine that has evolved significantly, allowing it to automate complex, repetitive tasks typically handled by SOC teams. Unlike traditional automation tools that focus solely on sandboxing or alert enrichment, Intezer proactively interprets threats, makes intelligent decisions, and offers actionable recommendations. This enhances incident response efficiency and reduces analyst fatigue by enabling faster, more accurate threat investigation and resolution in modern cybersecurity environments.

Intezer offers a comprehensive SOC automation solution that operates continuously to prioritize alerts, analyze threats, and initiate response actions around the clock. By leveraging intelligent automation, advanced threat detection, and guided remediation, Intezer significantly reduces the burden on security teams. This allows analysts to avoid time-consuming investigations of false positives and redundant manual processes, enabling faster, more accurate incident response. At the heart of the platform is Intezer Analyze, a unified malware investigation tool that supports static, dynamic, and genetic analysis across a wide range of file types. It assists SOC and incident response teams in rapidly identifying malware behavior, mapping threats to known malware families, extracting IoCs, and aligning with MITRE ATT&CK tactics and techniques. The tool also provides downloadable YARA rules for custom threat detection, with a free community edition available for initial exploration.

Additionally, Intezer Transformations empowers malware analysts and threat hunters with a streamlined, integrated analysis environment. It enables fast classification of suspicious files or endpoints, reduces response time, and consolidates disparate tools into one cohesive workflow. Intezer ensures secure, automated triage of threats, delivering verified and actionable alerts. It integrates seamlessly into existing workflows, offering immediate operational value without disrupting established security processes.

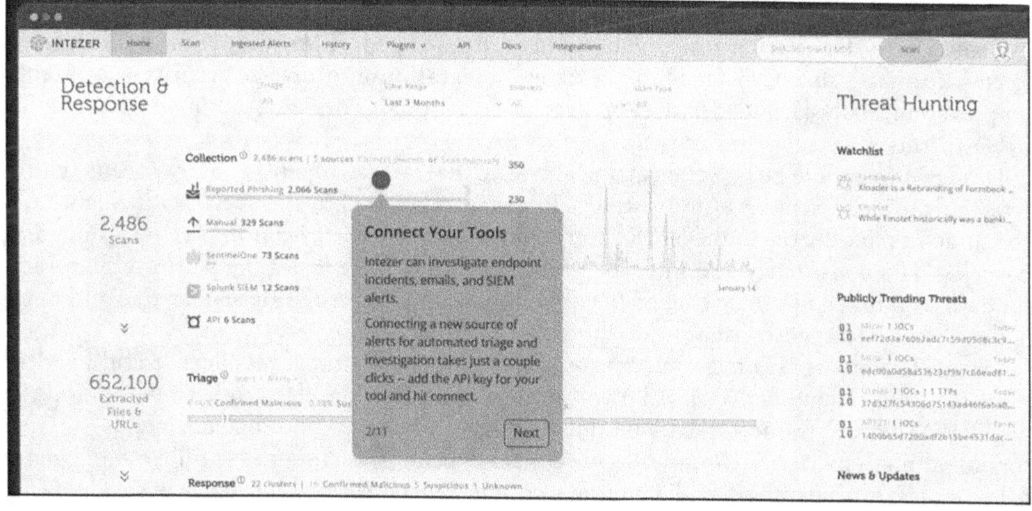

Figure 4.4 Intezer.

4.2.6 MISP threat sharing

MISP [6], initially introduced as the Malware Information Sharing Platform, is a collaborative, open-source solution tailored for the systematic sharing and analysis of CTI. Designed with community participation at its core, it enables organizations to collect, store, and distribute information related to cybersecurity incidents in a structured and efficient manner. MISP supports a wide range of data formats and observables, promoting interoperability across security teams and platforms. By fostering real-time information exchange, it helps strengthen situational awareness and accelerates threat detection and response efforts within and across organizations. Initiated by CIRCL (Computer Incident Response Centre Luxembourg), MISP supports the collection, analysis, storage, and dissemination of threat intelligence associated with malware, cyberattacks, and security incidents.

The platform enables security professionals to correlate IoCs across various sources by linking attributes to specific attack vectors, malware families, or adversarial campaigns. Its design primarily serves the needs of SOC analysts, cybersecurity teams, malware researchers, and IT professionals by offering tools that streamline threat intelligence workflows. As the platform matured, MISP expanded its focus beyond malware, incorporating fraud detection, vulnerability reporting, and threat event aggregation. It now encompasses an ecosystem of supporting tools and extensions, including PyMISP for automation, standardized taxonomies, and predefined warning lists. These additions enhance its interoperability with other systems and promote standardized data sharing practices. MISP's core mission is to strengthen collaborative cybersecurity efforts by enabling seamless information sharing across organizations. It integrates easily with various security infrastructures such as SIEMs, log analyzers, and Intrusion Detection Systems (IDS) (Network-based NIDS or Host-based HIDS), making it a vital tool in proactive cyber defense.

4.2.7 OpenCTI – Open CTI platform

OpenCTI [7] initiative represents a sophisticated and collaborative effort aimed at enhancing the way organizations handle CTI. Designed as a flexible and open-source platform, it enables structured collection, contextual analysis, and efficient dissemination of threat data. The project originated from a partnership between CERT-EU, which supports cybersecurity within European Union institutions, and ANSSI, France's national authority on information system security. By offering a modular architecture and support for standardized threat intelligence formats, OpenCTI facilitates seamless integration into diverse security ecosystems, empowering analysts and decision-makers with actionable insights to pre-empt evolving cyber threats.

Designed to handle both technical and strategic threat data, OpenCTI allows security professionals to store, structure, and visualize information related to cybersecurity incidents and threat actors. It adheres to the STIX2 (Structured Threat Information Expression) standard, ensuring data consistency and interoperability. Figure 4.5 illustrates the platform features a modern web-based interface backed by a powerful GraphQL API, offering flexible and interactive threat intelligence visualization and exploration.

OpenCTI supports seamless integration with other major threat intelligence and incident response tools, including MISP (Malware Information Sharing Platform), TheHive, and the MITRE ATT&CK framework. Its modular design and extensibility make it highly suitable for threat analysts, SOC teams, and cyber defense centers seeking to centralize intelligence feeds, correlate observables, and maintain a comprehensive threat knowledge base. OpenCTI ultimately empowers organizations to make informed security decisions and enhance their threat detection and response capabilities.

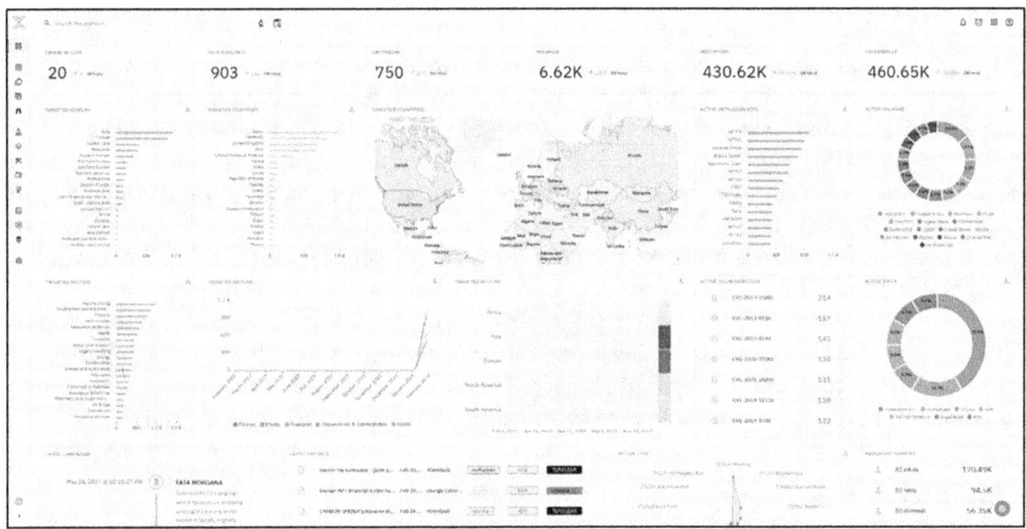

Figure 4.5 OpenCTI.

This platform integrates several critical components designed to enhance the detection, analysis, and response to cybersecurity threats. Central to its framework are modules that collect and aggregate data from diverse sources, including network logs, endpoint telemetry, open-source feeds, and proprietary intelligence. This data is normalized and enriched to provide context such as geolocation, threat actor attribution, and behavioral patterns, which aids analysts in identifying emerging threats and attack vectors. Additionally, the platform incorporates real-time correlation engines and behavioral analytics to detect anomalies indicative of malicious activity. Automation features, such as playbooks and threat scoring, streamline response efforts and reduce analyst workload. Integration with external tools like Security Information and Event Management (SIEM) systems, IDS, and ticketing platforms ensures cohesive and timely threat mitigation. Through these elements, the platform supports a proactive security posture by transforming raw data into actionable insights.

- OpenCTI delivers linked operational and strategic intelligence information through a uniform data model based on STIX2 standards.
- Automated workflows: The engine automatically draws logical conclusions to provide insights and real-time connections.
- Integration with the information technology ecosystem: Its open-source design enables simple integration with any native or third-party system.
- Advanced visual analytics enable security professionals to depict entities and their interrelations, including hierarchical or embedded associations, through dynamic and customizable visual formats.
- Analytical capabilities are enhanced by ensuring that every data point and threat indicator is traceable to its source, supporting effective assessment, prioritization, and refinement during the threat intelligence process.
- OpenCTI operates as a comprehensive CTI framework, offering robust integration options through its Python and Go APIs, complemented by an intuitive and feature-rich web-based interface.

4.2.8 Pulsedive

Pulsedive [8] is an open-source community-driven threat intel platform that offers a comprehensive approach to analyzing and enriching IoCs. By aggregating data from multiple open-source feeds, the platform enhances the contextual value of IPs, domains, and URLs using a built-in risk-scoring engine, as displayed in Figure 4.6. This helps users assess the potential threat level of each indicator. Pulsedive supports the submission, scanning, and enrichment of IoCs, while also providing risk factors that clarify why specific indicators are flagged as high-risk. It offers a centralized and real-time overview of emerging threats and malicious activities. The platform allows users to conduct in-depth searches of indicators using filters such as type, value, associated threat feeds, attributes, properties, risk level, and last seen timestamps. Threat-based searches can also be performed using parameters like threat name, aliases, categories, feed sources, and observed behavior. This functionality aids analysts in correlating, updating, and prioritizing threat intelligence for proactive cybersecurity measures.

4.2.9 VirusTotal

VirusTotal [9] is an advanced online platform that leverages the power of more than 92 antivirus engines and domain/URL reputation services to analyze suspicious files and links, as shown in Figure 4.7. It extracts relevant threat indicators using a range of integrated analysis tools. Users can upload files directly from their local machines via a browser or choose alternative submission methods such as desktop applications, browser plugins, and a RESTful public API. Among these, the web interface is prioritized for scanning tasks within public submissions. The API, which operates over HTTP, allows developers to automate file or URL submissions using any programming language, making it versatile for integration in custom workflows. Likewise, suspicious URLs can be submitted not only through the web portal but also via the same browser extensions and API, ensuring flexibility and ease of use for cybersecurity professionals and researchers. This service enhances threat intelligence by providing detailed reports on potential malware or phishing threats.

When a file, URL, or domain is submitted to a platform like VirusTotal, the results of the scan are not only returned to the person who submitted it but are also shared with trusted

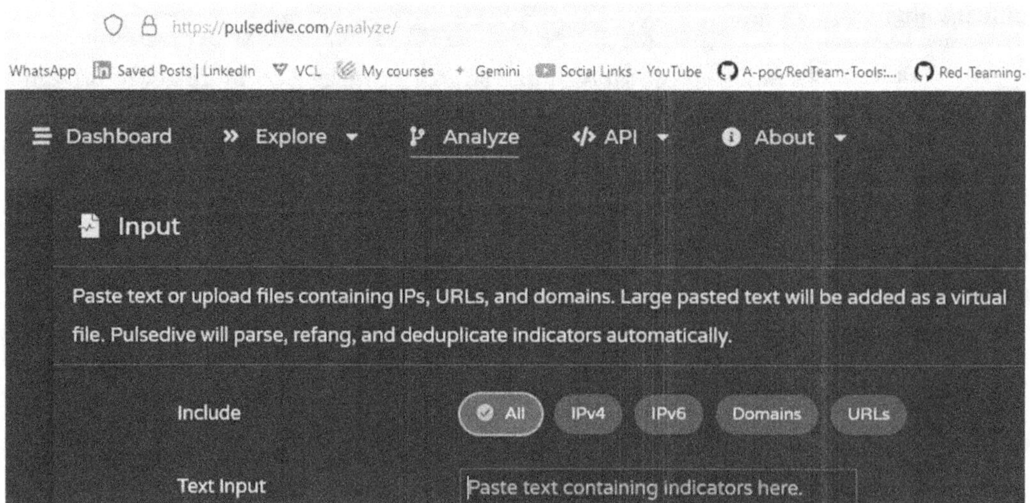

Figure 4.6 PulseDive.

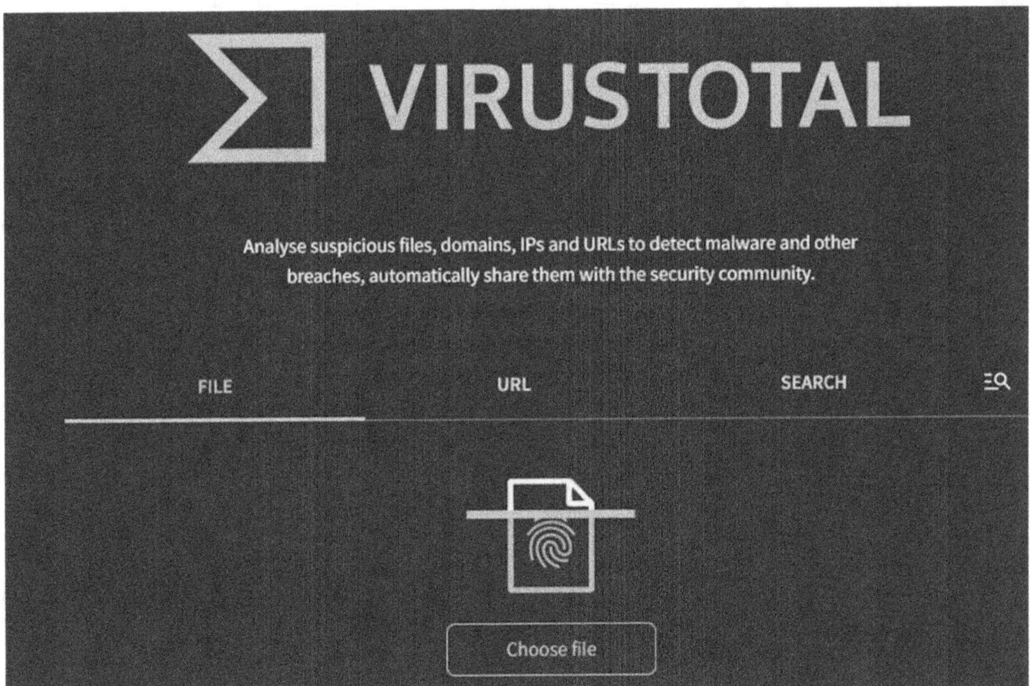

Figure 4.7 VirusTotal.

cybersecurity partners. These partners leverage the data to enhance their own threat detection systems. As a result, every submission contributes to the global effort to strengthen cybersecurity defenses and broaden threat intelligence coverage. VirusTotal's core scanning feature supports a variety of other capabilities, such as enabling user interaction through community comments and shared insights about files and URLs. This interactive platform is particularly effective in detecting malicious payloads and identifying false positives, files mistakenly flagged as threats. When a file is flagged by an antivirus engine, VirusTotal informs the user and shows the specific detection label. In the case of URLs, it categorizes them based on risk types such as phishing, malware distribution, or suspicious behavior. In the context of Threat Hunting, the process begins with gathering samples, followed by static feature extraction and dynamic behavioral analysis. This produces rich datasets. To make sense of this data, cybersecurity analysts apply clustering and correlation techniques. These methods help identify patterns, link related threats, and uncover potential IOCs.

4.3 CLUSTERING AND CORRELATION

Clustering is the next step after extracting features and behaviors (static and dynamic) from malware samples. This step stores them in an intelligent way so that the samples are classified according to the different features and behaviors that were extracted earlier. The goal is to group elements according to their shared characteristics and similarities. This helps analysts identify related threats and understand the scope of an attack campaign and classify malware based on Features and Behaviors extracted:

- Based on Static Features: Timestamp, Imphash, Ssdeep, Digital Certs…
- Based on Properties: Downloaded, Backdoor, Ransomware, Keylogger

This helps connect all the information together to make some sense to associate this information to understand the attack flow. For example, by using Graph databases display relationships between nodes for unstructured data. This is a collection of nodes and edges using NoSQL Databases. Imagine you have a list of IP addresses identified as malicious after hunting.

- Clustering – It is grouping these IPs based on geographic location, associated domains, or malware signatures. This could reveal a coordinated attack originating from a specific region or targeting a particular set of websites.
- Correlation – Identifies the relationships between different pieces of CTI data. Correlation helps analysts connect the dots, understand the bigger picture of an attack, and potentially identify the threat actor behind it.

Or let's say you have intel about a phishing campaign targeting a specific industry.

- Hunting involves gathering email content, malicious URLs, and compromised user credentials.
- Clustering categorizes these into various groups.
- Correlation analyzes the cluster to find connections between these elements, analysts can understand the attack flow, identify potential victims, and potentially link the campaign back to a known threat group. This can involve answering questions like:
  - Where are the threat actors located?
  - Who is sponsoring them?
  - What sectors or industry are they targeting?
  - What is their C2 Infrastructure? Ports used, OS, Binary, Scripts.
  - TTPs followed.
    - Initial compromise.
    - Privilege escalation.
    - Persistence.
    - Lateral movement.

4.4 ATTRIBUTION

In CTI, attribution refers to the systematic collection and examination of data linked to a cyber incident or hostile action.

- Identify names/groups.
- Find location of attacker or intermediary.
- Targets – financial/government institutions, nuclear/power plants, aerospace.
- Countries involved – North Korea ➔ South Korea, China & Russia ➔ US/EU.
- Data type – none, just destructive (MBR wiper), political, activists, Intellectual property.
- Exfil strategy – SSL-only, Fake SSL, using Diffie-Hellman key exchange.

This resulting identity includes attacker information as presented in Table 4.1.

For example, Syrian C2 servers are usually located in the same country and have Arabic & English language enabled in the OS which displays the behavior. The goal is to locate the threat actors behind the malicious clusters identified. The process typically involves the following steps:

Table 4.1 Attacker and location information

Attacker info	Location info
Attacker's Name, Alias, Email, social media ID and any related accounts.	Physical (geographic) or virtual location such as an IP address or Ethernet address. Hosting provider, TOR exit node IPs

1. Incident Response: The first step in the attribution process is incident response. This involves identifying and responding to a security incident, such as a data breach, malware infection, or network intrusion. Incident response teams will typically collect evidence and gather information about the incident to determine the scope and impact of the attack.
2. TTP Analysis: After the immediate threat has been neutralized, CTI specialists proceed with an in-depth examination of the attacker's TTPs. This process entails studying the specific tools, strategies, and operational patterns employed during the breach. The primary objective is to uncover distinctive features or behavioral signatures within the attack that might help attribute it to a specific threat actor or group.
    a. Initial Compromise → Spear Phishing, Water Hole attacks, Spams or USB infections.
    b. Privilege Escalation → Zero-day attacks (Stuxnet, Duqu) nation-state sponsored.
    c. Hack Tools → Pwdump, Pass-the-hash.
    d. Persistence → staying inside the system for long time w/o detection
        i. Registry
        ii. Rootkit
        iii. Backdoor
        iv. COM Object Hijacking
    e. Lateral Movement → Pivot once inside, scan & spread into local network to compromise other systems.
        i. Port Scans → protocols and services
        ii. Map Network
        iii. Man-in-the-middle attack – sniff and intercept info.
        iv. Remote Access → R-Services (RDP, VNC, SSH, FTP, Reverse Proxy)
    f. Credential Harvesting →
        i. Steal NTLM Hashes
        ii. Steal plain text passwords from logs, code, or memory.
        iii. Deploy Keylogger
3. Identification of Compromise Indicators and Intelligence Gathering: Following the initial analysis, investigators focus on uncovering IOCs, specific artifacts that signal malicious behavior. These may include suspicious IP addresses, file signatures, registry changes, or unusual domain queries. Security analysts draw on curated threat intelligence sources, including commercial feeds and publicly available data, to recognize recurring tactics, techniques, or infrastructure. Such intelligence helps establish context and may reveal links to known threat actors or campaigns.
4. Tracing and Attribution of the Attack: Once sufficient evidence has been compiled, efforts shift toward attributing the cyber incident to its source. This phase involves synthesizing technical, behavioral, and contextual indicators to determine the actor behind the operation. Attribution may rely on a blend of digital forensic evidence, insider reports, and insights from intelligence organizations. In some cases, it includes geolocation techniques or fingerprinting specific tools or malware strains to narrow down the origin to entities or regions.

Attribution plays a vital role in the domain of CTI, as it equips organizations with a deeper understanding of the actors responsible for malicious activities. Uncovering the identity or affiliation of an attacker offers critical insights into their underlying motives, skill level, and strategic objectives. This awareness enables security teams to tailor their defense mechanisms more effectively and anticipate potential threats with greater precision. However, attributing cyberattacks remains a highly intricate and demanding process due to several compounding factors:

1. Evolving Adversarial Tactics: Threat actors are continuously advancing their techniques, employing sophisticated methods to obscure their activities and evade digital forensics. This level of operational security makes it exceedingly difficult to trace incidents back to their true origin.
2. Deceptive Strategies (False Flags): Some attackers deliberately plant misleading evidence or mimic the tactics of other groups to obscure their identity – a tactic known as a false flag operation. Such deception not only complicates the attribution process but also risks misdirecting retaliatory or defensive actions.
3. Insufficient Intelligence: In certain scenarios, investigators may lack the requisite data to confidently identify the responsible party. This is especially common when dealing with novel attack vectors or actors operating under deep cover, such as well-resourced nation-state groups using zero-day exploits or custom malware.
4. Geopolitical and Legal Complexities: Assigning blame in cyberspace often carries significant diplomatic consequences. Governments may choose to withhold attribution to avoid provoking geopolitical tensions, engaging in retaliatory action, or straining international relations – particularly when accusations involve state-sponsored entities.

For example, if an organization can attribute an attack to a specific nation-state, they may be able to develop a better understanding of that nation-state's geopolitical motivations and cyber capabilities. Understanding who is behind a cyberattack, commonly referred to as attribution, plays a crucial role in developing defense mechanisms tailored to the specific TTPs of hostile entities, especially those affiliated with nation-states. Through the analysis of TTPs observed in past intrusions, organizations can detect recurring behavioral patterns and align them with known threat actors. This analytical approach not only uncovers the adversary's preferred tools and strategies but also sheds light on their broader objectives, enabling a more precise and contextual response.

One of the primary benefits of attribution in CTI is the enhancement of incident response capabilities. When defenders can accurately identify the nature of the attacker and their intent, they are in a better position to react swiftly and with greater precision. Such insights can significantly limit the damage inflicted during an attack by disrupting the adversary's timeline and operations. Moreover, understanding whether the threat stems from a highly resourced nation-state or an opportunistic lone actor allows organizations to allocate their response efforts accordingly, ensuring that critical resources are concentrated where they are most needed.

Attribution also serves as a catalyst for cooperation among different organizations. Sharing intelligence related to attackers' identities, behaviors, and campaign patterns facilitates a collaborative approach to cybersecurity. This exchange can include joint response plans, coordinated detection rules, or mutual access to threat intelligence feeds. Collective defense, built on shared attribution insights, ultimately leads to a more robust and informed posture across entire sectors or regions.

Beyond immediate tactical responses, attribution has long-term strategic value. It enables organizations to accumulate intelligence about attackers' capabilities, preferred entry points, and evolving methodologies. This knowledge can then inform proactive measures to strengthen network defenses and anticipate future threats. In terms of risk management, attribution helps organizations rank threats by severity and urgency. By discerning which actors pose the most substantial risk, security teams can prioritize mitigation efforts and adjust their protective strategies to reflect the threat landscape realistically. Furthermore, there are significant legal and geopolitical implications tied to attribution. Knowing who is responsible for a cyberattack allows governments and private entities to take appropriate actions, whether through legal channels or diplomatic engagement. This accountability can act as a deterrent, signaling to malicious actors that their behavior has consequences and that digital aggression will provoke a response.

Attribution also empowers proactive cybersecurity practices like threat hunting. By tracing attacks back to specific individuals or groups, defenders can move beyond passive monitoring and actively search for related IOC or lingering malicious activity within their environments. Thus, attribution is a cornerstone of modern cyber defense. It provides the contextual intelligence necessary to adapt defensive strategies, enhances the efficiency of incident handling, supports legal accountability, and fosters collaborative resilience. As adversarial tactics grow more complex and concealed, the ability to accurately identify perpetrators will become even more indispensable in safeguarding digital infrastructures and national interests.

4.5 TRACKING

After we have gathered the information about the attacker, it is very important to find out what they are doing or what he/they are up to, adding new tools, create new malware variants, or use new IP or domains, which shows how the attacker is evolving. Although this phase is like the hunting phase (where we searched for malware samples/phishing domains, etc.) but in this phase we search for new info with context and focus (as we already know the attack techniques, tools, features, and behavior of the attacker). This information is required to be provided to the LEAs. The goal is to anticipate new attacks and identify new variants proactively using PassiveDNS. Passive DNS (PDNS) is a technique used in CTI to gather information about attackers and their infrastructure by passively monitoring and collecting DNS data. Unlike traditional DNS lookups, where your computer actively queries a server, Passive DNS collects data from various sources on the internet that record DNS requests and responses. This data includes Domain names, IP addresses, Timestamps, Other DNS record types (MX, NS, etc.) PDNS doesn't interact with the DNS system itself, making it a stealthy way to collect information.

PDNS provides valuable insights for tracking criminals and their activities:

- Identifying Malicious Domains: Criminals often register domains with short lifespans for phishing attacks or malware distribution. PDNS can reveal these domains by tracking historical associations between IP addresses and domains. A sudden change in IP address for a domain can be a red flag.
- Mapping Attack Infrastructure: PDNS helps identify relationships between different domains and servers used by attackers. By analyzing historical data, security professionals can uncover a network of malicious infrastructure used for coordinated attacks.
- Tracking Malware C2 Servers: Criminals often use DNS to communicate between infected devices and their command and control (C2) servers. PDNS can help identify these C2 servers by tracking unusual domain resolution patterns.
- Investigating Incidents: During an incident investigation, PDNS data can be used to identify related domains and servers that may have been involved in the attack. This can help security teams understand the scope of the attack and identify potential entry points.

Benefits of passive DNS in CTI:

- Early Warning: PDNS can reveal malicious activity before traditional methods like blacklists.
- Historical Context: By analyzing historical data, PDNS helps uncover patterns and connections that might be missed in real-time analysis.
- Hidden Infrastructure: PDNS can reveal infrastructure hidden behind techniques like domain flux (frequent IP changes).
- Other ways are using:
  - Lookups: since we extracted features, behavior, location, IP, URLs, Strings, Certs we now use Yara Rules, ImpHash, SSdeep.
  - OSINT: find attacker's email address → spear phishing emails, attachments – search for similar features.
  - Hacking Forums: gain.

4.6 TAKE DOWN

All the efforts done till date in various phases (Hunting, Features, Behaviors, Clustering, Correlation, Attribution, and Tracking) finally provided to the LEAs to decide to "Take Down" the malicious infra and arrest the criminals. This will stop the malicious activities from spreading like new IPs/Domains. The goal is to dismantle the organized crime operations also called Sinkhole as a technique to disrupt communications between the malicious actor and compromised user devices or even redirect the malicious C2 attacker's server to the cybercell/researcher's analysis server. The aim is to stop infections from the C2 server as part of a joint effort with LEAs, ISPs, and Data center/hosting providers helping with logs for legal actions, as shown in Figure 4.8. But at times this is not possible due to territorial boundaries

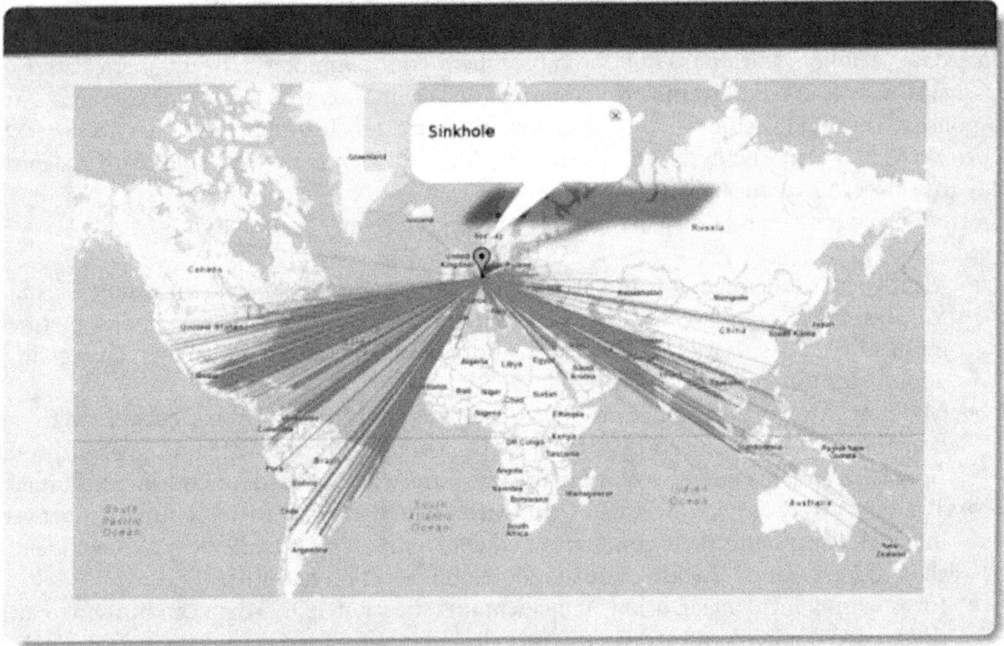

Figure 4.8 Bots connecting to Sinkhole.

or Political and Global Economic rivalries, for example China, Havana, North Korea, Russia will not listen to US, India, Interpol, or Europol.

The Sinkhole process involves the following steps:

1. Identification: Security researchers identify malicious domains or IP addresses used by attackers, typically command and control (C&C) servers for malware or botnets.
2. DNS Redirection: Collaboration occurs with domain registrars or internet service providers (ISPs) to redirect traffic destined for those malicious addresses. Change IP address of C2 server in DNS.
3. Sinkhole Server: A controlled server, the "sinkhole," is set up to receive the redirected traffic. This server can be:
   a. Informational: simply collects data on infected devices trying to connect, providing valuable intel on the attack scope and potential victims.
   b. Deceptive: might mimic the malicious server, preventing further communication and potentially disrupting attacker operations.

Benefits of Sinkhole:

- Disrupts Attacker Communication: By cutting off communication, attackers lose control of infected devices and can't launch further attacks or steal data.
- Gathers Attack Intelligence: Analyzing traffic logs on the sinkhole server reveals information about infected devices, malware variants, and attacker tactics. This intel helps improve future takedowns and threat detection.
- Protects Users: By redirecting traffic away from malicious servers, users are prevented from unknowingly downloading malware or having their data stolen.

4.7 CONCLUSION

This chapter provides a comprehensive view into the operationalization of CTI, emphasizing its pivotal role in identifying, understanding, and disrupting adversarial behavior in real-time. By integrating various intelligence sources, from open-source platforms to advanced commercial tools, organizations can enhance their situational awareness and mount proactive defenses against sophisticated threats. The methodologies, including clustering, correlation, attribution, tracking, and eventual takedown, demonstrate a structured approach to handling cyber threats from detection to disruption. Each phase builds upon the previous one, allowing security teams to connect isolated indicators into a cohesive narrative that reveals the attacker's intent, methods, and infrastructure. The importance of collaboration between organizations, law enforcement, and global threat-sharing communities has been highlighted as a critical element in the takedown process. Tools like Passive DNS and sinkholing offer practical means to anticipate attacks and dismantle hostile operations, while attribution techniques provide insights into the adversary's identity, motivations, and geopolitical affiliations. As threat actors evolve, so too must the defenders. Operationalizing CTI is not a one-time action but an ongoing process that requires adaptability, strategic foresight, and collective effort. When effectively implemented, it transforms reactive defense postures into intelligent, proactive operations that can safeguard digital ecosystems with greater resilience.

MULTIPLE CHOICE QUESTIONS

1. A financial SOC receives daily raw threat feeds, but analysts complain that 70% of alerts do not align with their internal asset criticality. Meanwhile, the CTI team discovers that incident responders rarely use the weekly threat reports designed for executives. Leadership insists that CTI "is not providing actionable value," despite significant investment. Which CTI lifecycle stage is most clearly failing?

   A. Collection
   B. Requirements
   C. Dissemination
   D. Feedback

   Correct Answer: B
   Reason: Requirements define *who needs what intelligence for what purpose*. Misalignment across SOC, IR, and leadership indicates poor PIR creation. Why others are wrong:
   - A: Collection is downstream of bad requirements.
   - C: Even perfect reporting is useless if requirements are wrong.
   - D: Feedback helps refine, but the root is requirement failure.

2. A SOC receives intel about a new ransomware variant targeting RDP services. Even though the CTI team shared IoCs, analysts still fail to detect early beaconing. Investigation shows that EDR correlation rules were never updated and the SOC playbooks did not include the new TTPs shared by CTI. What breakdown occurred?

   A. CTI was not effectively operationalized into security controls
   B. The CTI team produced inaccurate intelligence
   C. The SOC has poor staffing ratios
   D. The ransomware IoCs were expired

   Correct Answer: A
   Reason: The IoCs and TTPs were provided, but SOC controls/playbooks were not updated, which is a classic operationalization failure. Why others are wrong:
   - B: No indication intel was wrong.
   - C: Staffing irrelevant.
   - D: IoCs are new, not expired.

3. A multinational retail chain sees increasing credential-stuffing attacks, supply-chain skimming, and card-not-present fraud. Executives ask CTI to "give us everything on cybercrime," while SOC analysts request specific intelligence related to payment systems. CTI leadership attempts to define PIRs but finds conflicting expectations. Which approach best aligns with CTI best practices?

   A. Define the PIR only based on SOC's needs
   B. Consolidate cross-department needs and map them to specific intelligence goals
   C. Ignore executive requests due to lack of technical detail
   D. Create a single PIR covering all cybercrime activity

   Correct Answer: B
   Reason: PIRs represent *organizational* priorities, not single-team interests. Needs must be consolidated and made specific. Why others are wrong:
   - A: PIRs must be enterprise wide.
   - C: Executive needs matter, even if vague.
   - D: PIRs must be specific, not broad.

4. A CTI analyst receives three intelligence sources: (1) a dark-web leak site claiming access to corporate credentials, (2) a paid TI provider giving structured reporting, and (3) a social media rumor about a new APT exploiting cloud APIs. Leadership asks for an assessment. What should the analyst prioritize?

   A. Rank sources based on trust, validation ability, and relevance
   B. Prioritize the dark-web leak because it is the most "critical"
   C. Treat all sources as equally credible
   D. Ignore unstructured sources entirely

   Correct Answer: A
   Reason: CTI operationalization requires source scoring (trustworthiness, relevance, reliability). Why others are wrong:
   - B: Dark-web claims require verification.
   - C: Not all intel is equal.
   - D: Social media can contain valuable leads when validated.

5. During an incident, forensic analysts discover encoded PowerShell logs suggesting lateral movement. The CTI team references historical TTPs and links the behavior to a known APT that previously targeted the same sector. The IR team updates containment actions based on CTI insights. Which CTI maturity behavior does this reflect?

   A. Tactical-only CTI
   B. Strategic CTI only
   C. Fusion-center style intelligence integration
   D. Ad-hoc CTI

   Correct Answer: C
   Reason: Fusion requires bidirectional interaction: forensics → CTI → incident response. Why others are wrong:
   - A: Tactical CTI alone wouldn't integrate with DFIR outcomes.
   - B: Strategic intel is long-term, not IR-oriented.
   - D: This is structured, not ad-hoc.

6. A CTI team maps recent phishing, credential theft, and privilege escalation events to ATT&CK techniques. They identify gaps in detection for T1059, T1078, and T1550. The SOC adjusts detection rules accordingly. This scenario demonstrates which CTI operational capability?

   A. Reporting
   B. Intelligence-driven detection engineering
   C. Infrastructure threat mapping
   D. Strategic threat attribution

   Correct Answer: B
   Reason: ATT&CK mapping → detection engineering is a core operational CTI function. Why others are wrong:
   - A: Reporting is just output, not detection tuning.
   - C: Not about attacker infrastructure.
   - D: No attribution being performed.

7. A regional ISAC shares malicious IP addresses used in DDoS attacks. However, when integrated into the company's firewall, it blocks many legitimate API partners. Post-mortem analysis shows the intel lacked contextual details like TTL or confidence score. Which intel quality attribute was missing?

    A. Timeliness
    B. Accuracy & context
    C. Completeness
    D. Actionability

    Correct Answer: B
    Reason: Context (confidence, TTL, false-positive likelihood) is crucial for operational blocking. Why others are wrong:
    - A: Timely intel can still be low-quality.
    - C: It was not incomplete – just lacking context.
    - D: It was actionable, but incorrectly so.

8. A CTI team tracks more than 40 external intel feeds but continuously fails to answer business questions. Analysts admit they rarely use most feeds, and correlation rules decay because feeds do not map to PIRs. What is the correct remediation?

    A. Replace all feeds with free OSINT
    B. Use a Collection Management Framework (CMF) to align feeds with PIRs
    C. Ignore PIRs and focus only on threat feeds
    D. Remove all feeds except paid ones

    Correct Answer: B
    Reason: CMF ensures feeds map to validated collection requirements directly. Why others are wrong:
    - A: OSINT alone is insufficient.
    - C: PIRs drive intelligence – not the other way.
    - D: Paid feeds are not inherently better.

9. The CTI team produces 30-page technical reports filled with IoCs, ATT&CK diagrams, and memory forensics details. Executives consistently ignore these reports, saying they do not support business decision-making. What adjustment is needed?

    A. Increase technical details
    B. Add more IoCs and sandbox results
    C. Restructure reports for strategic-level communication
    D. Reduce reporting frequency

    Correct Answer: C
    Reason: Executives require *risk-focused*, not technical, reporting. Why others are wrong:
    - A and B worsen the issue.
    - D irrelevant; the problem is format, not volume.

10. During an intrusion, CTI analysts recognize early reconnaissance stages through anomalous scanning. They advise SOC to implement preemptive blocking of suspected C2 domains. IR isolates the host before lateral movement occurs. What CTI value is demonstrated?

    A. Post incident digital forensics
    B. Threat intelligence applied across the Kill Chain
    C. Compliance-driven operations
    D. Attribution to a known adversary

Correct Answer: B

Reason: CTI enabled defensive action at multiple Kill Chain points (recon → C2 → lateral movement prevention). Why others are wrong:

- A: Not a forensics scenario.
- C: No regulatory angle.
- D: No attribution done.

11. A company implements automated enrichment of IoCs using STIX/TAXII feeds. However, analysts find the automated rules are tagging outdated indicators and generating false positives, overwhelming the SOC. What is the likely root cause?

    A. The SOC lacks machine learning technology
    B. The CTI automation pipeline lacks TTL & confidence scoring checks
    C. STIX/TAXII cannot handle modern IoCs
    D. Automation replaces the need for analysts

    Correct Answer: B

    Reason: Proper operationalization requires TTL and confidence filtering to avoid stale/low quality IoCs. Why others are wrong:

    - A: ML unrelated.
    - C: STIX/TAXII handle modern IoCs fine.
    - D: Analysts remain necessary.

12. During a breach, IR discovers persistence using registry Run keys. CTI maps this behavior to historical campaigns of a financially motivated group known for double-extortion ransomware. The IR team uses this info to predict next-stage actions and stops exfiltration attempts. What CTI benefit is this?

    A. Historical reporting only
    B. Threat anticipation
    C. Asset prioritization
    D. Vulnerability mapping

    Correct Answer: B

    Reason: CTI enabled prediction of attacker *future actions*. Why others are wrong:

    - A: Not just historic.
    - C, D: Not relevant here.

13. SOC analysts ingest TI feeds containing thousands of IPs. They ask CTI whether adding all IPs to firewall blocklists is safe. CTI warns them that the feed includes sink holed domains, research honeypots, and benign scanning nodes. Which CTI principle is being applied?

    A. Blind indicator blocking
    B. Context-driven enrichment
    C. Strategic threat forecasting
    D. Threat actor attribution

    Correct Answer: B

    Reason: Enrichment provides context so analysts understand *which indicators should be acted upon*. Why others are wrong:

    - A is what they *should avoid*.
    - C doesn't involve IoCs.
    - D not about attribution.

14. A CTI program is evaluated six months after deployment. Despite limited workforce, the SOC shows a 40% reduction in alert triage time and a higher accuracy in detecting TTPs mapped to key PIRs. What metric best supports CTI maturity improvement?

    A. Number of IoCs collected
    B. Reduction in Mean Time to Detect (MTTD)
    C. Size of the CTI team
    D. Threat reports published per month

    Correct Answer: B
    Reason: MTTD directly reflects operational detection improvements driven by CTI.
       Why others are wrong:
    - A meaningless volume metric.
    - C unrelated to effectiveness.
    - D quantity ≠ quality.

15. A SOC analyst escalates an alert for domain "abc-cloudsync.net." CTI analysts realize this domain was previously tagged as benign but now appears in C2 infrastructure for a new campaign. However, there is no workflow for rapid reclassification of indicators. The organization responds too slowly. What should be implemented?

    A. Automated IoC ingestion without review
    B. A feedback loop between SOC and CTI for indicator reassessment
    C. Removal of CTI as a separate function
    D. Rely only on external ISAC alerts

    Correct Answer: B
    Reason: Operational CTI requires fast feedback cycles to update indicator validity.
       Why others are wrong:
    - A increases false positives.
    - C eliminates intelligence value.
    - D reduces visibility.

REFERENCES

1. AlienVault, "AlienVault - Open threat exchange," 2026. https://otx.alienvault.com/dashboard/new
2. "CTI4SOC: Ultimate solution to SOC analyst's biggest challenges - SOCRadar® Cyber Intelligence Inc.," SOCRadar® Cyber Intelligence Inc., Jan. 26, 2023. Accessed Jul. 4, 2025. https://socradar.io/cti4soc-ultimate-solution-to-soc-analysts-biggest-challenges
3. Docguard.io, "Docguard | Detects suspicious files!," *Docguard.io*, 2025. Accessed Jul. 4, 2025. https://app.docguard.io/examples
4. "GreyNoise visualizer," *Greynoise.io*, 2025. Accessed Jul. 4, 2025. https://viz.greynoise.io
5. "Autonomous SOC product tour," *Intezer*, Apr. 8, 2025. Accessed Jul. 4, 2025. https://intezer.com/autonomous-soc/product-tour
6. MISP, "MISP features and functionalities," MISP Open Source Threat Intelligence Platform & Open Standards for Threat Information Sharing, 2026. https://www.misp-project.org/features
7. "OpenCTI - Cyber threat intelligence platform," *Opencti.io*, 2025. https://demo.opencti.io/dashboard
8. P. LLC, "Threat intelligence - Pulsedive," *pulsedive.com*. https://pulsedive.com
9. VirusTotal, "VirusTotal," *Virustotal.com*, 2019. https://www.virustotal.com/gui/home/upload

Chapter 5

Malware analysis in practice

5.1 INTRODUCTION

Malware, an abbreviation for malicious software [1], is any program or script intentionally created to damage systems, compromise data, or interfere with regular computer functions. This exists as binary executables or malicious scripts that operate with the intent to infiltrate, damage, or exploit devices, networks, or users. Malware is a central weapon in the arsenal of cyber attackers and plays a significant role in executing a range of malicious activities that can severely impact individual users, businesses, and even national infrastructure.

There are various types of malwares, each engineered to serve different malicious objectives. Trojans are among the most deceptive types; they disguise themselves as legitimate applications to trick users into installing them. Once inside the system, they can steal data, delete files, or provide attackers with backdoor access. Remote Access Trojans (RATs) [2] take this further by allowing attackers to remotely control the victim's device, often enabling keylogging, screen capturing, or deploying additional malware. Ransomware, on the other hand, encrypts files or entire operating systems, demanding payment from the user to regain access. This form of extortion has become increasingly prevalent in targeted attacks. Droppers are specialized malware whose sole purpose is to download or install additional malicious components from the attacker's command-and-control (C2) server [3]. They act as facilitators, ensuring the complete delivery of the malicious payload.

Malware serves several malicious purposes, with some of the most common uses being surveillance, theft, and destruction. Spyware, keyloggers, and RATs are often employed to silently monitor user behavior, collect login credentials, or capture sensitive information. In cases of data exfiltration, droppers may include scripts that create covert communication channels such as HTTP tunnels or traffic over non-standard ports, allowing attackers to quietly steal data from compromised systems. Ransomware is used to lock or encrypt vital data, leveraging that control to demand ransoms from victims under threat of permanent data loss. Some droppers also contain destructive payloads designed to cause operational chaos. For instance, they may delete system files, overload memory or CPU resources, or disable critical services, effectively crashing the system or rendering it unusable.

Malware remains a persistent and evolving threat, used to spy, steal, extort, and destroy. Its multifaceted nature and adaptability make it a preferred tool for cybercriminals, and understanding its types and functions is crucial for any cybersecurity defense strategy. In Security Operations Center (SOC) [4], different teams receive malware – malicious IPs, Domains, C2 Servers. Files. In a modern cybersecurity landscape, responding to malicious artifacts requires a coordinated effort from multiple specialized teams to minimize damage and restore normal operations. When harmful files or behaviors are detected within an IT environment, teams must analyze their negative impact and implement strategies to remediate the system. SOC analysts serve as the frontline defenders of an organization's cybersecurity, continuously

DOI: 10.1201/9781003730583-5

monitoring system logs and responding to alerts triggered by Security Information and Event Management (SIEM) tools, often on a 24/7 basis. Their job is to detect suspicious activity in real time and escalate incidents when necessary. Incident Response (IR) [5] teams step in once a threat is confirmed, focusing on containment, eradication, and recovery actions to restore the affected environment and prevent further compromise.

Parallel to this, threat hunting teams take a proactive approach by searching for hidden threats that may have bypassed automated defenses. They search for signs of potential threats, like harmful IP addresses, unusual domain names, or recognized malware file hashes, which are commonly known as Indicators of Compromise (IoC) [6]. These indicators are then passed on to IT or security administrators for enforcement through firewalls, intrusion detection systems, SIEM platforms, and endpoint protection tools. Malware Analysts play a critical role in understanding the technical structure and behavior of malicious code. They reverse-engineer malware to uncover how it operates, what systems it targets, and how it communicates with the attacker's infrastructure. This information supports the development of patches or detection signatures used by antivirus vendors, security software developers, or operating system and application maintainers.

The process of malware analysis aims to extract as much relevant information as possible from a sample to understand its purpose and effects. Analysts seek to determine the type of malware, whether it's a trojan, ransomware, worm, or spyware, and identify the operating systems and applications it targets. The analysis reveals how the infection occurred, such as through a phishing email, malicious link, or software exploit. It also uncovers the malware's communication patterns, such as attempts to reach out to command-and-control servers, and highlights specific IoCs like registry changes, file modifications, or unauthorized data access. These insights are critical for developing effective defensive strategies and ensuring such incidents are prevented in the future. Ultimately, this collaborative and analytical approach helps organizations strengthen their cyber resilience and recover quickly from attacks.

5.2 MALWARE ANALYSIS PROCEDURE

Malware analysis is a critical task in cybersecurity that must be conducted with utmost caution to prevent any unintentional harm to production systems or networks. To ensure safety and effectiveness, it is essential to analyze malware in a controlled and isolated environment that mimics a real-world system while containing potential threats. One of the most reliable setups for this purpose is the use of virtual machines (VMs). Analysts often utilize specialized operating system distributions such as REMnux, which is tailored for reverse engineering and malware analysis. These environments are typically hosted on platforms like VMware or VirtualBox and may run Windows 10 or 11, depending on the malware's intended target environment. This virtualized setup allows for a flexible and safe examination without affecting the host system.

In addition to local virtual environments, cloud-based malware analysis platforms offer scalable and secure alternatives. These services are designed to simulate system behavior and log every interaction that the malware attempts, providing detailed insights into its functionality without exposing internal infrastructure. A key step in safe malware analysis is to restrict or completely block internet access within the sandboxed environment. This prevents the malware from reaching out to its command-and-control (C2) servers, which are often used by attackers to send instructions, download additional payloads, or exfiltrate data. Cutting off these communication channels ensures that the malware cannot interact with its external handlers during the analysis process.

To gain meaningful insights, it is also essential to have robust monitoring and logging mechanisms in place. Analysts should configure the system to log all activities, such as outbound IP addresses, attempted domain name resolutions, and connections to suspicious URLs.

These logs are crucial for identifying the malware's behavior patterns and for tracing the origin or network infrastructure involved in the attack. Importantly, malware must never be tested on actual user or production machines. A dedicated system, referred to as a sandbox, must be used to safely execute and observe the malware. This isolated environment ensures that even if the malware attempts destructive actions or network propagation, the damage is contained and does not spread beyond the analysis setup.

Types of Malware Analysis:

1. Static Malware Analysis is the process of analyzing the malware without opening or executing the malware → sneak peek from a window/door. The objective is to extract as many metadata as possible (limited) attributes to draw an image of the malware – Hash, Strings, PE Headers.

2. Dynamic Malware Analysis is a critical technique in modern cybersecurity, designed to observe and understand the behavior of a potentially malicious file by executing it within a controlled, isolated environment – often referred to as a sandbox. Unlike static analysis, which examines the code without running it, dynamic analysis focuses on what the malware does when it is allowed to operate. This method provides deep insights into the functional attributes of malware, revealing how it interacts with the system, what changes it attempts to make, and how it communicates with external entities once executed.

   The primary goal of dynamic malware analysis is to uncover behavioral patterns that may not be visible through signature-based or static analysis methods. By executing the file and monitoring its runtime behavior, analysts can detect suspicious activities such as unauthorized file modifications, unexpected use of system resources, or abnormal network connections to unknown or blacklisted domains. Additionally, the process may involve examining the memory usage, API calls, registry changes, and attempts to escalate privileges. This level of scrutiny allows security teams to identify zero-day threats or polymorphic malware that traditional detection methods might miss due to their constantly changing code.

   Since the analysis is based on behavior rather than relying on known signatures or hash values, it can effectively identify malicious files even if they have been heavily modified or are completely new. This makes dynamic analysis a powerful tool in proactive threat detection, especially in environments where adversaries frequently deploy customized or evolving threats. A major benefit of this method is its capability to identify malware that is either new or deliberately hidden. However, dynamic analysis is not without its limitations. One of the main drawbacks is the potential for false positives, benign applications may sometimes be flagged as malicious due to their complex or unusual behavior during execution. Moreover, sophisticated malware may detect the sandboxed environment and modify its behavior to avoid detection, which can hinder the effectiveness of the analysis. Additionally, running unknown files in a virtual environment requires resources and time, making it less suitable for rapid, large-scale scanning. Thus, dynamic malware analysis is a valuable strategy for uncovering and understanding emerging threats through behavioral assessment. While it may have challenges such as false positives and evasion tactics, its strengths in detecting novel and adaptive malware make it an essential component of a robust cybersecurity defense framework.

3. Code Analysis is the process of reverse engineering the malware assembly code – read inside the exe, study the instructions.

4. Behavioral Analysis monitors and analyzes the activities of the malware after execution, which involves checking the working of malware for processes created, registry entries made, C2/IP/Domain network connections attempted.

5.3 STATIC ANALYSIS

This chapter focuses on Static malware analysis – analyze malware w/o executing it, which involves.

5.3.1 Identify filetype

To determine the true nature of a file, it's essential to go beyond its visible extension and inspect the internal file signature embedded within its header. This is especially important when dealing with files across various operating systems like Windows, Linux, or macOS, and understanding whether the architecture is 32-bit or 64-bit. For Windows specifically, executable files such as .exe and .dll are based on the Portable Executable (PE) format. A genuine PE file typically begins with the hexadecimal signature 4D 5A, which translates to the ASCII characters MZ, followed by a message like This program cannot be run in DOS mode, confirming its structure.

Cyber attackers often disguise malicious executables using misleading file extensions to evade detection, for example, renaming Evil.exe to Evil.doc, Evil.ps1 to Evil.jpg, or Evil.py to Evil.txt. This double-extension technique can deceive users and even bypass basic security filters if file headers are not examined. To validate a file's authenticity and header signature, a hex editor is indispensable. On a Windows VM, download and install HxD, which is a light-weight yet powerful hex editor. Opening a .txt file in HxD reveals its true structure, which can help distinguish between legitimate and disguised malicious files, as displayed in Figure 5.1.

The file named "GoogleEarthProSetup.exe" is subsequently opened. Upon inspection, it is identified as a "Portable Executable" (PE) file, a format commonly used in Windows operating systems. This classification is visually confirmed and detailed in Figure 5.2, which provides supporting evidence for the file's structural format and behavior.

5.3.2 Identify malware

This is generated by applying the Hash function to the malware sample. Hash is a unique identifier value (a fixed-size string/fingerprint). Hash is a signature-based approach to check the value from disclosure sites or databases for known malwares, maintained by anti-virus/

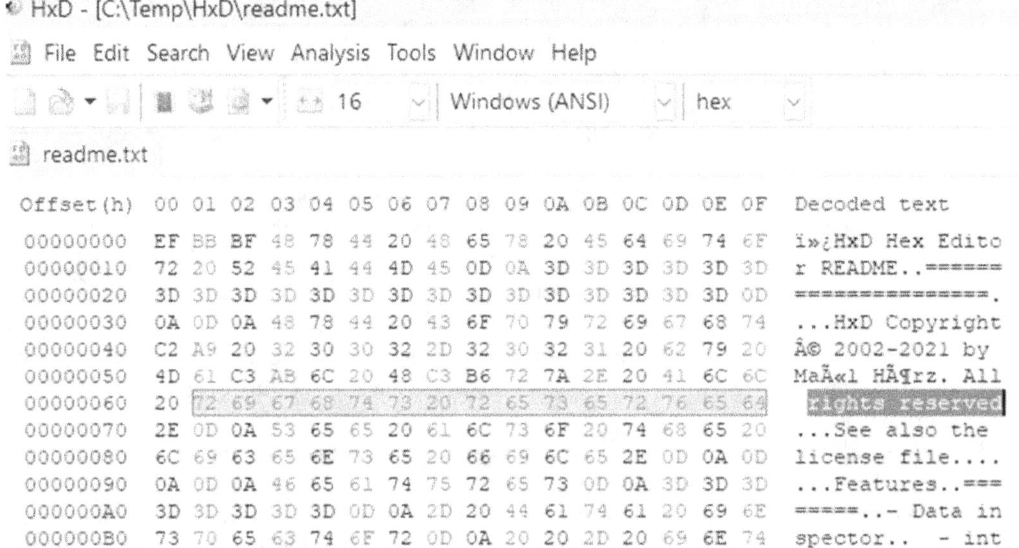

Figure 5.1 Open text file in hex editor.

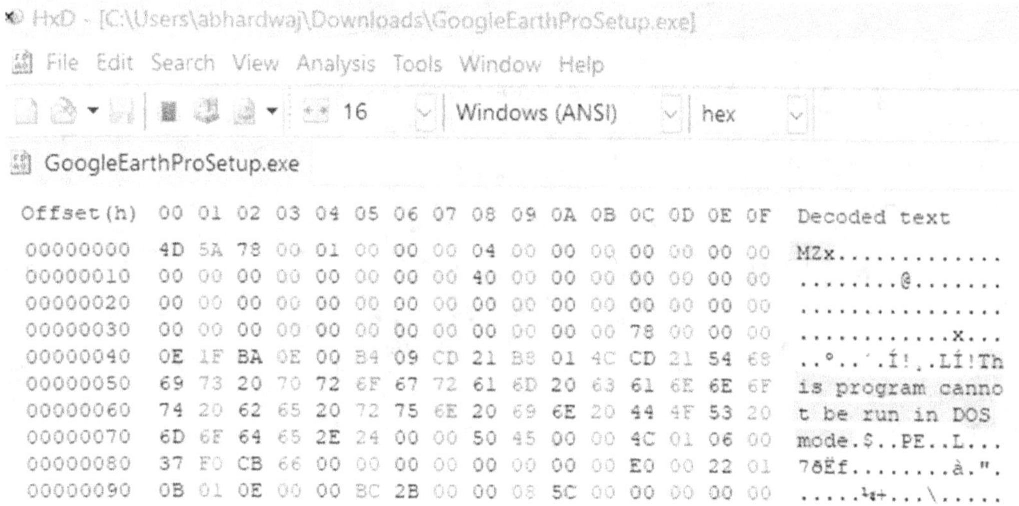

Figure 5.2 Portable executable binary.

anti-malware vendors if they have it as an entry. Hash function is applied to a file to generate a unique cryptographic value for the file content. This hash is compared against a database of known malware hashes. If there's a match, the file is flagged as malicious. Hashes can only detect malware that has already been identified and added to the database. It is ineffective against new or mutated malware. Hashing algorithms used are MD5, SHA-1, and SHA256 to give a unique digest known as fingerprint. For example, finding the Hash of a file is used to validate its properties and check if it is malicious.

To determine the hash value of a file, reliable hash tools should be utilized. Several applications are available for this purpose. Hashtab, which can be installed from the Implbits website, integrates seamlessly with file properties to display hash values. Another effective tool is MultiHasher, available from Abelhadigital, which supports a wide range of hash algorithms. Additionally, HashMyFiles, provided by NirSoft, offers a lightweight utility for computing file hashes with ease. Once the hash value is obtained, the file can be uploaded to VirusTotal, a trusted online platform for malware analysis and threat detection, as illustrated in Figure 5.3.

Check file hash and basic level details for the reported malware, as shown in Figure 5.4.

Then click the Behavior tab to find more details, as illustrated in Figure 5.5.

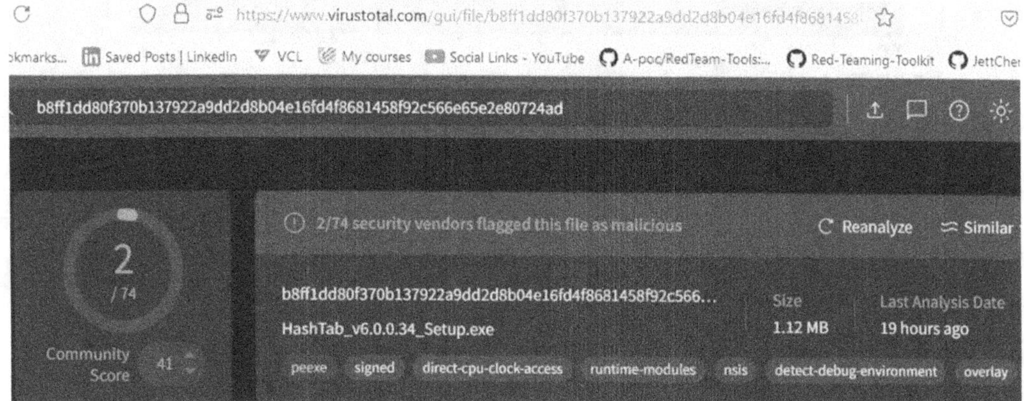

Figure 5.3 Upload malware file to VirusTotal.

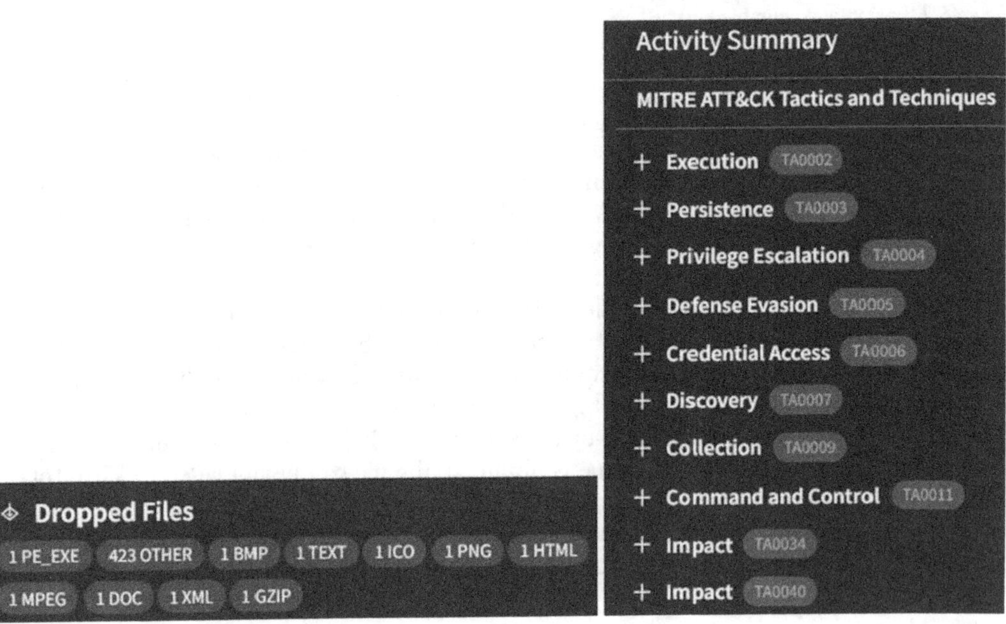

Figure 5.4 Reported details about Malware file.

Figure 5.5 File behavior revealed.

5.3.3 Strings

This gives a glimpse of what the malware can do like perform API Calls using OS functions to contact C2 servers, add registry entries, which also shows the nature of malware. This involves retrieving readable characters and meaningful words from within the malware, helping to reveal its functionality by filtering out random or nonsensical strings. For this, look for the File name, URL/Domains/IPs it tries to connect, API Calls made.

5.3.4 Imports

Malware uses various OS functions to perform specific work instead of writing code from scratch. Keep an eye for the following:

- RegQuery → Returns a list of the next tier of subkeys and entries that are located under a specified subkey in the registry.
- URLDownloadFile → downloads a file from a specified URL to the local workstation's Internet cache or to a specified location.
- InternetOpenA → Initializes an application's use of the WinINet functions.

5.4 MALWARE ANALYSIS USING VIRTUAL MACHINE

There are several malware analysis-based VM OS prepackaged with malware analysis tools, two of which are discussed below.

5.4.1 Flare-VM OS

FLARE-VM is a specialized framework designed to streamline the setup and management of a comprehensive reverse engineering environment on Windows-based VMs. It provides a curated suite of reverse engineering, malware analysis, and forensic tools through an automated installation process. Available for download via its GitHub repository (https://github.com/mandiant/flare-vm), FLARE-VM simplifies what would otherwise be a complex and time-consuming process of individually sourcing and configuring multiple tools, as illustrated in Figure 5.6.

The architecture of FLARE-VM is built upon two key Windows technologies. First, it uses Chocolatey, a widely adopted package manager for Windows that facilitates the installation of software through simple PowerShell-based scripts. Each package in Chocolatey is a ZIP archive containing installation instructions, which automates the process of downloading, installing, and configuring specific applications. Second, Boxstarter is employed to enhance automation further by allowing fully scripted and repeatable environment setups. Boxstarter utilizes Chocolatey packages to perform complete software deployments, making it particularly useful for provisioning standardized analysis environments. Together, these make

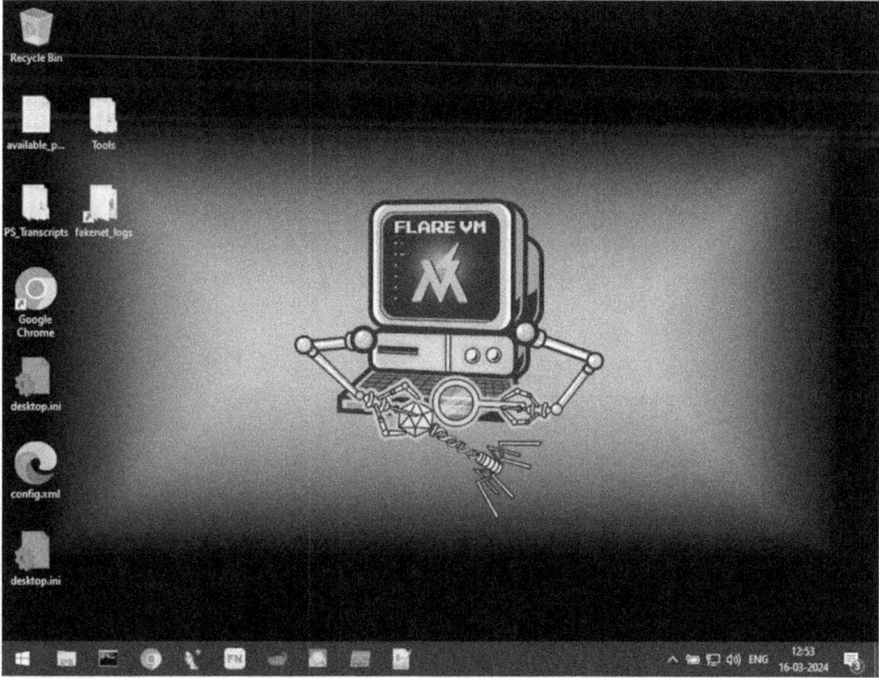

Figure 5.6 Flare VM.

FLARE-VM an efficient and scalable solution for analysts and researchers who need consistent, up-to-date reverse engineering workspaces. The automated and script-driven nature of its setup not only saves time but also minimizes human error in configuring complex toolchains.

5.4.2 Remnux VM OS

Download Remnux as a VM from https://remnux.org/ as an OWA file for Oracle Virtual Box and import the appliance as shown in Figure 5.7.

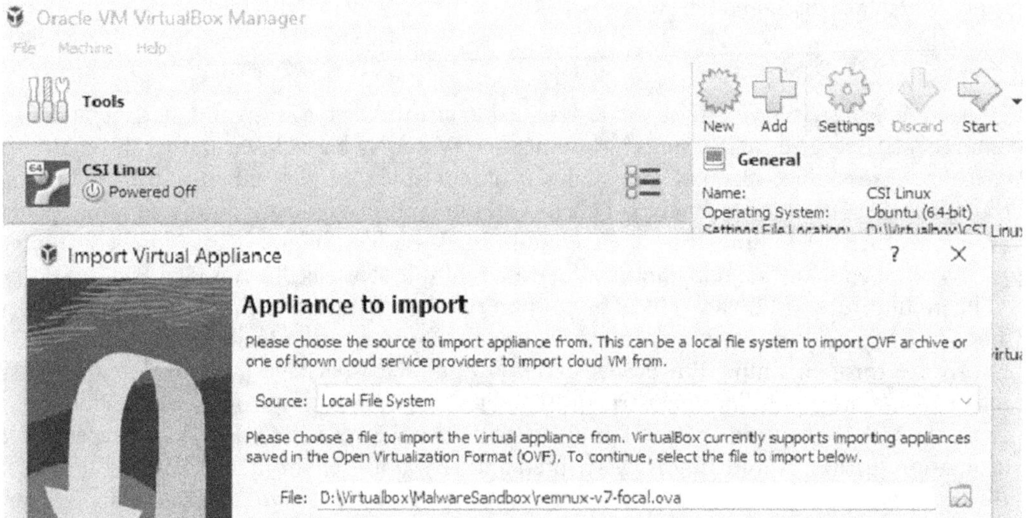

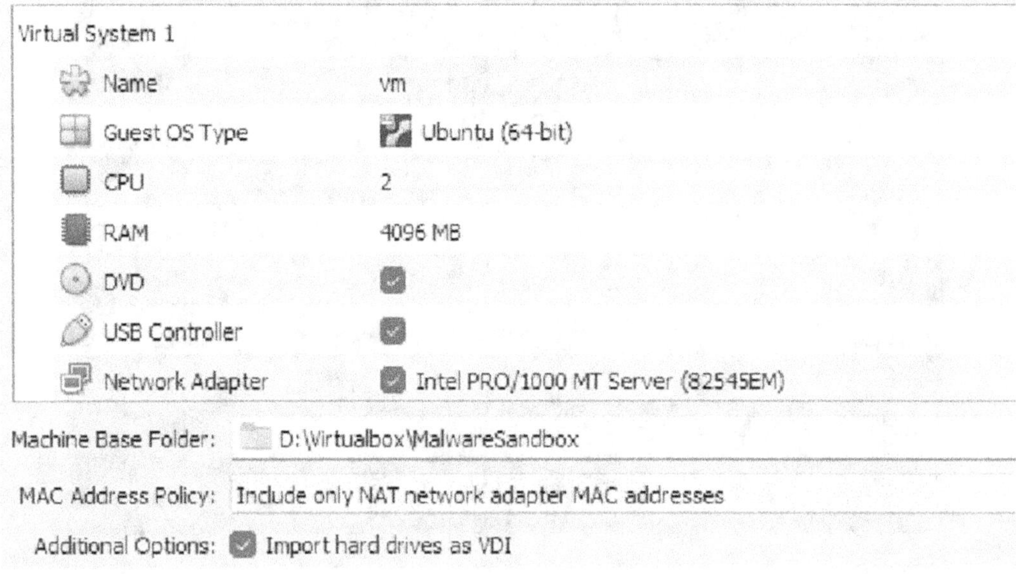

Figure 5.7 Remnux VM.

Figure 5.8 Remnux OS tools.

Start the Remnux VM and login as user "**remnux**" with password "**malware**" and view the preinstalled tools as shown in Figure 5.8.

5.5 MALWARE ANALYSIS TACTICS

5.5.1 Wireshark

Wireshark is a widely utilized open-source protocol analyzer that allows users to capture and inspect network traffic in real time. It supports the Packet Capture (PCAP) format, making it a valuable resource for IT professionals in diagnosing a variety of network-related issues. In cybersecurity contexts, Wireshark is frequently employed to analyze traffic patterns associated with malware activity, including instances of malware distribution, data exfiltration, and command-and-control (C2) communications, many of which exploit web traffic as a medium. Despite its robust capabilities, the tool's default column layout may not effectively highlight suspicious web-based activity. To enhance the visibility of such threats, users can customize the column settings within Wireshark, tailoring the interface to suit specific investigative needs. Before utilizing the tool, it is necessary to install it by accessing the official download page at https://www.wireshark.org/download.html. With proper configuration, Wireshark becomes a powerful instrument for both network diagnostics and threat analysis.

Once installed, customizing the column display can significantly enhance usability, as the default configuration offers extensive information that may not align with specific analytical requirements. Adjusting the columns allows for a more tailored inspection of packet data. A packet capture (PCAP) file should be downloaded from a trusted GitHub repository to observe Wireshark's default interface in action. Upon opening the PCAP file, the standard layout becomes visible, as illustrated in Figure 5.9, providing a basis for further customization.

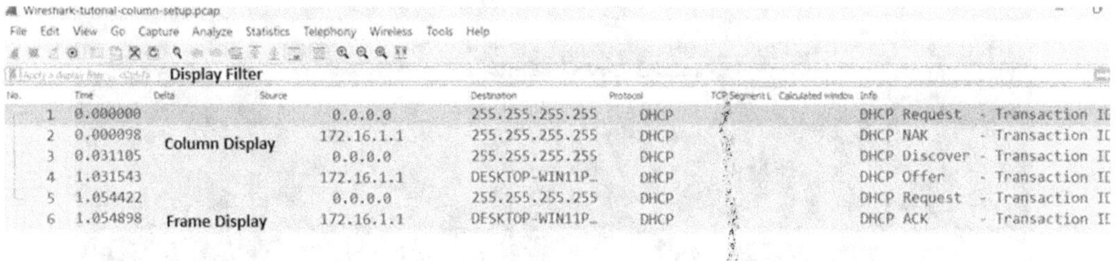

Figure 5.9 Wireshark GUI.

To standardize the timestamp format, the display settings must be adjusted to reflect Coordinated Universal Time (UTC). To adjust the time display settings for accurate data interpretation, begin by accessing the *View* menu and selecting *Time Display Format*. Within this menu, modify the format from "Seconds Since Beginning of Capture" to "UTC Date and Time of Day." This change ensures the time data aligns with real-world timestamps. Furthermore, to maintain consistency across the dataset, it is recommended to adjust the time resolution setting from *Automatic* to *Seconds*. This step refines the temporal granularity of the displayed information. Both adjustments contribute to a standardized and precise presentation of time data, as demonstrated in Figure 5.10.

Certain columns in network analysis tools, such as No., Protocol, and Length, may not be essential for routine tasks. Streamlining the interface by removing these can improve clarity and focus. This can be done by right-clicking on the header of the column to be removed and selecting the Remove this Column option from the context menu. As demonstrated in Figure 5.11, this method helps in customizing the workspace to suit specific analytical needs more efficiently.

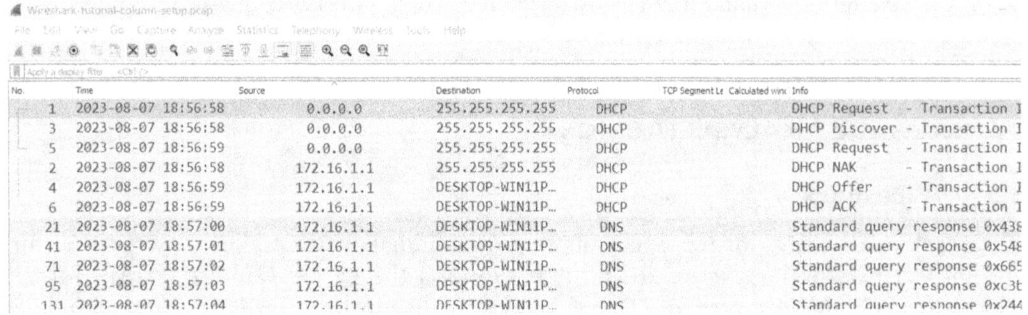

Figure 5.10 Name resolution and time customization.

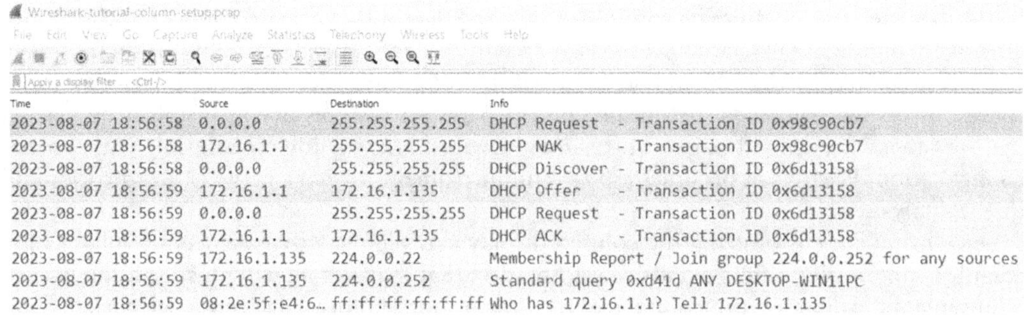

Figure 5.11 Edited columns.

To incorporate essential columns such as Source Port and Destination Port, it is necessary to select the specific information fields labeled as "src.port" and "dst.port." These parameters are typically used to identify the originating and target ports involved in network communication. As illustrated in Figure 5.12, this selection enables a more detailed analysis of traffic flow by including port-specific data, which is critical for effective network monitoring, threat detection, and forensic investigation in cybersecurity contexts.

To ensure the proper visualization of data in Wireshark, it is essential to adjust the display alignment of values according to specific formatting needs. Depending on the nature of the information being analyzed, values can be aligned to the left, right, or center. This customization enhances clarity and interpretability, especially when dealing with complex network traffic. The display should be configured to match the desired format, as illustrated in Figure 5.13, allowing for more accurate and organized data presentation during analysis.

To simplify the interface and reduce on-screen detail, the "Packet Bytes" window can be hidden from view. This can be accomplished by navigating to the "View" menu and deselecting the "Packet Bytes" option. This action effectively removes the lower panel displaying the raw data associated with selected packets. Such a step is useful when the focus is on higher-level packet information, rather than low-level hexadecimal or ASCII content. Figure 5.14 illustrates this process within the network analysis environment.

To analyze domains accessed via unencrypted HTTP traffic, a custom column can be added in Wireshark using specific frame-level data. Begin by entering the filter expression http.request in the display filter bar to isolate HTTP request packets as shown in Figure 5.15. After the filtered results appear, select the first packet displayed. In the detailed view pane, expand the section labeled Hypertext Transmission Protocol to explore HTTP-specific attributes.

☐	Calculated window size	Custom
☑	Info	Information
☑	Source Port	Source port
☑	Destination Port	Destination port

Figure 5.12 Add source and destination port columns.

Time	Source	Source Port	Destination	Destination Port	Info
2023-08-07 18:56:58	0.0.0.0	bootpc	255.255.255.255	bootps	DHCP Request - Transaction ID 0x98c90cb7
2023-08-07 18:56:58	172.16.1.1	bootps	255.255.255.255	bootpc	DHCP NAK - Transaction ID 0x98c90cb7
2023-08-07 18:56:58	0.0.0.0	bootpc	255.255.255.255	bootps	DHCP Discover - Transaction ID 0x6d13158
2023-08-07 18:56:59	172.16.1.1	bootps	172.16.1.135	bootpc	DHCP Offer - Transaction ID 0x6d13158
2023-08-07 18:56:59	0.0.0.0	bootpc	255.255.255.255	bootps	DHCP Request - Transaction ID 0x6d13158
2023-08-07 18:56:59	172.16.1.1	bootps	172.16.1.135	bootpc	DHCP ACK - Transaction ID 0x6d13158

Time	Source	Source Port	Destination	Destination Port	Info
2023-08-07 18:56:58	0.0.0.0	bootpc	255.255.255.255	bootps	DHCP Request - Transaction ID 0x98c90cb7
2023-08-07 18:56:58	172.16.1.1	bootps	255.255.255.255	bootpc	DHCP NAK - Transaction ID 0x98c90cb7
2023-08-07 18:56:58	0.0.0.0	bootpc	255.255.255.255	bootps	DHCP Discover - Transaction ID 0x6d13158
2023-08-07 18:56:59	172.16.1.1	bootps	172.16.1.135	bootpc	DHCP Offer - Transaction ID 0x6d13158
2023-08-07 18:56:59	0.0.0.0	bootpc	255.255.255.255	bootps	DHCP Request - Transaction ID 0x6d13158
2023-08-07 18:56:59	172.16.1.1	bootps	172.16.1.135	bootpc	DHCP ACK - Transaction ID 0x6d13158

Figure 5.13 Adjusted view.

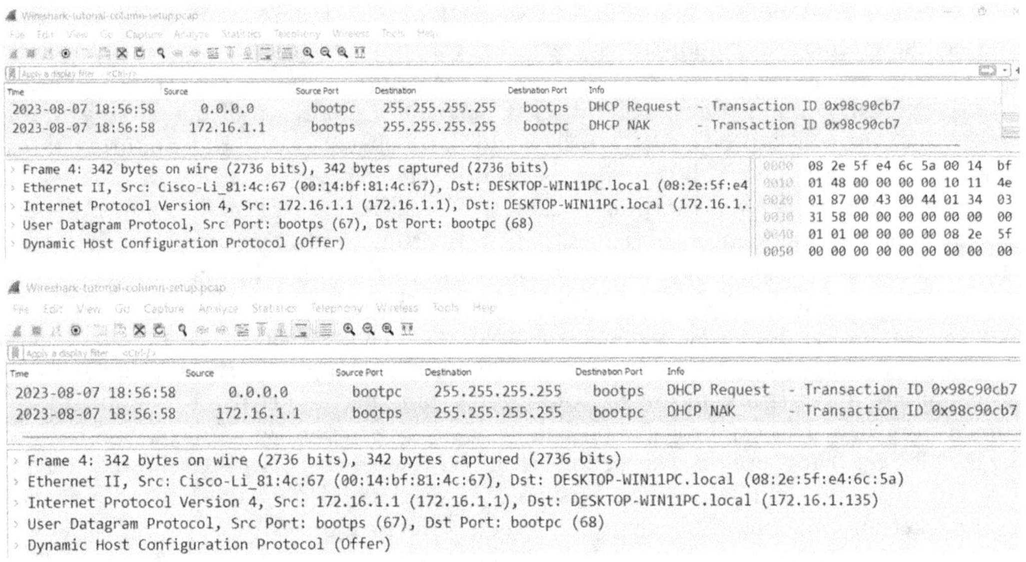

Figure 5.14 Hiding detailed packet bytes view.

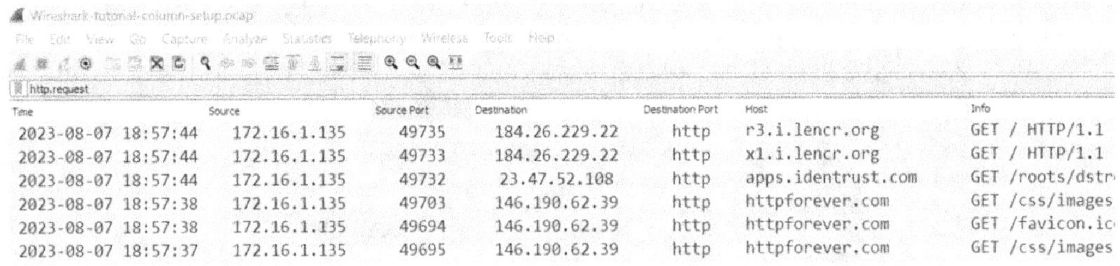

Figure 5.15 Filter for HTTP traffic.

Locate the line containing the Host field, which typically includes recognizable domain names such as msftconnecttest. Upon identifying this line, left-click to highlight it, then right-click to open a context menu. From the available options, choose Apply as Column. This action adds the domain name as a separate, easily viewable column in the packet list interface.

To analyze domains involved in encrypted HTTPS web traffic, a tailored column can be created in Wireshark for efficient tracking. Begin by ensuring the filter bar is cleared and then input the command tls.handshake.type eq 1 to isolate relevant handshake packets. Upon executing the filter, select the initial frame displayed in the results. Proceed by expanding the section labeled Transport Layer Security, which contains details of the encrypted session. Within this section, navigate to and expand the layer titled TLSv1.2 Record Layer: Handshake Protocol: Client Hello. Further details can be accessed by expanding the segment labeled Handshake Protocol: Client Hello. This process enables detailed inspection of domain information embedded within the client hello message, facilitating encrypted traffic analysis as shown in Figure 5.16.

In the detailed frame information section of the analysis tool, scroll down until you locate the line beginning with "Extension: server_name." Once found, expand this line to reveal its contents. Within this extension, identify and further expand the entry labeled "Server Name: Indication extension." Performing this action will result in the automatic addition of a new

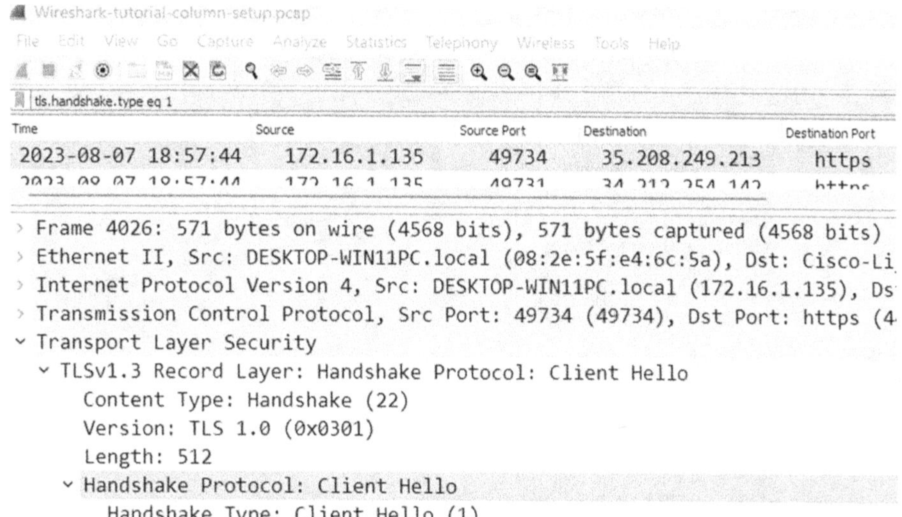

Figure 5.16 Filter for HTTPS traffic.

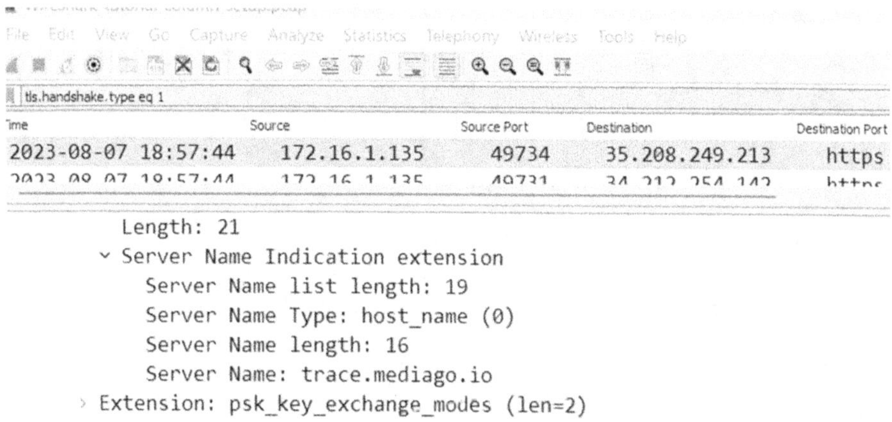

Figure 5.17 Check for server name.

column in the packet details pane. This new column, labeled "Server Name," will appear adjacent to the previously created "Host" column. The updated column structure, including the new Server Name field, is visually represented in Figure 5.17.

Beneath the main section, one will observe a line indicating the server's name, specifically labeled as *trace.mediago.io*. To proceed, the user should left-click on this line to highlight it. Following this, a right-click will open a contextual menu from which the option *Apply as Column* must be selected. This action is illustrated in Figure 5.18, demonstrating how the entry is transformed into a column within the data view for subsequent analysis.

To effectively monitor both HTTP and HTTPS traffic within a network capture, analysts can utilize specific filters in Wireshark. By applying the appropriate filter expression, it becomes possible to isolate and observe relevant web communication patterns. For instance, using the filter expression http.request or tls.handshake.type eq 1 enables the detection of initial HTTP requests as well as the TLS handshake processes that signal the beginning of

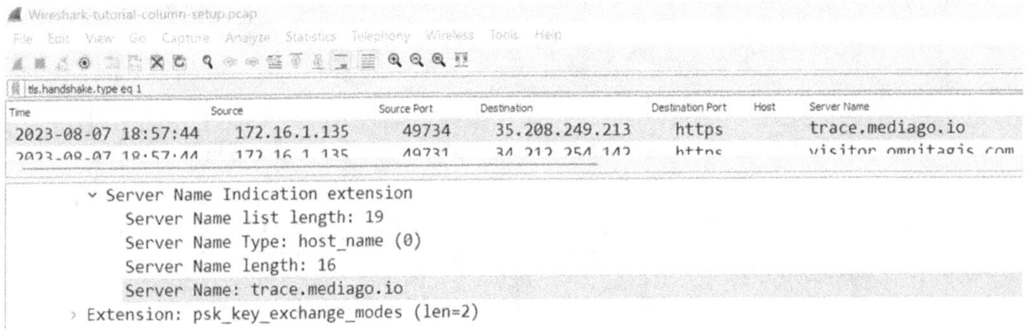

Figure 5.18 Apply data as column.

Figure 5.19 Filter for both HTTP and HTTPS traffic.

encrypted HTTPS sessions. This approach ensures that any domains or endpoints involved in the captured web traffic are reflected in the updated "Host" column, providing critical insight into network activity. Figure 5.19 illustrates this filtering method and its practical application within the Wireshark interface.

5.5.2 IP addresses

An IP (Internet Protocol) address is a numerical identifier assigned to a computer to communicate with other systems and the outside world. IP address is used to identify a host or network interface and display its location. IP addresses can be both public and private. In order for a device to establish communication over the internet, it must utilize both a public and a private Internet Protocol (IP) address. These two types of addresses play distinct yet interconnected roles in facilitating secure and functional network access. The private IP address is used within the local network, enabling communication among devices such as computers, smartphones, and printers connected to the same router. However, when a device attempts to access resources beyond the local network, such as websites or cloud services, this private address is not directly transmitted over the internet.

Instead, the network's router, typically managed by an Internet Service Provider (ISP), substitutes the private IP address with a public IP address that is assigned to the entire local network. This translation, often handled by Network Address Translation (NAT), acts as a protective mechanism that conceals the internal IP configurations from external entities.

By doing so, it safeguards the devices within the private network from direct exposure to the internet and permits multiple devices to share a single public IP address when accessing online resources. For instance, in a home network environment using Reliance Jio's Wi-Fi service, a device may be assigned a private IP address such as 192.168.29.114, as illustrated in Figure 5.20. This address enables the device to interact with others within the same Local Area Network (LAN), while its external communication is facilitated through the ISP's designated public IP address. This configuration underscores the dual-layered structure of IP addressing that underpins secure and efficient internet connectivity in contemporary networked systems.

The external IP address, visible to the broader internet, is typically an IPv6 format such as 2405:xxxx:xxxx::/xx. This globally unique identifier facilitates communication across networks and is essential for routing internet traffic effectively. Figure 5.21 provides a visual representation of this IPv6 address configuration in a real-world scenario.

Using a VPN, while locally I am in Dehradun, but virtually I am in England as validated in Figure 5.22.

```
Wireless LAN adapter Wi-Fi:

   Connection-specific DNS Suffix  . :
   IPv6 Address. . . . . . . . . . . : 2405:201:6804:426a:5666:de0:9858:ef77
   Temporary IPv6 Address. . . . . . : 2405:201:6804:426a:e52b:1425:68f8:3eb3
   Link-local IPv6 Address . . . . . : fe80::f560:2b79:ebb2:afd8%22
   IPv4 Address. . . . . . . . . . . : 192.168.29.114
   Subnet Mask . . . . . . . . . . . : 255.255.255.0
   Default Gateway . . . . . . . . . : fe80::aada:cff:fe3b:2f49%22
                                       192.168.29.1
```

Figure 5.20 Check IP version 4 and version 6 address.

Your IP Address	Country
2405:201:6804:426a:e52b:1425:68f8:3eb3	India

Coordinates	ISP
30.29203, 78.02043	Reliance Jio Infocomm Limited

Domain	Net Speed
ril.com	DSL

Weather Station	Mobile Carrier
Dehradun (INXX0140)	Jio

Elevation	Usage Type
621m	(MOB) Mobile ISP

Figure 5.21 IP address and geo-coordinates.

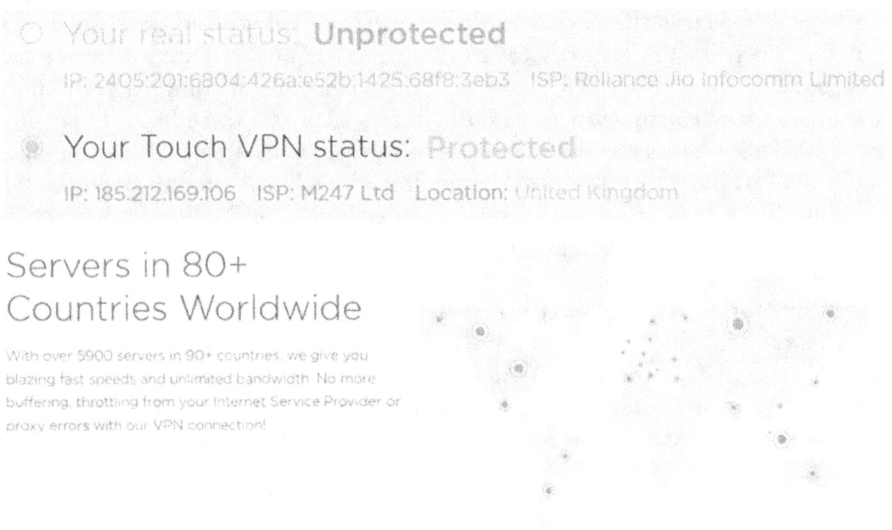

Figure 5.22 Virtual location using VPN.

5.5.3 Three way handshake

In network communications, the Transmission Control Protocol (TCP) plays a crucial role in guaranteeing the reliable delivery of data between two devices, such as a personal laptop and a remote server, across the Internet or a local network. Establishing a stable connection between these systems is achieved through a process known as the three-way handshake, which comprises three sequential steps: the initiation of synchronization (SYN), the server's response with a synchronization acknowledgment (SYN-ACK), and the client's final acknowledgment (ACK). This handshake ensures both devices are prepared for data exchange and agree on initial parameters. To observe this process in action, one can utilize a network protocol analyzer such as Wireshark. By capturing live network traffic and applying a filter such as tcp.port == 80, it becomes possible to analyze HTTP-based communication, as illustrated in Figure 5.23.

5.5.4 SSL handshake

The "SSL" in SSL Handshake is Secure Sockets Layer (SSL) security protocol is old (Netscape 1995), and people rarely use it these days. Servers and devices these days use Transport Layer Security (TLS) (early 2000) but some people continue to call this step as SSL Handshake which is negotiation about how two systems will communicate, and transfer information called "SSL Session."

Network traffic from any HTTPS-enabled website can be captured using Wireshark. To isolate relevant encrypted communication data, the traffic should be filtered using the SSL display filter. This process, illustrated in Figure 5.24, enables a focused examination of secure session packets transmitted between the client and the server.

5.5.5 Wireshark filters

5.5.5.1 Search for a specific IP Address in the network packet dump

Initiate the Wireshark application and allow it to run a live packet capture for approximately 10 to 15 seconds. During this period, network traffic data will be collected and displayed in

Filter: `tcp.port == 80`

No.	Time	Source	Source Port	Protocol	Destination	Destination Port	Info
21	2024-09-18 12:36…	2405:201…	61892	TCP	2404:6800:4002:81f…	http	61892 → http(80) [ACK] Seq=1 Ack=1 Win=514 Len=1
23	2024-09-18 12:36…	2404:680…	http	TCP	2405:201:6804:426a…	61892	http(80) → 61892 [ACK] Seq=1 Ack=2 Win=261 Len=0 S
504	2024-09-18 12:36…	2405:201…	61943	TCP	2600:1901:0:38d7::	http	61943 → http(80) [SYN] Seq=0 Win=64800 Len=0 MSS=1
510	2024-09-18 12:36…	2600:190…	http	TCP	2405:201:6804:426a…	61943	http(80) → 61943 [SYN, ACK] Seq=0 Ack=1 Win=65535
511	2024-09-18 12:36…	2405:201…	61943	TCP	2600:1901:0:38d7::	http	61943 → http(80) [ACK] Seq=1 Ack=1 Win=132352 Len=
512	2024-09-18 12:36…	2405:201…	61943	HTTP	2600:1901:0:38d7::	http	GET /canonical.html HTTP/1.1
515	2024-09-18 12:36…	2600:190…	http	TCP	2405:201:6804:426a…	61943	http(80) → 61943 [ACK] Seq=1 Ack=304 Win=66816 Len
516	2024-09-18 12:36…	2600:190…	http	HTTP	2405:201:6804:426a…	61943	HTTP/1.1 200 OK (text/html)

| 504 | 2024-09-18 12:36… | 2405:201… | 61943 | TCP | 2600:1901:0:38d7:: | http | 61943 → http(80) [SYN] Seq=0 Win=64800 Len=0 MSS=1 |

```
> [Expert Info (Chat/Sequence): Connection establish request (SYN): server port 80]
  .... .... ...0 = Fin: Not set
  [TCP Flags: ··········S·]
Window: 64800
[Calculated window size: 64800]
Checksum: 0xc8d9 [unverified]
[Checksum Status: Unverified]
Urgent Pointer: 0
v Options: (12 bytes), Maximum segment size, No-Operation (NOP), Window scale, No-Operation (NOP), No-Operation (NOP), SACK permittec
  v TCP Option - Maximum segment size: 1440 bytes
      Kind: Maximum Segment Size (2)
      Length: 4
      MSS Value: 1440
  > TCP Option - No-Operation (NOP)
  > TCP Option - Window scale: 8 (multiply by 256)
```

Figure 5.23 Filter for specific port.

Filter: `ssl`

No.	Time	Source	Source Port	Protocol	Destination	Destination Port	Server Name	Info
1	2024-09-18 13:13…	52.198.2…	https	TLSv1.2	192.168.29.114	63424		Application Data
33	2024-09-18 13:13…	192.168…	57893	QUIC	34.117.188.166	https	contile.service…	Initial, DCID=15aa0092538c0034, S
43	2024-09-18 13:13…	192.168…	63463	TLSv1.3	34.149.100.209	https	firefox.setting…	Client Hello
51	2024-09-18 13:13…	34.149.1…	https	TLSv1.3	192.168.29.114	63463		Server Hello, Change Cipher Spec
53	2024-09-18 13:13…	34.149.1…	https	TLSv1.3	192.168.29.114	63463		Application Data
58	2024-09-18 13:13…	34.117.1…	https	QUIC	192.168.29.114	57893		Handshake, DCID=23f3d0, SCID=f5a2
79	2024-09-18 13:13…	192.168…	64257	QUIC	34.110.138.217	https	merino.services…	Initial, DCID=70526a5fda75c7d0, S
83	2024-09-18 13:13…	192.168…	63424	TLSv1.2	52.198.223.169	https		Application Data
91	2024-09-18 13:13…	34.110.1…	https	QUIC	192.168.29.114	64257		Handshake, DCID=6a6ccf, SCID=f052
122	2024-09-18 13:13…	192.168…	63424	TLSv1.2	52.198.223.169	https		Application Data
123	2024-09-18 13:13…	192.168…	63463	TLSv1.3	34.149.100.209	https		Change Cipher Spec, Application C
125	2024-09-18 13:13…	192.168…	63463	TLSv1.3	34.149.100.209	https		Application Data
134	2024-09-18 13:13…	2405:201…	63467	TLSv1.2	2600:1901:0:92au::	https	content-signatu…	Client Hello
149	2024-09-18 13:13…	192.168…	63468	TLSv1.3	34.110.138.217	https	merino.services…	Client Hello
150	2024-09-18 13:13…	34.149.1…	https	TLSv1.3	192.168.29.114	63463		Application Data, Application Dat
152	2024-09-18 13:13…	34.149.1…	https	TLSv1.3	192.168.29.114	63463		Application Data
154	2024-09-18 13:13…	192.168…	63463	TLSv1.3	34.149.100.209	https		Application Data
161	2024-09-18 13:13…	2600:190…	https	TLSv1.2	2405:201:6804:426a…	63467		Server Hello
163	2024-09-18 13:13…	2600:190…	https	TLSv1.2	2405:201:6804:426a…	63467		Certificate, Server Key Exchange,
169	2024-09-18 13:13…	2405:201…	63467	TLSv1.2	2600:1901:0:92a9::	https		Client Key Exchange, Change Ciphe
173	2024-09-18 13:13…	2405:201…	64862	QUIC	2404:6800:4002:813…	https	www.google.com	Initial, DCID=6cb38ef439abcfb4c5,

Figure 5.24 Filter for SSL traffic packets.

real time, similar to the illustration provided in Figure 5.25, offering insights into ongoing communication exchanges across the monitored network interface.

To locate the system's IP address, access the search bar and open the Command Prompt (CMD). Enter the command ipconfig to retrieve network configuration details. The IP address assigned to the system will appear in the output. As illustrated in Figure 5.26, the observed IP address is 10.3.7.132.

To analyze specific network traffic in Wireshark, enter the filter expression ip.addr == 10.3.7.132 or substitute it with the relevant private IP address. As illustrated in Figure 5.27, this filter isolates all packets that either originate from or are directed toward the specified IP, aiding focused inspection.

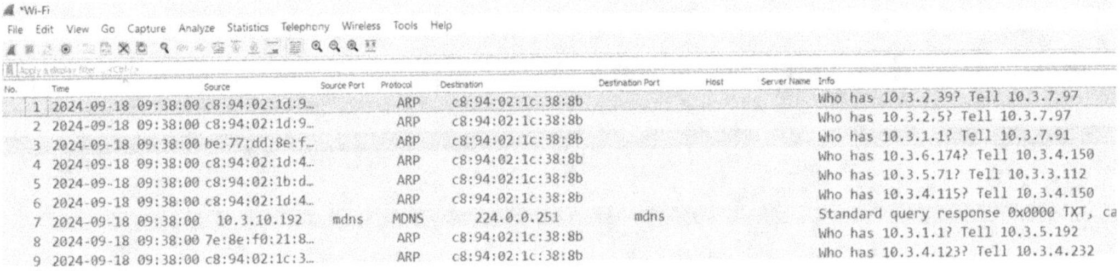

Figure 5.25 Wireshark packet capture.

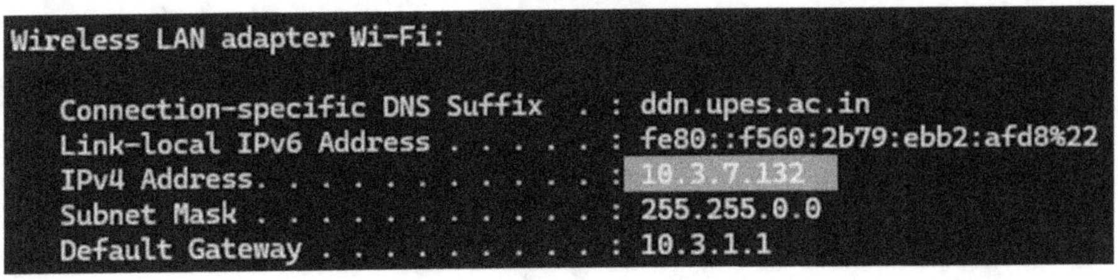

Figure 5.26 Check for IP address.

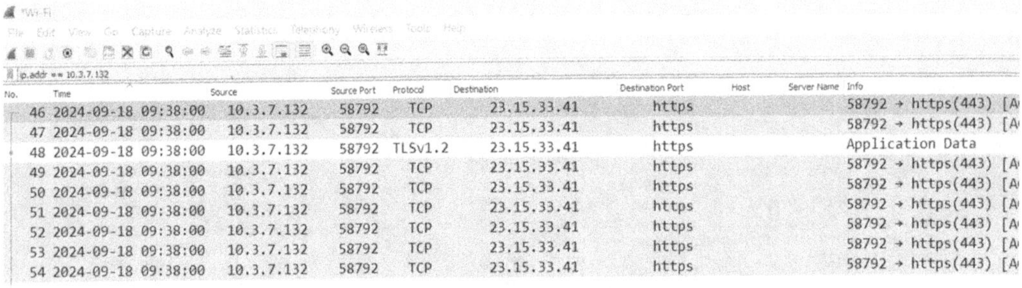

Figure 5.27 Filter for specific IP address.

5.5.5.2 Search for a specific port number

To filter and analyze HTTP traffic within the same captured data stream, the expression tcp.
port == 80 can be applied. This command isolates packets transmitted over port 80, which is
commonly used for HTTP communication. The filtered output, as illustrated in Figure 5.28,
provides a focused view of web traffic.

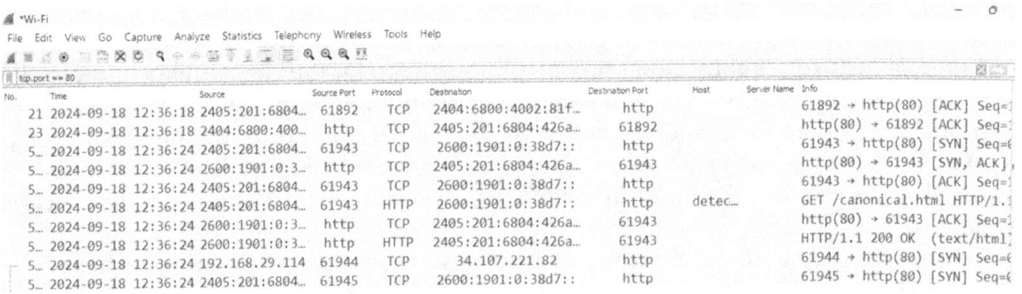

Figure 5.28 Filter for port 80.

5.5.5.3 Search for a specific keyword or word in the traffic dump

To filter and examine specific HTTP traffic within the same captured dataset, the frame matching expression abc can be applied. This method isolates relevant packets, facilitating focused analysis. As illustrated in Figure 5.29, this targeted approach enhances visibility into HTTP communication patterns, streamlining traffic inspection and protocol-level diagnostics.

5.5.5.4 Export objects (files) from PACP

In the analysis of network packet captures (pcap) linked to suspicious activities, cybersecurity analysts often extract embedded objects such as malware binaries for detailed inspection. Certain malware targeting Windows systems may be transmitted via unencrypted HTTP traffic. For instance, Figure 5.30 illustrates extracted objects from a sample pcap filtered using http.request.

Two HTTP GET requests were made to the domain smart-fax.com. The first request terminated with the .doc extension, suggesting that it potentially delivered a Microsoft Word document. The second request ended with the .exe extension, indicating that it likely retrieved a Windows executable file. To further examine the contents of the Word document, it can be extracted from the HTTP object list. This is done by navigating to the File menu, selecting Export Objects, then choosing HTTP, and finally saving the desired object, as demonstrated in Figure 5.31. Such extraction aids in forensic analysis and malware detection.

To analyze upload these files to VirusTotal and other malware analysis portal, create your report.

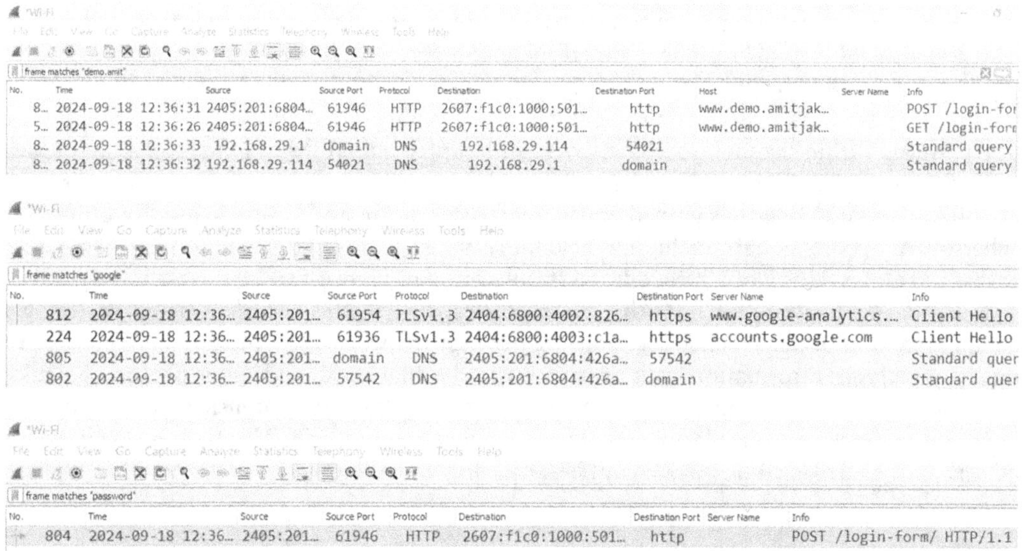

Figure 5.29 Filter for specific keyword.

Figure 5.30 PACP dump with objects and files.

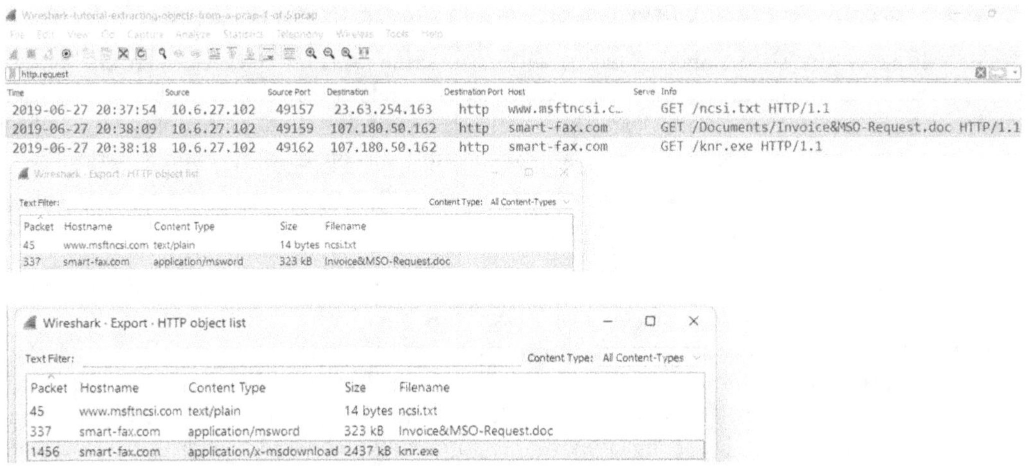

Figure 5.31 Select object from packets.

5.5.6 NetworkMiner

NetworkMiner is a widely adopted, open-source tool designed for conducting network forensics by analyzing captured network traffic. It is capable of extracting a variety of artifacts, including files, images, email communications, and even credentials such as passwords from packet capture (PCAP) files. In addition to offline analysis, NetworkMiner also supports live traffic monitoring by sniffing data directly from a network interface. One of its core features is the ability to compile detailed metadata for each IP address encountered during traffic analysis, thereby creating an inventory of network hosts. This host-based view facilitates passive asset discovery and provides valuable insights into device-to-device communication patterns within the monitored network. Although originally developed for the Windows operating system, the tool is also compatible with Linux environments. Since its initial release in 2007, NetworkMiner has gained widespread recognition and is now regularly utilized by cybersecurity professionals, including incident response teams and law enforcement agencies across the globe. This global usage trend is illustrated in Figure 5.32.

When a PCAP file is opened, the recorded network traffic becomes visible, offering a detailed account of packet exchanges during the capture period. As illustrated in Figure 5.33, this data includes information such as source and destination IP addresses, protocols, packet size, and timestamps, enabling comprehensive traffic analysis and forensic investigation.

A comprehensive collection of malware packet capture (PCAP) files is available at https://www.netresec.com/?page=PcapFiles, offering valuable resources for network forensic

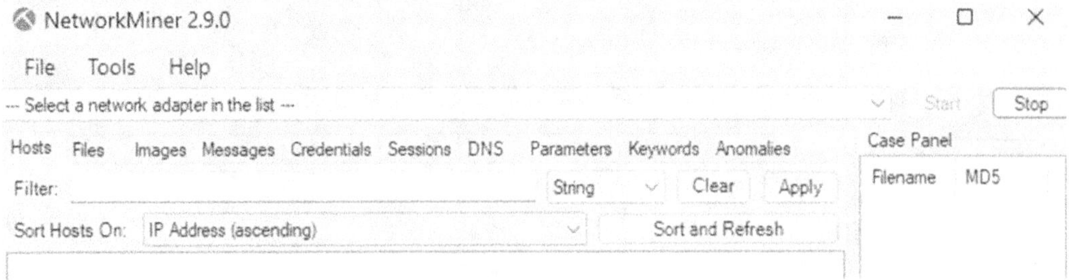

Figure 5.32 NetworkMiner GUI.

NetworkMiner 2.9.0

File   Tools   Help

--- Select a network adapter in the list ---

Hosts (10) Files (3) Images Messages Credentials Sessions (4) DNS (8) Parameters (155) Keywords Anomalies

Filter:

Sort Hosts On: IP Address (ascending)

10.6.27.1
10.6.27.102 [Rutherford-PC] [RUTHERFORD-PC] (Windows)
10.6.27.255
23.63.254.163 [a1961.g2.akamai.net] [www.msftncsi.com.edgesuite.net] [www.msftncsi.com] (Other)
23.63.254.176 [a1961.g2.akamai.net] [www.msftncsi.com.edgesuite.net]
23.105.131.229 [dunlop.hopto.org] (Other)
107.180.50.162 [smart-fax.com] (Other)
131.107.255.255 [dns.msftncsi.com]
224.0.0.252
255.255.255.255

Figure 5.33 Open network traffic dump.

NetworkMiner 2.9.0

File   Tools   Help

--- Select a network adapter in the list ---

Hosts (74) Files (374) Images Messages Credentials (11) Sessions (499) DNS (506) Parameters (9350) Keywords Anomalies

Show Cookies   Show NTLM challenge-response   Mask Passwords

Client	Server	Protocol	Username
10.0.19.14 [DESKTOP-5QS3D5D]	188.166.154.118 [oceriesfornot.top]	HTTP Cookie	__gads=3546287305:1:14094:123; _gat=10.0.19044.64; _
10.0.19.14 [DESKTOP-5QS3D5D] [DESKTOP-5QS3D5D.b...	10.0.19.9 [BURNINCANDLE] [BURNINCANDLE-DC] [bum...	Kerberos	patrick.zimmerman
10.0.19.14 [DESKTOP-5QS3D5D] [DESKTOP-5QS3D5D.b...	10.0.19.9 [BURNINCANDLE] [BURNINCANDLE-DC] [bum...	Kerberos	patrick.zimmerman
10.0.19.14 [DESKTOP-5QS3D5D] [DESKTOP-5QS3D5D.b...	10.0.19.9 [BURNINCANDLE] [BURNINCANDLE-DC] [bum...	Kerberos	patrick.zimmerman

Figure 5.34 Analyze network PCAP file.

analysis. Alternatively, the PCAP file utilized in the previous example may be examined using NetworkMiner, following the methodology demonstrated in Figure 5.34, to extract and interpret network-based artifacts linked to malicious activity.

5.5.7 FakeNet

FakeNet is a specialized network simulation utility developed for Windows environments, primarily aimed at facilitating dynamic malware analysis. Its core function involves intercepting and redirecting all outbound network traffic, whether originating from hardcoded IP addresses or domain name resolution requests back to the local machine (localhost). This redirection mechanism ensures that even evasive or network-dependent malware remains active and observable during analysis. To support this, FakeNet emulates a range of common network protocols, including DNS, HTTP, and SSL, thereby maintaining the illusion of a legitimate external network environment for the malicious software. Additionally, it offers a Python-based extension interface, enabling security researchers to develop and integrate custom protocol handlers tailored to specific threats or investigative needs. Beyond protocol emulation, FakeNet is equipped to monitor traffic on any network port and can generate packet capture logs locally, providing a comprehensive view of the malware's communication

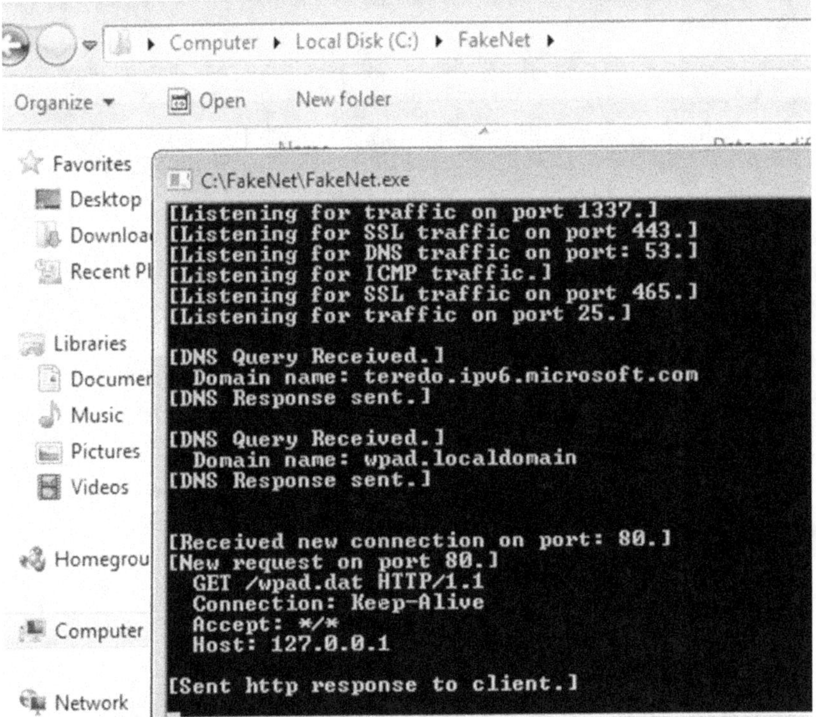

Figure 5.35 FakeNet traffic.

behavior. This combination of features makes FakeNet a valuable asset in the toolkit of cybersecurity professionals conducting in-depth threat assessments.

Use a Windows OS VM (Win7 Pro OS). Disconnect Internet, set your LAN card → Host only. Unzip and run FakeNet with Administrator privileges, this modifies the DNS settings for that VM and allows others to begin connections and immediately you can see tons of requests. This simulates an Internet connection as shown in Figure 5.35.

If you try to open any web portal (Facebook, Gmail) it gives you the webpage below as if the website is accessible as displayed in Figure 5.36.

The FakeNet command interface provides detailed insights into network connections initiated by potentially suspicious processes. It displays the destination of each connection, including associated IP addresses or domain names, the application used to initiate the

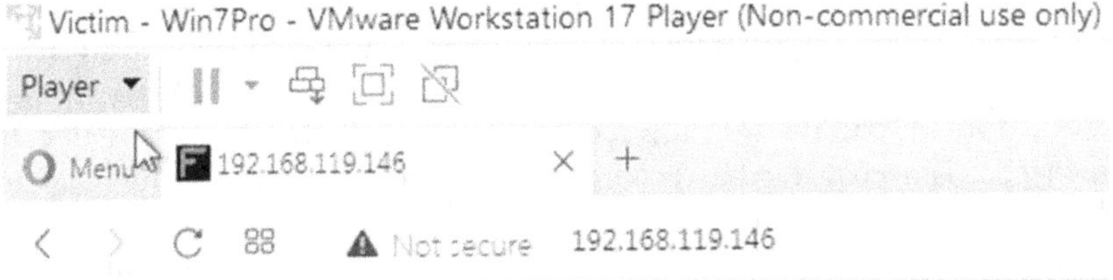

Figure 5.36 Allowing DNS & web access via FakeNet.

```
The format for the options are:
'PacketDumpOptions DumpPackets:XXX Fileprefix:XXXX
'DNSOptions ModifyLocalDNS:XXX
'InvasiveOptions EnableDummyService:XXX RedirectAllTraffic:XX MaxListeners:##
'OutputOptions DumpHTTPPosts:XXX DumpOutput:Yes Fileprevix:XXXX

'These are the default global options
```

Figure 5.37 Edit Config file for saving traffic dump.

```
  ┌─(kali㉿kali)-[~]
  └─$ sudo nmap -sV -O 192.168.119.146
Starting Nmap 7.94SVN ( https://nmap.org ) at 2024-09-14 17:15 +06
Stats: 0:01:34 elapsed; 0 hosts completed (1 up), 1 undergoing Service Scan
Service scan Timing: About 57.14% done; ETC: 17:18 (0:01:00 remaining)
Stats: 0:03:19 elapsed; 0 hosts completed (1 up), 1 undergoing Script Scan
NSE Timing: About 99.46% done; ETC: 17:18 (0:00:00 remaining)
Nmap scan report for 192.168.119.146
Host is up (0.0011s latency).
Not shown: 979 closed tcp ports (reset)
PORT       STATE  SERVICE         VERSION
25/tcp     open   smtp?
80/tcp     open   http
135/tcp    open   msrpc           Microsoft Windows RPC
139/tcp    open   netbios-ssn     Microsoft Windows netbios-ssn
443/tcp    open   ssl/https
445/tcp    open   microsoft-ds    Microsoft Windows 7 - 10 microsoft-ds (workgroup: WORKGROUP)
465/tcp    open   ssl/smtps?
554/tcp    open   rtsp?
```

Figure 5.38 NMAP scan for windows VM.

traffic, such as Firefox and the specific port or protocol employed. For comprehensive traffic analysis, the configuration file *FakeNet.cfg* must be modified. Specifically, the parameter DumpOutput should be set to Yes in place of its default placeholder value. This enables the saving of all captured traffic into a PCAP file. The recorded data can then be analyzed using packet inspection tools such as Wireshark, as illustrated in Figure 5.37.

To verify the open ports on the VM running FakeNet, access the Kali Linux environment and perform a network scan using the NMAP tool. This procedure, illustrated in Figure 5.38, allows for the identification of active services and listening ports, ensuring proper visibility into the system's exposed interfaces.

5.6 MALWARE ANALYSIS WITH CLOUD-BASED PORTALS

Use cloud portal to understand the basics of malware analysis.

5.6.1 ANY.RUN

ANY.RUN is an advanced cloud-based platform designed for cybersecurity professionals to detect, monitor, and analyze potential threats through URLs or files as shown in Figure 5.39. Functioning as an interactive malware analysis sandbox, it enables real-time inspection and manipulation of threat behaviors, offering deeper visibility into malicious activity and a 15-day trial version is available.

For the environment setup, a Windows operating system was selected along with specific versions of commonly used web browsers to closely reflect typical end-user configurations. To enhance the realism of the analysis, pre-installed software suites, including productivity tools like Microsoft Office, were incorporated, thereby replicating authentic usage scenarios.

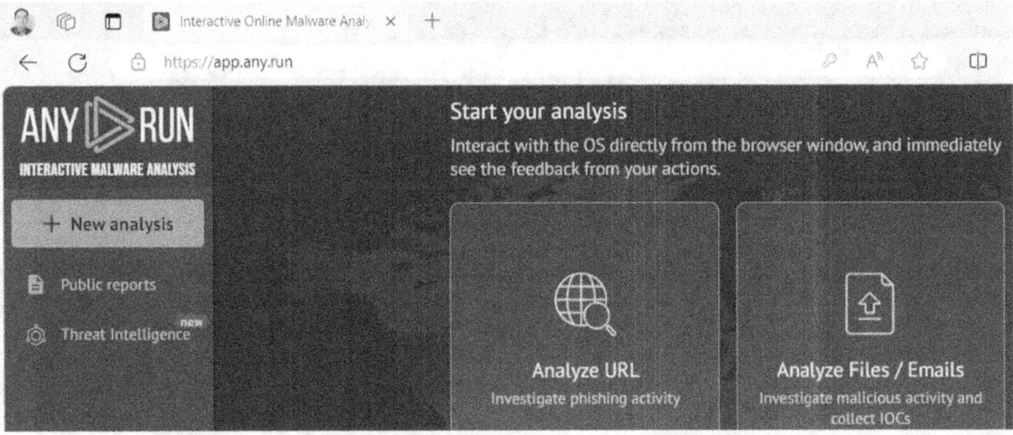

Figure 5.39 Any.Run GUI portal.

Figure 5.40 Any.Run network options.

Figure 5.40 illustrates the network configuration included a HTTPS Man-in-the-Middle (MITM) proxy, enabling the interception and inspection of encrypted traffic. This facilitated detailed observation of malware communications with command-and-control (C2) infrastructure. Additionally, FakeNet was employed to simulate network responses, effectively detecting malware with worm-like behavior or attempts to connect to non-functional or deceptive external servers.

5.6.2 Hybrid-analysis

The community is provided access to a complimentary malware analysis platform built upon the Falcon Sandbox framework, which facilitates comprehensive static and dynamic inspection of submitted files. Falcon Sandbox is recognized for its advanced analytical capabilities and modular, flexible architecture. This adaptability allows it to be deployed in various configurations, ranging from large-scale automated systems capable of analyzing thousands of samples via a straightforward REST API, to more focused implementations such as web-based services for digital forensics, incident response, or enterprise-level self-service portals. An example of such an implementation is depicted in Figure 5.41.

Thanks to its user-friendly interface and extensive integration features with a wide range of technology platforms, Falcon Sandbox effectively enhances the incident response workflows and overall security infrastructure within SOCs. Its adaptability and robust analytical capabilities have made it a trusted tool among diverse cybersecurity stakeholders. Today, it is widely utilized by SOC teams, Computer Emergency Response Teams (CERTs), Digital

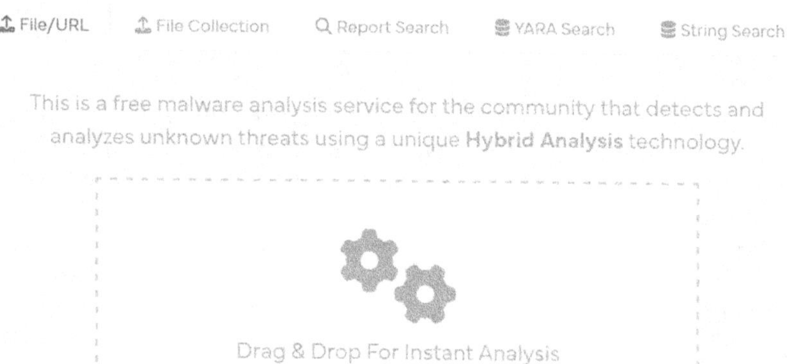

Figure 5.41 Hybrid analysis portal.

Forensics and Incident Response (DFIR) professionals, IT security and forensic laboratories, academic researchers, and global threat intelligence service providers, underscoring its critical role in modern cyber defense operations.

Multiple S&P 100, Fortune 500 and U.S. government agencies are using Falcon Sandbox and enjoying it every day.

5.6.3 FileScan.IO

Filescan.io represents a modern malware analysis platform designed to thoroughly examine files and URLs for potential threats. It supports the scanning of various file types, including executables, documents, and scripts, aiming not just to detect malware but to deeply analyze file behavior and extract IoCs. This helps in identifying larger attack patterns, as displayed in Figure 5.42.

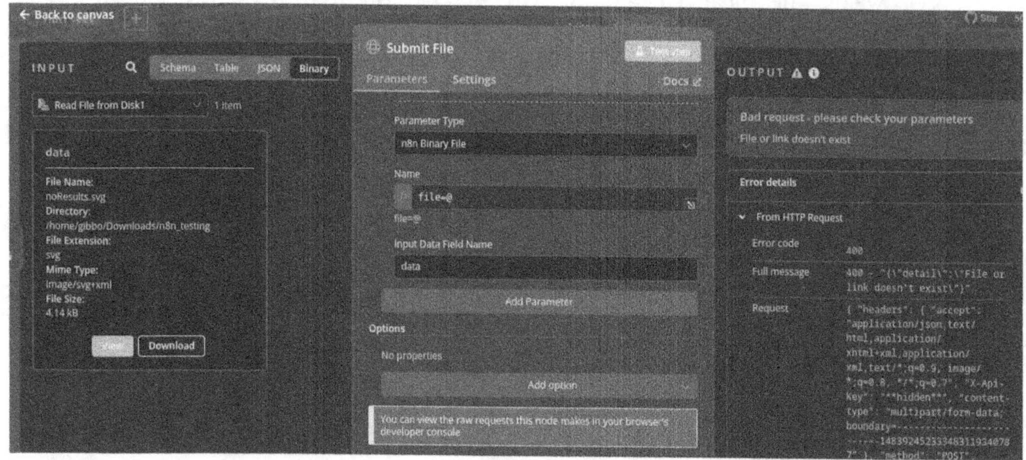

Figure 5.42 Filescan IO analysis.

The platform is known for its speed and efficiency, requiring fewer system resources compared to traditional tools. Filescan.io operates under a freemium model, offering basic functionality for free, with advanced features available through paid plans. Developed by OPSWAT, a recognized name in cybersecurity, the platform may be challenging for beginners due to its detailed technical reports. It may also flag suspicious, yet non-malicious files, necessitating careful interpretation.

5.7 CONCLUSION

Malware analysis remains a cornerstone of modern cybersecurity defense strategies, providing critical insight into how malicious software operates, spreads, and impacts digital ecosystems. This chapter has detailed the structured methodologies employed in both static and dynamic malware analysis, highlighting the importance of safe environments, such as VMs and sandboxes, to prevent inadvertent damage during investigations. It has also illustrated the utility of open-source and commercial tools in extracting meaningful IoCs, essential for threat detection and remediation. As cyber threats continue to evolve in sophistication and frequency, cloud-based analysis platforms like ANY.RUN, Hybrid Analysis, and Filescan.io have emerged as vital resources, offering scalable, real-time visibility into malware behavior. The integration of such platforms with traditional tools enables a more comprehensive and collaborative approach to threat intelligence. Practical techniques like file signature validation, hash comparison, string analysis, and network traffic monitoring further enhance the analyst's ability to detect and understand novel malware strains. The collaborative effort of SOC analysts, incident responders, and malware researchers ensures an adaptive, layered defense capable of addressing both known and unknown threats. Overall, the knowledge and practices outlined in this chapter equip cybersecurity professionals with the tools and workflows necessary to anticipate, identify, and mitigate malicious activity effectively. These skills not only support incident response efforts but also play a pivotal role in building more resilient and secure information systems in an increasingly hostile digital landscape.

MULTIPLE CHOICE QUESTIONS

1. During an investigation, a SOC analyst receives a suspicious file named "invoice.jpg," but when viewed in Windows Explorer, it has a large file size of 4 MB. Opening it in HxD reveals a hex header beginning with 4D 5A, followed by the text *"This program cannot be run in DOS mode"*. VirusTotal shows several detections identifying it as a trojan dropper. What technique is the malware using?

    A. Polymorphic obfuscation
    B. Double-extension masquerading
    C. Payload encryption
    D. DLL side-loading

    Correct Answer: B
    Why correct: The chapter discusses attackers disguising EXEs as .jpg/.doc by editing only the extension, while the header still shows MZ (PE file). Why others are wrong:
    - A: No code mutation described.
    - C: Nothing indicates encryption.
    - D: DLLs not involved.

2. A Windows VM running FLARE-VM receives a suspicious binary. Analysts generate MD5, SHA1, and SHA256 hashes using HashMyFiles and MultiHasher. The MD5 matches a known ransomware family in multiple databases, but SHA256 does not. Despite this mismatch, VirusTotal shows 50+ detections marking it malicious. What is the best interpretation?

   A. It is a false positive
   B. The file is new malware, unrelated to known families
   C. This is a minor variant sharing enough similarity for detection
   D. VirusTotal has corrupted metadata

   Correct Answer: C
   Why correct: Hash-based detection fails on slight modifications; multi-engine behavioral detections still classify it correctly. Why others are wrong:
   - A: 50+ engines disagree.
   - B: MD5 match points to same lineage.
   - D: VirusTotal does not corrupt hashes.

3. A suspicious executable is detonated inside a Windows 10 sandbox, but no registry changes, network calls, or file modifications occur. Analysts notice the malware exits instantly. A strings review reveals references to "VMware," "VirtualBox," and "sandboxie.dll." What is happening?

   A. Malware is corrupt and cannot run
   B. Malware is detecting sandbox artifacts and aborting
   C. Network block rules prevented execution
   D. The sample is actually benign

   Correct Answer: B
   Why correct: Chapter explains malware detecting sandboxes and altering behavior as an evasion method. Why others are wrong:
   - A: Strings clearly show anti-VM logic.
   - C: Even offline malware will show system modifications.
   - D: Malicious strings indicate intent.

4. Analysts run FakeNet-NG inside a Windows VM. A sample launches and immediately begins attempting DNS lookups, HTTPS connections, and HTTP GET requests, all redirected to localhost. The malware continues execution normally, logging output to PCAP even with no internet access. What characteristic of FakeNet is being used?

   A. Network packet encryption
   B. Protocol emulation to trick malware
   C. Dynamic DLL injection
   D. Behavioral sandboxing

   Correct Answer: B
   Why correct: FakeNet creates fake DNS, HTTP, SSL responses to simulate an internet connection, allowing malware to "think" the network is real. Why others are wrong:
   - A: FakeNet does not encrypt malware traffic.
   - C: No DLL injection described.
   - D: Sandbox is separate – FakeNet is only network simulation.

5. Static analysis of a dropper reveals imports including URLDownloadFileA, InternetOpenA, and RegSetValueExA. Network analysis shows attempts to download a second-stage payload. No encryption observed. Which malware role does this best match?

   A. Worm designed for lateral movement
   B. Dropper used for multistage payload delivery
   C. Ransomware already encrypted files
   D. Keylogger silently stealing data

   Correct Answer: B
   Why correct: The imports and behavior (download + registry changes) match a classic dropper, as defined in the chapter. Why others are wrong:
   - A: No propagation behavior.
   - C: No encryption activity.
   - D: Keyloggers require hook APIs.

6. A malware analyst inspects a suspicious EXE in HxD and confirms MZ/PE signatures, but further inspection shows corrupted section headers and unusual entropy patterns. When loaded into a debugger, it crashes instantly. What does this most likely indicate?

   A. Benign software damaged during download
   B. Packed or obfuscated malware
   C. Incorrect CPU architecture
   D. Wrong file type mislabeling

   Correct Answer: B
   Why correct: Packed malware intentionally modifies section sizes, header structures, and entropy – classic signs. Why others are wrong:
   - A: Entropy patterns imply intentional packing.
   - C: Architecture mismatch triggers error messages, not high entropy.
   - D: It *is* a PE file.

7. A PCAP from an infected endpoint shows two HTTP GET requests to smart-fax. com, retrieving a .doc followed by a .exe. Exporting objects reveals the EXE contains high-entropy data and embedded macros inside the DOC. What attack chain does this represent?

   A. Worm propagation
   B. Email-based malware delivery
   C. Drive-by download attack
   D. Multistage dropper via HTTP

   Correct Answer: D
   Why correct: PCAP directly shows HTTP GET → malicious DOC → EXE payload, matching a staged dropper infection. Why others are wrong:
   - A: No scanning/spread.
   - B: No evidence of email.
   - C: Not browser-based exploit.

8. Inside ANY.RUN, analysts detonate a malware sample. Within seconds, it spawns PowerShell, modifies Run registry keys, and attempts TLS connections using SNI indicators. FakeNet responses keep malware active. What phase of analysis is most valuable here?

   A. Static analysis only
   B. Behavioral analysis during sandbox execution
   C. Manual debugging via assembly breakpoints
   D. TLS certificate reverse engineering

   Correct Answer: B
   Why correct: ANY.RUN gives real-time process creation, registry changes, and network indicators – behavioral analysis. Why others are wrong:
   - A: Static alone can't reveal registry changes.
   - C: Not using a debugger.
   - D: SNI insight is useful but secondary.

9. A suspicious file is uploaded to Hybrid Analysis. The platform shows "high threat score," "file persistence detected," and "connecting to suspicious TLDs." The community report labels it as a trojan. Hybrid Analysis is acting primarily as:

   A. A static hash comparison system
   B. A dynamic behavioral sandbox
   C. A network firewall emulator
   D. A binary decompiler

   Correct Answer: B
   Why correct: Hybrid Analysis (Falcon Sandbox) focuses on dynamic behavior scoring. Why others are wrong:
   - A: It does more than hashing.
   - C: It doesn't emulate firewalls.
   - D: Not focused on de-compilation.

10. Static analysis using the strings utility finds references to URLs, "cmd.exe," "powershell.exe," "RegDeleteValue," and unusual domain names ending with .ru. What conclusion is most accurate?

    A. Files contain harmless debug strings
    B. Likely a trojan that executes commands and modifies registry
    C. The file is encrypted and unreadable
    D. A macOS-targeted malware

    Correct Answer: B
    Why correct: Strings show command execution + registry APIs + suspicious domains = trojan behavior. Why others are wrong:
    - A: Debug strings rarely include RU domains or registry editing.
    - C: Strings visible means it is *not* encrypted.
    - D: Windows-specific APIs.

11. A malware analyst runs a sample inside a VM but forgets to disable NAT internet access. Logs show the file successfully contacted a known C2 server. Which danger does this create?

   A. The malware will self-delete
   B. The malware may exfiltrate data or download live payloads
   C. The malware will corrupt the VM only
   D. Nothing – VMs are always safe

Correct Answer: B
Why correct: Chapter strongly warns to block internet access; real C2 contact can cause real damage. Why others are wrong:
- A: No reason for self-deletion.
- C: It can escape via network.
- D: VMs are not foolproof.

12. A PCAP is analyzed in NetworkMiner. It automatically extracted EXE files, images, and credentials. Host profiles show multiple outbound connections to high-risk geolocations. What is the main strength NetworkMiner provides here?

   A. Static code analysis
   B. Passive asset discovery and artifact extraction
   C. Live memory inspection
   D. Reverse engineering capabilities

Correct Answer: B
Why correct: NetworkMiner is designed for passive host profiling and file/credential extraction from PCAPs. Why others are wrong:
- A: It does not inspect code.
- C: It doesn't read live memory.
- D: Not used for reverse engineering.

13. An analyst filters tls.handshake.type eq 1. They extract the Server Name Indication (SNI) column and see repeated connections to trace.mediago.io. The malware attempts encrypted communication before payload execution. Which conclusion is accurate?

   A. The malware uses SNI for encrypted C2 traffic
   B. The malware is benign because SNI is normal
   C. The malware is performing LAN-only communication
   D. The malware is running without network access

Correct Answer: A
Why correct: Chapter explains extracting SNI from TLS to identify domains used for C2 connections. Why others are wrong:
- B: SNI to suspicious domains is not normal.
- C: TLS goes outside LAN.
- D: TLS handshake proves network activity.

14. FakeNet is running inside a Windows VM. From Kali Linux, the analyst performs an Nmap scan and sees ports 80, 443, and 53 open, even though the VM has no internet. What does this indicate?

   A. Malware opened these ports
   B. FakeNet is simulating commonly used network services
   C. Windows has a built-in web server
   D. Nmap malfunctioned

Correct Answer: B
Why correct: FakeNet emulates DNS/HTTP/SSL to trick malware into thinking the internet exists. Why others are wrong:
- A: No malware mentioned yet.
- C: Windows doesn't expose these ports by default.
- D: Nmap is accurate.

15. A malware team faces a large suspicious campaign. Analysts must triage 200 samples quickly. Running each sample in a local VM with REMnux would take hours. ANY.RUN and Filescan.io offer batch processing with cloud sandboxes. Which approach is most efficient?

    A. Analyze all samples in local VM for accuracy
    B. Use cloud-based sandboxing to scale triage
    C. Increase VM RAM for faster results
    D. Skip dynamic analysis entirely

Correct Answer: B
Why correct: Cloud solutions provide scalable, fast analysis as explained. Why others are wrong:
- A: Not scalable.
- C: RAM does not fix throughput.
- D: Eliminates crucial insights.

REFERENCES

1. "The future of ransomware: Inside Cisco Talos threat hunters," *Cisco*, May 2025. Accessed Jul. 15, 2025. https://www.cisco.com/site/in/en/learn/topics/security/what-is-malware.html#tabs-3823800186-item-755666231a-tab
2. Fortinet, "What is a remote access Trojan (RAT)?," *Fortinet*, 2022. https://www.fortinet.com/resources/cyberglossary/remote-access-trojan
3. R. Grimmick, "What is C2? Command and control infrastructure explained," *varonis.com*, Aug. 8, 2022. https://www.varonis.com/blog/what-is-c2
4. IBM, "Security operations center," *Ibm.com*, Nov. 24, 2021. https://www.ibm.com/think/topics/security-operations-center
5. J. Holdsworth and M. Kosinski, "What is incident response?" *Ibm.com*, Aug. 20, 2024. https://www.ibm.com/think/topics/incident-response
6. Fortinet, "Indicators of compromise (IOCs)," *Fortinet*, 2024. https://www.fortinet.com/resources/cyberglossary/indicators-of-compromise

Chapter 6

Mapping adversary

CTI frameworks

6.1 CTI FRAMEWORKS

In the digital age, cyberattacks have emerged as a serious threat to the integrity and security of information systems across all sectors. These hostile actions are deliberately carried out by malicious actors, commonly referred to as cybercriminals or hackers, who target computer networks, digital infrastructure, and other technology-driven environments. The primary objective behind such attacks is to gain unauthorized access, exfiltrate confidential or sensitive information, or cause significant disruption and damage to the targeted systems. To achieve their goals, attackers employ a wide array of techniques, including but not limited to phishing schemes, malicious software (malware), distributed denial-of-service (DDoS) assaults, ransomware, social engineering tactics, man-in-the-middle (MitM) interceptions, and brute force intrusions. The consequences of these cyber intrusions are far-reaching and can be devastating.

Victims ranging from individuals and private corporations to public institutions and governments experience substantial financial setbacks, loss of personal or proprietary data, and, in extreme cases, the breakdown of essential services and critical infrastructure. The evolving nature and increasing sophistication of cyberattacks underscore the urgent need for robust cybersecurity measures and continuous vigilance. The stages of a Cyberattack include the steps as illustrated in Figure 6.1.

Reconnaissance is the initial stage of a cyberattack is reconnaissance. In this stage, hackers gather intelligence or information on a potential target. In this phase of a cyber intrusion, threat actors begin by gathering intelligence from openly accessible platforms and public-facing digital spaces. Popular sources for this reconnaissance include social networking and employment platforms such as LinkedIn, Facebook, Twitter, and job portals like Indeed. These data-rich environments provide attackers with valuable insights into a target's identity, geographic location, digital infrastructure, associated service providers, and even technical configurations. The primary intention at this phase is to identify active hosts and discern exploitable vectors within the target's ecosystem.

Following this intelligence-gathering phase, adversaries transition into the resource development or weaponization stage. At this juncture, the attackers begin crafting or acquiring the necessary tools and capabilities required for successful penetration. This might involve purchasing or renting cloud-based servers or physical hardware, developing custom malware, or repurposing existing malicious code. The goal is to create a robust operational toolkit that can breach and compromise the target's digital infrastructure, service accounts, or connected devices.

Once adequately equipped, the attackers proceed to the initial access phase, where the goal is to infiltrate the target environment. This is often achieved through a variety of attack vectors such as social engineering tactics, phishing emails, brute force credential attacks, or

DOI: 10.1201/9781003730583-6

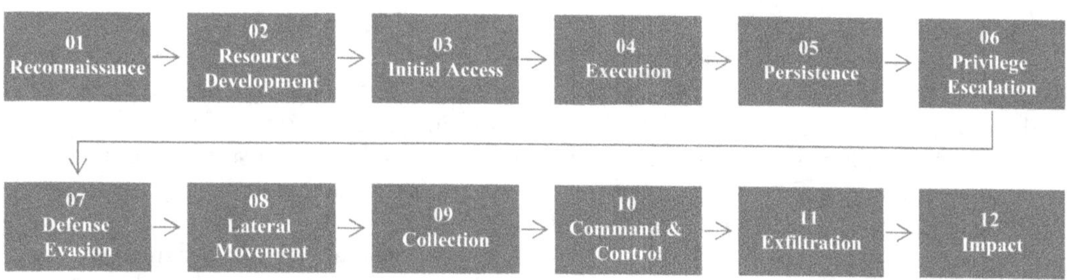

Figure 6.1 Cyberattack steps.

compromising exposed elements in the supply chain or web-facing infrastructure. This entry point marks the beginning of unauthorized access into the victim's network.

Upon gaining entry, adversaries initiate the execution phase, during which malicious payloads are deployed within the environment. These payloads may exploit built-in services, shared modules, containerized applications, or accessible APIs to run harmful scripts or commands. The attackers aim to achieve specific objectives while minimizing noise or anomalies that might alert defensive mechanisms.

Maintaining long-term access is crucial for adversaries, and this is achieved during the persistence phase. Here, techniques are employed to ensure continued control over the compromised environment, even if credentials are changed or systems rebooted. This might involve creating new administrative accounts, installing backdoors, disabling firewall rules, or deploying persistence mechanisms that reinitiate access upon system startup.

To deepen their hold, attackers often escalate privileges within the compromised environment. The privilege escalation stage allows them to gain higher-level permissions, typically reserved for system administrators or power users. With elevated access, attackers can manipulate system configurations, bypass restrictions, and expand their control to other components of the network.

Simultaneously, the attackers engage in defense evasion strategies to avoid detection by security systems and monitoring tools. These techniques include disabling or tampering with antivirus software, deleting system logs, encrypting or obfuscating payloads, and disguising malicious code as legitimate processes. The intent is to remain invisible to incident responders and automated detection systems for as long as possible.

As they continue their intrusion, attackers begin to move laterally across the network. The lateral movement phase involves pivoting from the initially compromised system to other devices, applications, or servers within the organization's network. This lateral spread allows them to identify and access more sensitive resources, such as databases containing intellectual property, financial information, or critical operational data.

At the collection stage, attackers consolidate the information they have accessed. This may include sensitive business data, trade secrets, personal information of employees or customers, and other classified digital assets. The data are methodically harvested and prepared for transfer, often prioritized based on its potential value or impact.

With control firmly established, adversaries initiate the command and control (C2) phase. This involves deploying C2 infrastructure that allows them to issue instructions, exfiltrate data, and remotely manage the compromised systems. Communication is typically maintained using encrypted channels, covert protocols, or obfuscated commands that help avoid triggering alarms.

Exfiltration phase marks the culmination of the attack. Here, all the collected data is covertly transferred from the victim's environment to an external location controlled by the attackers. This phase signifies a successful breach, where the threat actors achieve their ultimate objective of acquiring valuable or sensitive information for financial gain, strategic advantage, or further exploitation.

Impact is the final stage of a cyberattack, where hackers can corrupt or destroy sensitive and confidential data, modify configurations, or prevent services from being available.

In today's evolving cybersecurity landscape, organizations are increasingly recognizing the critical importance of CTI as a foundational element in safeguarding their digital infrastructure. CTI empowers security teams to prioritize their defensive efforts strategically, enabling both proactive and reactive measures against emerging cyber threats. One of the most pressing challenges in implementing effective CTI lies in managing the overwhelming influx of threat-related data generated from a variety of internal and external sources. To derive meaningful insights, organizations must first identify and select data streams that are most relevant and accessible to their specific operational context, acknowledging that threat intelligence is not a one-size-fits-all solution. The integration of both in-house telemetry and externally sourced threat information allows for the development of tailored intelligence frameworks that closely align with an organization's risk posture. This process demands skilled personnel capable of filtering, analyzing, and transforming raw data into actionable intelligence. Once refined, this intelligence must be efficiently communicated to appropriate stakeholders within the organization to enable timely and effective decision-making and incident response.

Given the diverse formats that threat data (Unstructured Data) comes in like threat reports in emails, IOCs from threat feeds, IP Address, Geolocation, Mobile number, Name, Email ID, Hashes, Malware in zip, Binaries, Social media tweets, (paper) press reports, web site scarped info, PDF/Excel, or Word documents – this data needs to be normalized and then analyzed. In the context of modern cybersecurity operations, a Threat Intelligence Platform (TIP) [1] plays a pivotal role by streamlining the collection, processing, and organization of threat-related data. These platforms automatically ingest vast amounts of information from diverse sources and standardize it into a consistent format, allowing security teams to interpret and act on it efficiently. The value of a TIP extends beyond simple data management, it enables contextual analysis that supports key operational functions such as alert prioritization, proactive threat hunting, and swift incident response. By offering relevant insights tailored to ongoing threats, TIPs help ensure that intelligence is not merely accumulated but effectively utilized. Crucially, to derive meaningful outcomes, it is essential to integrate such platforms with the existing security infrastructure. This seamless integration ensures that threat intelligence informs strategic and operational decisions, whether it's enhancing executive-level situational awareness or refining detection rules and defensive mechanisms. Through this process, threat data is transformed into a powerful tool for strengthening organizational resilience against evolving cyber risks.

Cyber Threat Intelligence (CTI) frameworks are essentially a roadmap for organizations to proactively defend against cyberattacks. They establish a structured approach to gathering information about potential threats, analyzing that data, and then using the insights to take action. Importance of CTI frameworks:

- Proactive Approach: Unlike reactive measures taken after an attack, CTI frameworks allow organizations to anticipate threats before they strike.
- Structured Methodology: These frameworks combine processes, technology, and human expertise to gather and interpret threat intelligence.
- Actionable Insights: By systematically collecting and analyzing data on cyber adversaries and their tactics, CTI frameworks provide actionable information to mitigate threats.

Although there are a lot of different CTI frameworks, three of the most common CTI frameworks are the MITRE ATT&CK, Cyber Kill Chain (CKC), and Diamond model.

6.2 MITRE ATT&CK FRAMEWORK

MITRE ATT&CK framework [2] introduced in 2015 serves as a comprehensive, descriptive model designed to catalog and analyze the behaviors and tactics employed by threat actors across various digital environments. Rather than offering a prescriptive defense mechanism, this framework provides a structured representation of how adversaries infiltrate and manipulate within systems, ranging from enterprise networks and cloud platforms to personal mobile devices and industrial control infrastructures. By systematically mapping out these techniques, MITRE ATT&CK enables cybersecurity professionals to better understand, anticipate, and respond to the evolving landscape of cyber threats.

ATT & CK = Adversarial Tactics, Techniques, & Common Knowledge.

This is considered a CTI framework, while it doesn't provide specific threat actor information like some CTI frameworks, it functions as a foundation for developing threat models and methodologies. MITRE ATT&CK catalogues real-world tactics, techniques, and procedures (TTPs) used by cyber attackers. This knowledge base allows defenders to identify how attackers operate and potentially predict their next moves. Security professionals leverage MITRE ATT&CK to develop threat models specific to their organization's environment. By mapping potential threats to the ATT&CK framework, they can prioritize vulnerabilities and tailor defenses.

ATT&CK framework is used to analyze raw threat intelligence data. By correlating indicators of compromise (IOCs) and attacker behaviors with ATT&CK techniques, security teams can gain valuable context and improve threat detection. Although MITRE ATT&CK itself doesn't provide specific details about individual threat actors, it serves as a foundational resource for CTI analysis and defense planning.

One of the most powerful aspects of the MITRE ATT&CK Framework lies in its ability to establish a unified language for describing adversarial behavior within the cybersecurity landscape. By offering a standardized taxonomy, the framework bridges the gap between various stakeholders, whether they are engaged in offensive security assessments or defensive threat mitigation. This shared structure enables professionals across different domains to articulate complex cyber threats in a consistent and comprehensible manner, even to individuals who may not possess deep technical expertise. Moreover, the framework's open and adaptable nature empowers organizations and researchers to tailor it according to their specific needs. They can expand upon the existing structure by defining custom TTPs, thereby aligning the framework more closely with unique threat environments or organizational objectives.

To get a better look at the ATT&CK Matrix [3] with Tactics that represent the high-level goals of the attackers. These tactics are further broken down into specific techniques that outline how attackers achieve those goals. This has real-time info shared by people about what the attackers perform step by step:

1. Reconnaissance: to gather information about a target network for planning future attacks.
2. Resource Development: obtain resources like tools or stolen credentials to be used in later attacks.
3. Initial Access: Techniques attackers use to gain a foothold on a victim's network.
4. Execution: Techniques that allow attackers to run malicious code on a compromised system.
5. Persistence: Methods attackers use to maintain access to a compromised system.

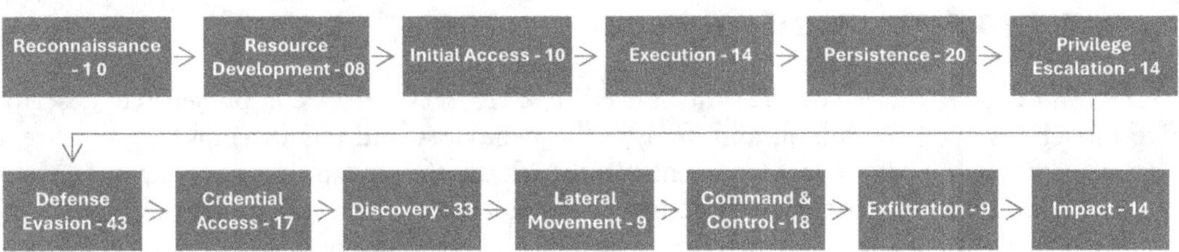

Figure 6.2 MITRE enterprise techniques.

6. Privilege Escalation: Techniques used to gain higher privileges within a compromised system.
7. Defense Evasion: Techniques that attackers use to bypass security controls.
8. Credential Access: Techniques used to steal credentials for accessing systems or data.
9. Discovery: Techniques used to find valuable data on a compromised system.
10. Lateral Movement: Techniques that allow attackers to move across a compromised network.
11. Command and Control (C2): to maintain communication with compromised systems.
12. Collection: Techniques used to gather data from a compromised system.
13. Exfiltration: Techniques used to transfer stolen data out of a compromised system.
14. Impact: Techniques used to cause damage or disruption to a compromised system.

Understanding these tactics and techniques can help security professionals better understand attacker behavior and improve their defenses, as displayed in
Figure 6.2.

6.3 MITRE CTI → GROUPS, SOFTWARE AND CAMPAIGNS

6.3.1 Groups

Groups [4] are activity clusters that are tracked by a common name in the security community. Analysts track these clusters using various analytic methodologies and terms such as threat groups, activity groups, and threat actors. Some groups have multiple names associated with similar activities due to various organizations tracking similar activities by different names. In the context of adversary classification, it is common for different organizations to define and categorize threat groups in ways that may not entirely align with one another. This can lead to partial overlaps or disagreements regarding the characterization of certain malicious actors or activity clusters.

To maintain consistency and clarity within its framework, the MITRE ATT&CK team adopts a broad definition of the term "Group." It encompasses any recognizable set of behaviors or threat actor patterns as identified by public sources or organizational analyses. When there is evidence of a connection or overlap between groups identified under different names by various entities, MITRE makes a concerted effort to reflect these relationships. These links are captured under the label "Associated Groups" on individual group pages – a term that has replaced the earlier use of "Aliases." This practice is intended to enhance situational awareness among cybersecurity analysts by highlighting potential correlations and naming conventions across different threat intelligence sources.

6.3.2 Software

The term Software [5] broadly refers to any code, whether proprietary, open-source, or system-native, that facilitates behaviors observed in adversarial campaigns. This encompasses everything from custom-built malicious programs to standard operating system (OS) utilities and widely available security tools. In many cases, the same software may be known by different names, depending on how various organizations track and label it. To enhance analytical clarity, efforts are made to reconcile these naming discrepancies by identifying overlaps, which are indicated as "Associated Software," a label previously known as "Aliases." This cross-referencing helps cybersecurity professionals maintain situational awareness, especially when tracking known threat behaviors across reports.

Each software entry in the ATT&CK framework is documented based on its observed or reported ability to execute specific techniques. These records are typically derived from open-source intelligence and public reporting, which means that the documented techniques do not necessarily represent the full range of a tool's capabilities, but rather what has been disclosed and verified through publicly accessible sources. When available, software entries are also linked to known adversary groups that have been documented using them in real-world attacks.

Software is generally categorized into two main types: *tools* and *malware*. Tools refer to applications that can be used by various actors, including defenders, penetration testers, red teamers, and adversaries, for either security or offensive purposes. These include both specialized programs not typically found on enterprise systems, such as Mimikatz or Metasploit, and standard system utilities like netstat, tasklist, or net, which are often already embedded within OSs. On the other hand, *malware* refers to software, whether commercial, custom-developed, or open-source, that is explicitly designed for malicious use by threat actors. Notable examples include PlugX and CHOPSTICK. The distinction between these categories is not always based on technical capability but rather on the intent and context of use.

6.3.3 Campaigns

Experts monitor and document intrusion activities through a variety of analytical frameworks, employing terms such as operations, intrusion sets, and campaigns [6] to categorize and interpret observed behavior. However, it is common for the same intrusion activity to be identified by multiple names, as different organizations may track the incidents independently and from distinct perspectives. In some cases, such malicious activity is not assigned a specific name at all, adding complexity to coordinated tracking efforts. Attribution of cyber intrusions can vary widely. Some attacks are clearly linked to known threat groups, while others remain unattributed due to insufficient evidence or operational anonymity. In sophisticated cyber operations, multiple actors, whether collaborating entities or entirely separate groups may each carry out specific functions, such as gaining initial access, deploying payloads, or conducting data theft.

To maintain consistency in its documentation, the MITRE ATT&CK team defines a *campaign* as a collection of intrusion events that occur within a defined timeframe and are directed at similar targets or share overarching objectives. When no public name is available for a particular intrusion, the ATT&CK framework assigns it a distinct identifier to ensure clarity and traceability. If the activity has already been referenced in public sources, MITRE retains the original name to maintain alignment with existing reports. For named Campaigns, the team makes a best effort to track overlapping names, which are designated as "Associated Campaigns" on each page, as we believe these overlaps are useful for analysts. Campaign entries will also be attributed to ATT&CK Group and Software pages, when possible, based on public reporting; unattributed activity will simply reference "threat actors" in the procedure example. Campaigns are mapped to publicly reported techniques, and original references are included.

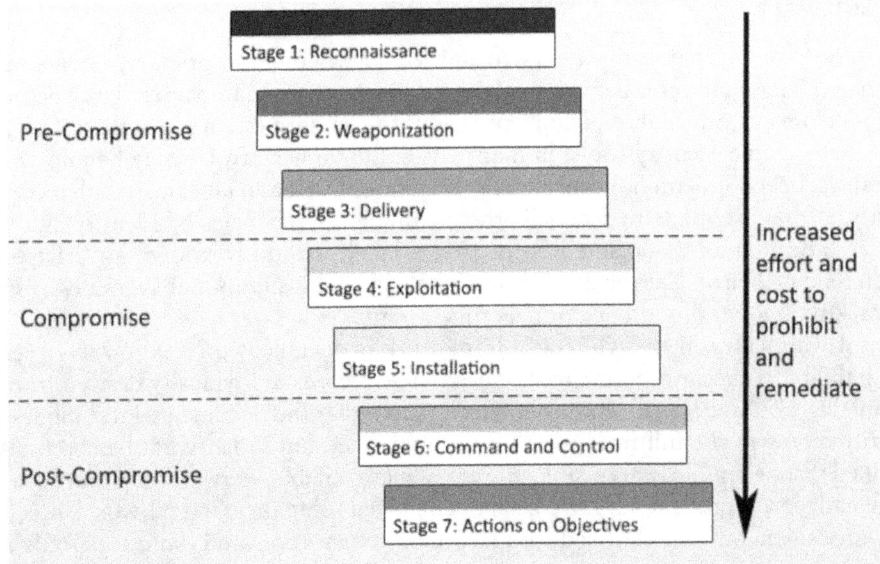

Figure 6.3 Att&ck navigator.

6.4 ATT&CK NAVIGATOR

ATT&CK Navigator [7] is an open-source tool designed to help users to explore and use the ATT&CK knowledge base as displayed in Figure 6.3. This is used to represent things like how well an organization is doing against the common attacks that are defined in MIRTE framework.

6.5 USE CASES

6.5.1 Use Case #1: ATT&CK navigator for CTI

Begin by accessing the MITRE ATT&CK Navigator and initiating a new layer within the Enterprise Matrix. This framework allows users to strategically organize cyber operations. For instance, a RED team can use it to simulate offensive tactics, while a BLUE team can develop defensive responses. Additionally, users may map the behavior patterns of specific Advanced Persistent Threat (APT) groups to better understand their typical techniques and procedures. as displayed in Figure 6.4. When planning a penetration test as part of RED team

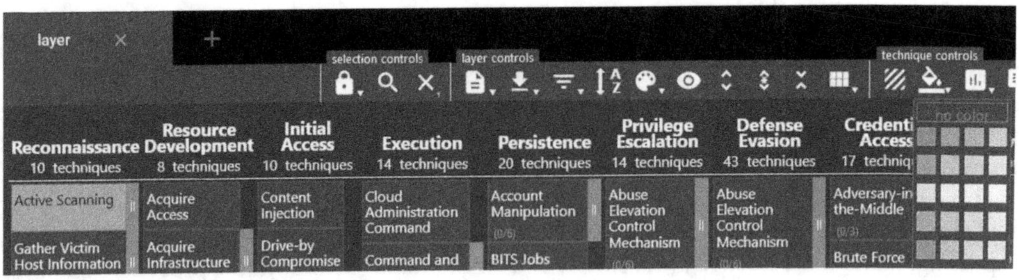

Figure 6.4 Select recon options.

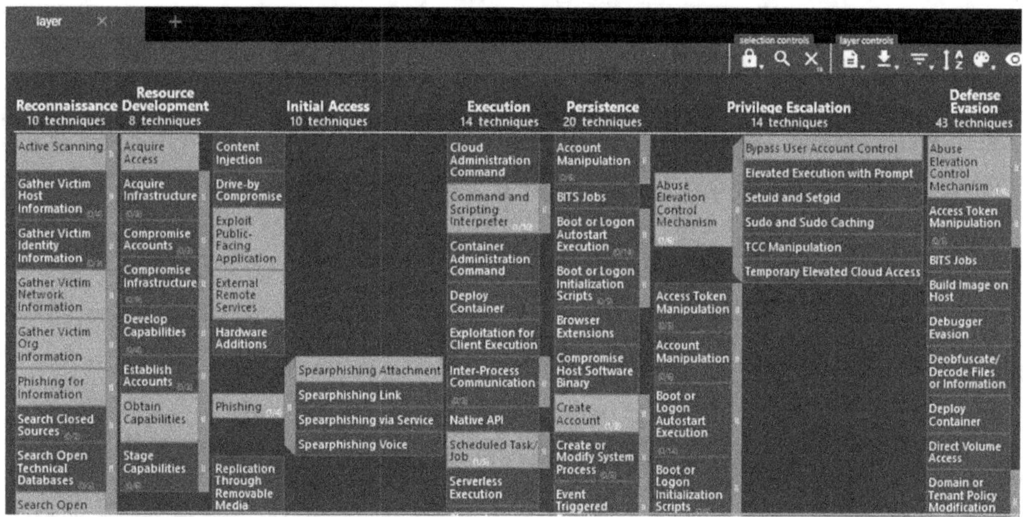

Figure 6.5 Select specific options.

activities, one might start by focusing on the "Reconnaissance" phase by selecting relevant techniques and marking them, such as with a green color, to signify active planning areas.

The manual selection process for Cyberattack, as illustrated in Figure 6.5, involves several tactical stages. It begins with reconnaissance through active scanning, collecting details about the target's network and organization, including phishing attempts and exploring publicly available websites. The attacker then develops resources by acquiring infrastructure and necessary tools. Gaining initial access follows, often by exploiting public-facing applications, remote services, or using phishing with malicious attachments. Once access is secured, execution occurs via command-line interfaces like Windows Command Shell. Persistence is established by creating local user accounts. Privilege escalation uses scheduled tasks, while defense evasion may involve bypassing user access control. Finally, credentials are accessed by dumping OS data, such as LSASS memory.

The next step involves emulating the behavior of a specific threat group, such as APT41. To begin this process, a new layer must be added. This is done by navigating to the search and multi-select option, as displayed in Figure 6.6, where APT41 is selected to incorporate the known tactics into the emulation framework.

Choose the threat group identified as APT41; this action will automatically populate the associated tactics used by APT41, as displayed in Figure 6.7. These tactics are pre-defined based on known patterns of behavior and operations linked to the group, streamlining the threat modeling process by aligning selections with this specific adversary's methods.

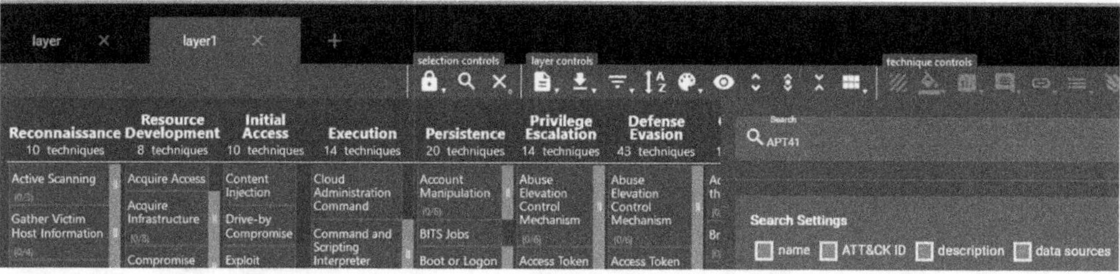

Figure 6.6 Emulate behavior of APT41.

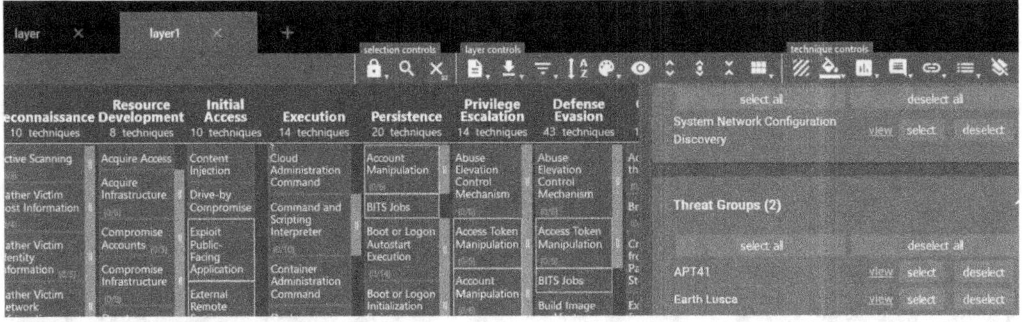

Figure 6.7 Auto-populate threat group tactics.

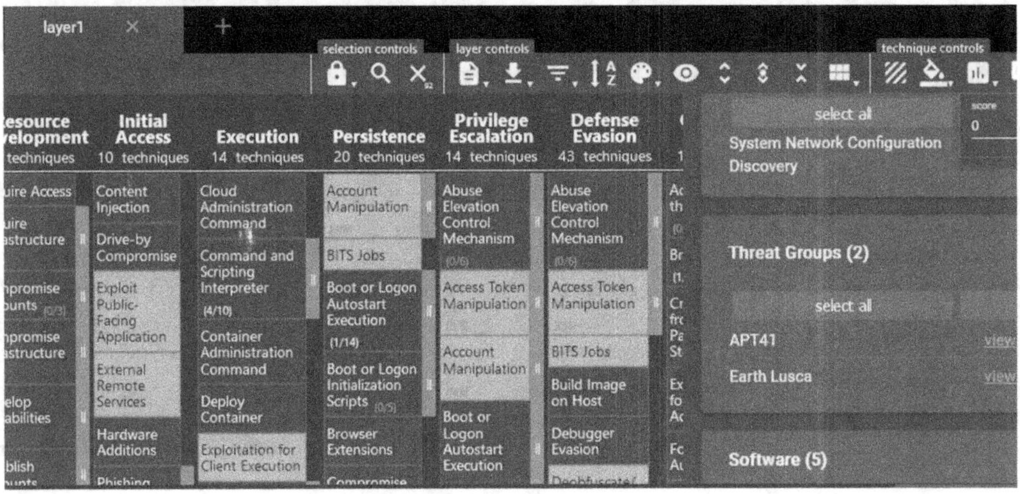

Figure 6.8 Predefined color scoring gradient.

Instead of manually applying colors, a predefined color scheme or scoring gradient can be selected, using a range from a base score of 0 to a high score of 100. By setting the gradient to 0 under the Score section, all known tactics employed by APT41 become visually distinguishable, as illustrated in Figure 6.8.

Based on the outcomes of the customized adversary emulation process, the scoring can be adjusted in alignment with the penetration testing strategy. This adaptive approach, as depicted in Figure 6.9, enables a more accurate evaluation of system vulnerabilities by reflecting specific testing objectives and simulated threat scenarios.

6.5.2 Use Case #2: Search for a specific adversary attacking finance-related institutions

To investigate cyber threats targeting financial institutions, begin by identifying specific adversary groups known to attack this sector. Once these threat actors are established, develop a comprehensive heat map outlining their techniques, tactics, and procedures. Figure 6.10 provides a structured framework for understanding and mitigating financial cybersecurity risks.

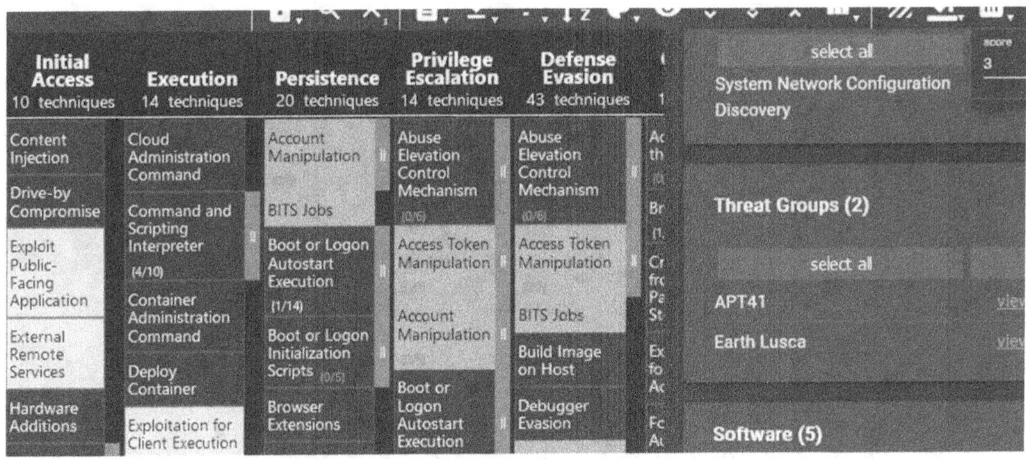

Figure 6.9 Adjust scoring.

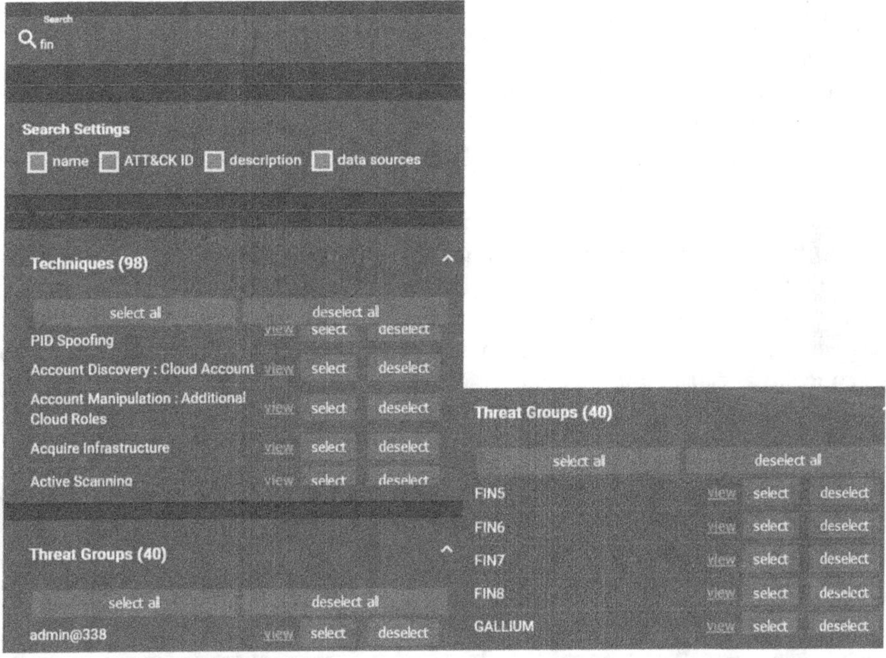

Figure 6.10 Search financial threat groups.

Within the FIN groups, the subgroup Fin6 was specifically chosen for detailed analysis. The corresponding layer was renamed appropriately to reflect this focus. A scoring system ranging from 0 to 3 was then applied to this layer, as illustrated in Figure 6.11, to evaluate and categorize relevant attributes.

Figure 6.11 Choosing specific financial threat group.

6.5.3 Use Case #3: Find and compare multiple adversaries attacking specific domains (finance institution)

Figure 6.12 presents a comparative assessment of various APTs targeting financial institutions, revealing distinct attack patterns across different threat layers. Notable groups such as FIN4 and FIN6 employ tailored tactics to infiltrate and exploit financial systems. Their operations span credential theft, data exfiltration, and financial fraud, highlighting complex, multilayered attack strategies.

To proceed, a new tab must be opened, and the option "Create Layer from Other Layers" should be selected. This action results in the automatic marking of existing layers, which become visually indicated, as demonstrated in Figure 6.13. The process helps distinguish the newly created layer from the original components.

To facilitate comparison between the layers, the Score Expression function is employed by combining layers (a+b). This process generates a new composite map that integrates the data from both layers, enabling visual and analytical assessment. The resulting output is illustrated in Figure 6.14, reflecting the merged spatial information.

Figure 6.15 presents the integrated visualization of both FIN4 and FIN5 mappings. This composite representation enables a comparative understanding of the two frameworks, highlighting their structural alignment and interdependencies. The unified depiction serves to enhance conceptual clarity and facilitates a more comprehensive analysis within the broader context of financial models.

Figure 6.12 Comparing two threat groups.

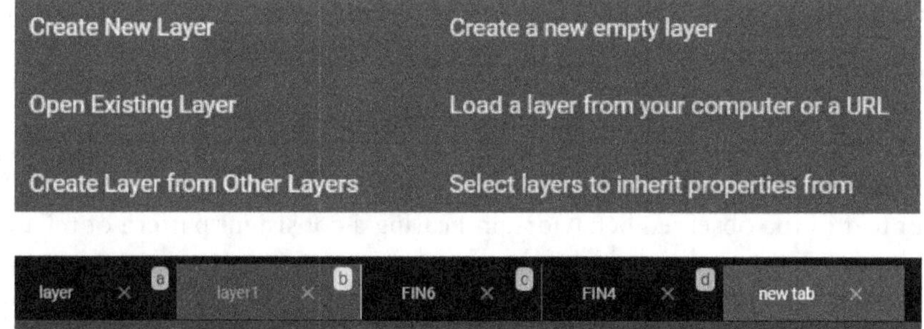

Figure 6.13 Add a new layer for comparison.

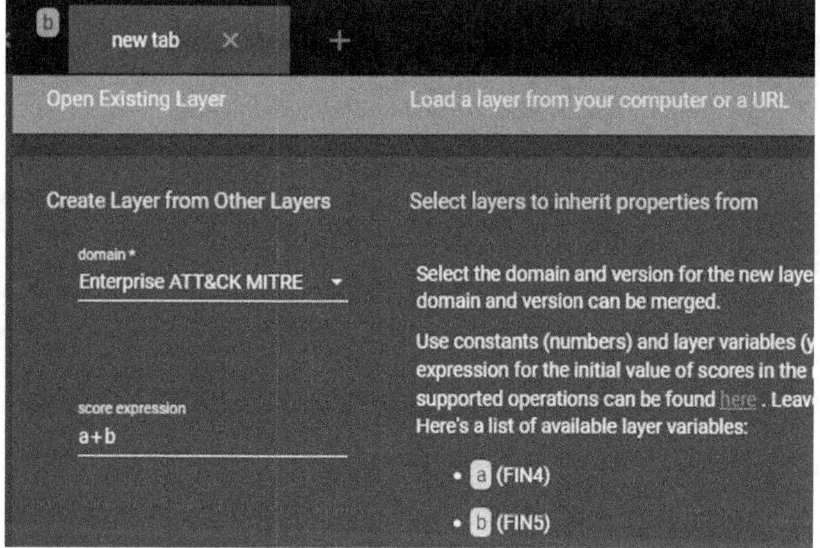

Figure 6.14 Score expression function.

Figure 6.15 Integrated visualization of both mappings.

Adopting the same color scheme applied in both Fin4 and Fin5 results in a visualization where techniques are represented by colors alongside numerical values. These numbers indicate the likelihood of each group employing a particular technique; lower values correspond to higher usage probability, as illustrated in Figure 6.16 of the analysis.

Figure 6.17 illustrates that the "Valid Account" technique is frequently employed by both parties as a shared method. Its widespread use highlights its strategic significance within the broader context of the observed behaviors, indicating a consistent pattern of reliance on this specific technique across multiple instances of activity.

The information presented can be effectively utilized by Security Operations Center (SOC) teams and OS administrators to enhance detection mechanisms within their security infrastructure. By incorporating this data into security control tools such as Security Information and Event Management (SIEM) systems, log analyzers, and Intrusion Detection/Prevention Systems (IDS/IPS), organizations can establish specific rules aligned with adversarial tactics.

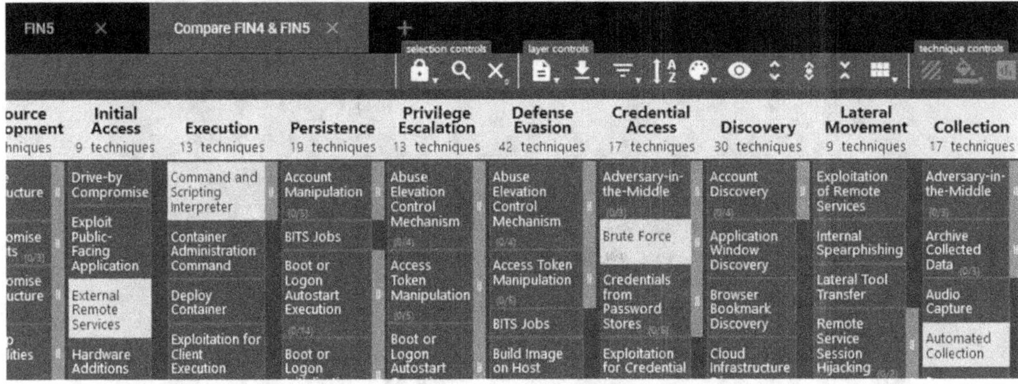

Figure 6.16 Customized visualization.

Figure 6.17 Valid account technique.

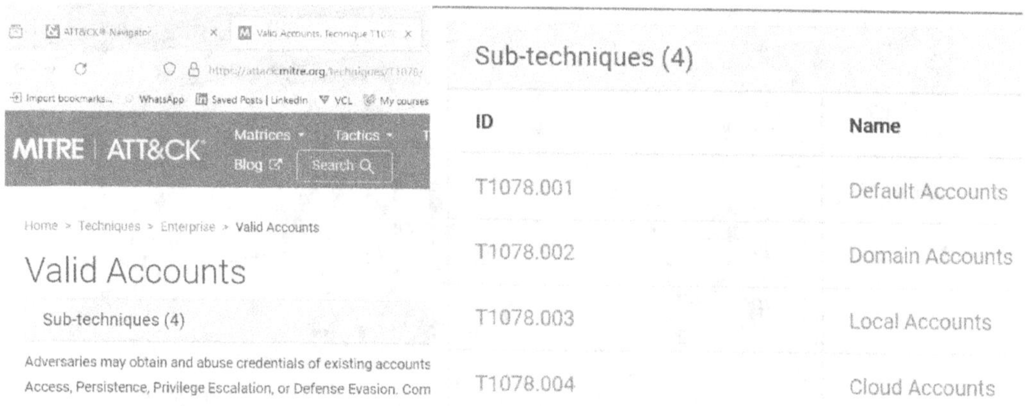

Figure 6.18 Visual mapping for operational intelligence.

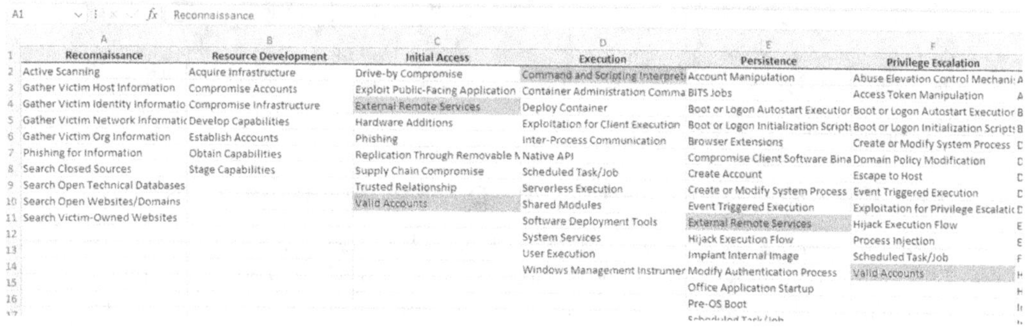

Figure 6.19 Data exported to excel format.

In particular, the "Valid Accounts" technique, along with its associated sub-techniques, can be referenced directly within the MITRE ATT&CK framework. This visual mapping, as illustrated in Figure 6.18, facilitates a clearer understanding of how to operationalize threat intelligence for proactive defense.

The data shown in Figure 6.19 is also available for export in Excel format, allowing for further analysis or documentation. This functionality enhances usability by enabling seamless transfer of tabular content into spreadsheet software, supporting extended evaluation, structured formatting, or integration with additional academic or technical datasets as required.

6.5.4 Use Case #4: Plot phishing email on MITRE ATT&CK framework

To analyze a phishing email within the context of the MITRE ATT&CK framework, a specific example of a potential phishing attempt can be selected, such as the GitHub phishing scenario available through trusted cybersecurity resources. Once the phishing email is identified, its characteristics and intended outcomes can be mapped onto the ATT&CK framework. This involves identifying the sequence of tactics and techniques likely to be employed by an attacker, including initial access through social engineering, user execution, and credential access. Figure 6.20 illustrates this mapping, demonstrating how the adversary's approach aligns with various stages of the framework to achieve malicious objectives.

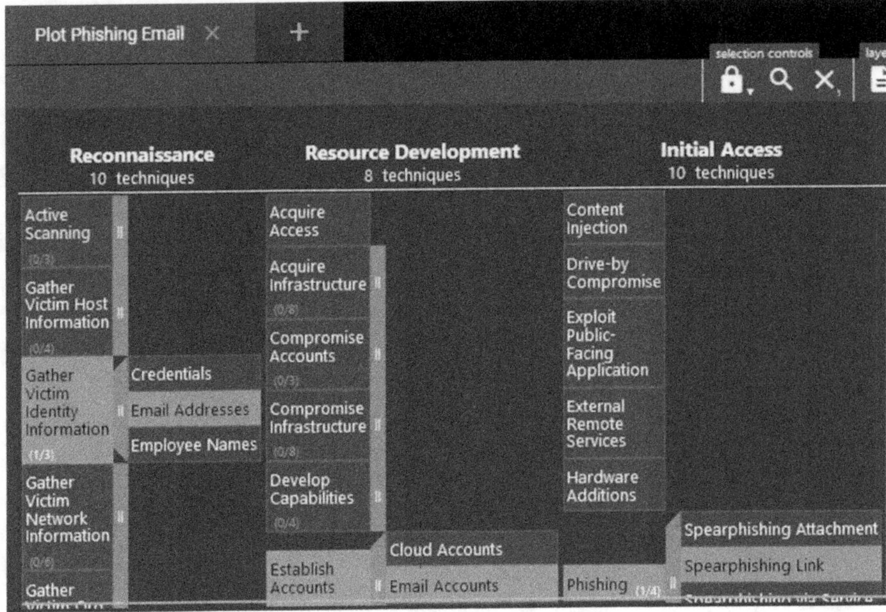

Figure 6.20 Analyze phishing emails.

6.5.5 Use Case #5: Use **MITRE D3FEND** for valid accounts attacks

To analyze the defense mechanisms against the "Valid Accounts" technique categorized under T1078, one should begin by accessing the MITRE D3FEND portal, available at https:// d3fend.mitre.org/. This platform serves as a comprehensive resource for exploring counter-measures mapped to specific adversary behaviors. Upon visiting the portal, initiating a search for the technique ID T1078 labelled as "Valid Accounts" will provide structured defensive insights, as illustrated in Figure 6.21. This lookup facilitates a deeper understanding of

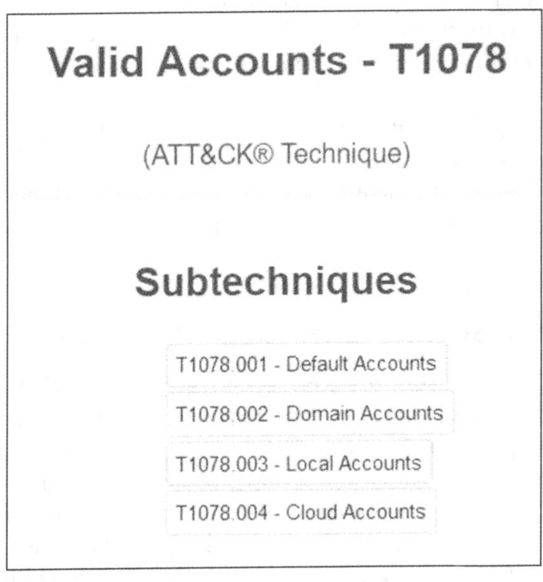

Figure 6.21 Analyze valid accounts technique.

detection and mitigation strategies associated with credential misuse, aiding in the formulation of robust cybersecurity defense postures within enterprise environments.

To address the exploitation of valid accounts by adversaries for unauthorized network access, a multifaceted mitigation strategy is essential. Enforcing strong authentication mechanisms such as multifactor authentication (MFA), implementing robust account monitoring, and adhering to the principle of least privilege can significantly reduce the risk of compromise. Regular audits of account activities, prompt revocation of unused credentials, and continuous behavioral analysis may help detect anomalies linked to credential misuse. Additionally, automated alert systems and login attempt throttling enhance security postures. Figure 6.22 illustrates the effectiveness of these mitigation measures, highlighting their impact on reducing unauthorized access through legitimate account credentials.

A robust password policy, as illustrated in Figure 6.23, serves as a foundational element in strengthening system security. By enforcing the use of complex and unique passwords, this approach significantly reduces vulnerabilities to unauthorized access, thereby enhancing overall cyber defense mechanisms and contributing to a more resilient digital infrastructure.

To examine the relationships stemming from valid accounts, multiple associated accounts are identified and illustrated in Figure 6.24. This analysis highlights the interconnected nature of these accounts, offering insights into user activity and potential behavioral patterns within the system, thereby supporting further investigation or anomaly detection in the dataset.

The outcomes related to system hardening, specifically focusing on authentication and authorization mechanisms, are examined and illustrated in Figure 6.25. This evaluation highlights the implementation and effectiveness of security configurations aimed at strengthening access control measures, ensuring that only verified and permitted entities can interact with the protected system environment.

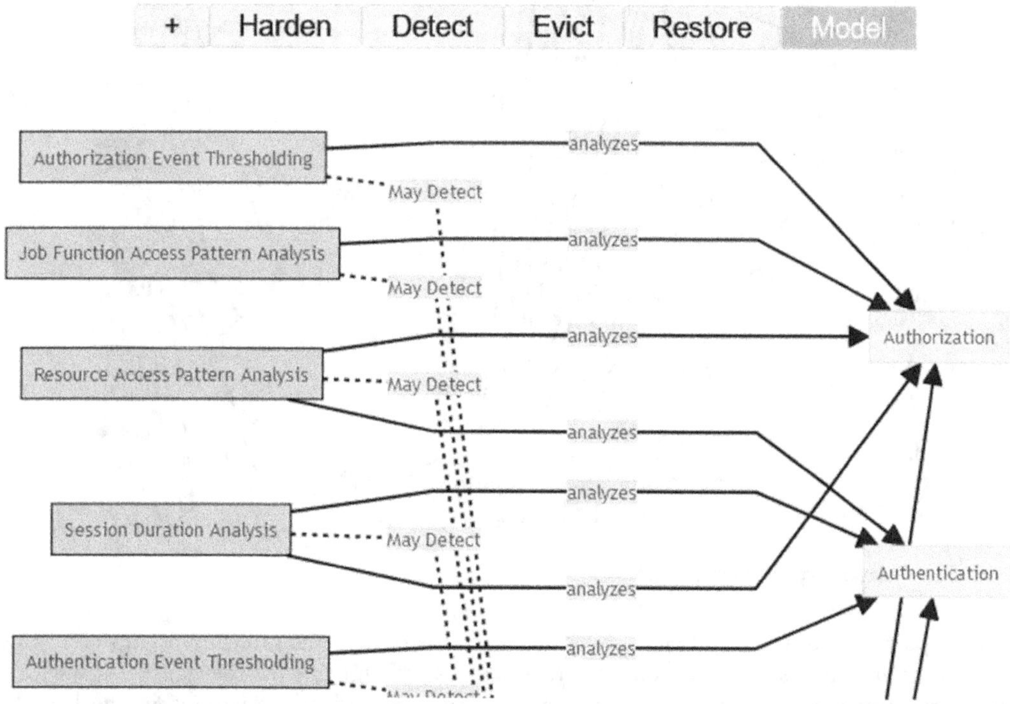

Figure 6.22 Mitigation options for exploitation of valid accounts.

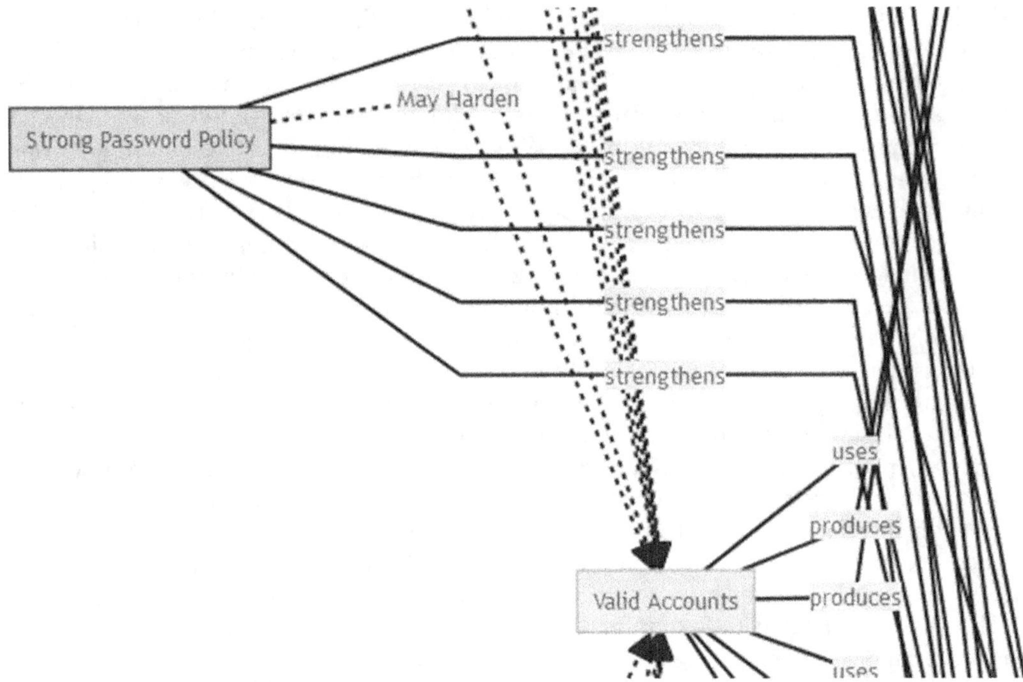

Figure 6.23 Option to use robust password policy.

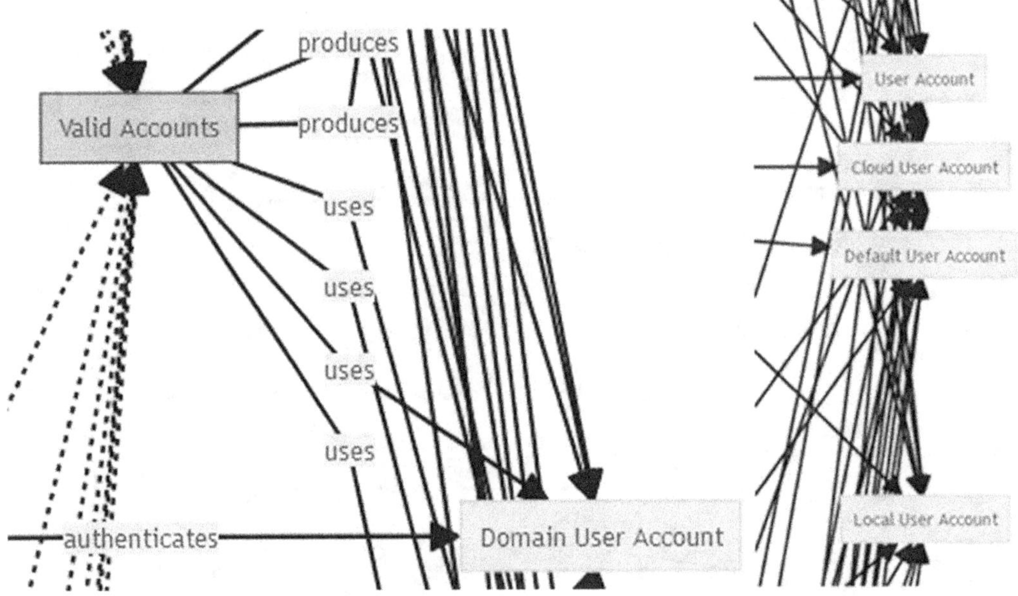

Figure 6.24 Relationships from valid accounts.

To explore any of the listed elements, refer to Figure 6.26, which outlines their definitions, operational mechanisms, and recommended actions. Engaging with the figure allows for a structured understanding of each component's function and relevance within the broader system or framework being discussed in this academic context.

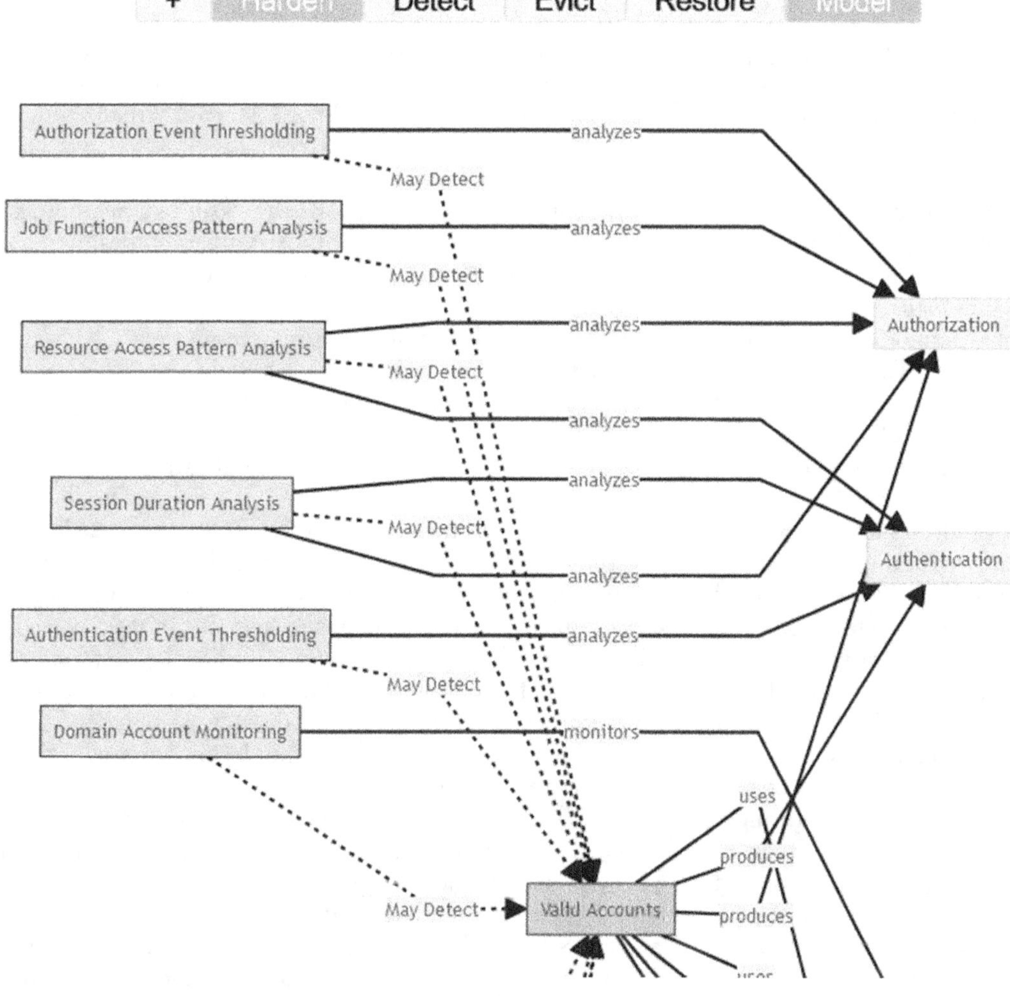

Figure 6.25 Authentication and authorization mechanisms.

Authentication Event Thresholding

D3-ANET

D3-ANET (Authentication Event Thresholding)

Definition

Collecting authentication events, creating a baseline user profile, and determining whether authentication events are consistent with the baseline profile.

How it works

Authentication event data is collected (logon information such as device id, time of day, day of week, geo-location, etc.) to create an activity baseline. Then, a threshold is determined either through a manually specified configuration, or a statistical analysis of deviations in historical data. New authentication events are evaluated to determine if a threshold is exceeded. Thresholds can be static or dynamic.

Actions

As a result of the analysis, actions taken could include:

- Account Locking
- Raising an alert

Figure 6.26 Explore listed elements.

6.6 CYBER KILL CHAIN

The CKC framework [8] breaks down cyberattacks into distinct stages, allowing defenders to identify the current stage of an attack and intervene. Imagine a cyberattack as a series of phases, like a kill chain. This framework, developed by Lockheed Martin, visualizes these phases:

- Reconnaissance: Attackers gather information about your systems and vulnerabilities.
- Weaponization: They develop or acquire tools to exploit those vulnerabilities.
- Delivery: The malicious payload is delivered to your system, often through phishing emails.
- Exploitation: The attackers leverage the vulnerability to gain access.
- Installation: They install malware to maintain control and steal data.
- Command and Control (C2): Communication channels are established for remote control.
- Actions on Objectives: Attackers achieve their goals, like data exfiltration.

By understanding these phases, security teams can focus their efforts on fortifying each stage and disrupting the attack chain. Originally conceptualized by Lockheed Martin in 2011 as part of a military-inspired strategy, the CKC provides a structured, sequential framework for analyzing the lifecycle of a cyberattack. Its primary objective is to help organizations recognize and interrupt malicious activities before they can cause significant harm. Often referred to as the cyberattack lifecycle, this model offers insight into how attacks unfold and highlights critical junctures where defenders can intervene to detect, disrupt, or prevent further intrusion. By dissecting the attack process into defined stages, the model enhances situational awareness and informs more proactive cybersecurity measures.

While the initial formulation of the kill chain comprised seven distinct stages, the framework has since evolved to reflect the growing complexity of modern cyber threats. Today, it commonly encompasses eight phases: reconnaissance, weaponization, delivery, exploitation, installation, command and control, actions on objective, and monetization. This extended version allows for a more nuanced understanding of contemporary attack strategies. Security professionals often rely on this model when addressing advanced and persistent threats, such as ransomware attacks and sophisticated data breaches, using it to strengthen organizational defenses at every point of potential vulnerability.

In the realm of cybersecurity, the concept of the "CKC" originates from military strategy, where it was initially used to describe the sequential phases involved in executing an attack. These phases traditionally encompassed target identification, planning, command issuance, and eventual target engagement or destruction. When adapted to the field of cybersecurity, the CKC serves as a strategic framework that outlines the distinct stages typically observed in a cyberattack. This includes steps such as reconnaissance, weaponization, delivery, exploitation, installation, command and control, and actions on objectives. By breaking down a cyberattack into identifiable and traceable phases, organizations are better equipped to understand, anticipate, and defend against both internal and external threats.

Rather than functioning as a security tool or software solution, the CKC operates as a conceptual model that assists cybersecurity professionals in predicting an attacker's next move. It provides a structured approach to understanding how a breach unfolds, which in turn enables quicker detection, response, and mitigation of potential incidents. Through mapping the progression of an attack, security teams can pinpoint vulnerabilities and assess the adequacy of existing defenses. Simulated exercises based on this model also serve a critical role in preparing teams for real-world scenarios. These simulations not only test an organization's

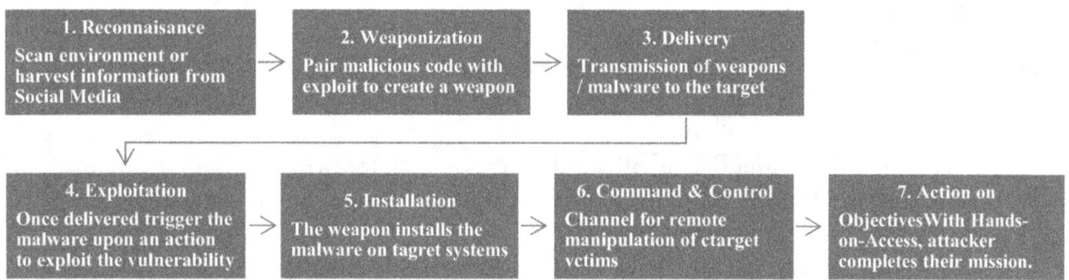

Figure 6.27 Stages of cyber kill chain.

response capabilities but also expose weaknesses in current security protocols, staff readiness, and technological safeguards. Consequently, the insights gained from employing the CKC framework can inform strategic decisions related to staff training, policy refinement, and the deployment or upgrade of tools such as endpoint detection systems, firewalls, or virtual private networks (VPNs). This holistic perspective fosters a proactive rather than reactive security posture, aligning organizational defenses with the evolving landscape of cyber threats.

Computer security teams at Lockheed Martin are the first to take this concept and apply it to information security, but the CKC continues to evolve with the changing nature of cyber threats. At the core of the CKC is the notion that cyberattacks often occur in phases and they can be disrupted through controls established at each phase as illustrated in Figure 6.27.

6.6.1 Phase 1: Reconnaissance

In the initial stage of a cyberattack, commonly referred to as the reconnaissance or observation phase – malicious actors focus on gathering intelligence about their intended targets. This preparatory stage plays a crucial role in shaping the subsequent steps of an attack. During this period, attackers engage in systematic research to understand the structure, behavior, and vulnerabilities of potential victims. They may examine publicly available data, analyze system architecture, or probe for weaknesses that could serve as points of entry. The depth and quality of information collected at this stage directly influence the precision and effectiveness of the attack that follows. The more comprehensive the reconnaissance, the greater the attacker's ability to tailor a strategy that evades detection and maximizes impact.

6.6.1.1 Example 1: Social media scraping

Attackers utilize social media platforms to gather information about a target organization and its employees. By scraping public profiles and posts, attackers identify:

- Employee names, titles, and departments.
- Company tools and technologies used (mentioned in bios or posts).
- Security practices (e.g., two-factor authentication mentions).
- Internal events or projects that could be leveraged in social engineering attacks.

Techniques involve:

- Attackers use automated scripts to harvest data from social media APIs or the open web.
- They manually browse profiles and groups to collect relevant information.

6.6.1.2 Example 2: Website network mapping

Attackers can map a target organization's network infrastructure by analyzing their website and online presence. This is performed using:

- DNS enumeration: Identifying all subdomains associated with the main domain.
- Port scanning: Probing publicly accessible IP addresses for open ports that can reveal services running on the network.
- Website fingerprinting: Analyzing website code and server responses to identify specific software versions used, which might have known vulnerabilities.

Techniques involved:

- Attackers leverage freely available tools like DNS interrogation tools and port scanners.
- They use specialized website fingerprinting services.

6.6.2 Phase 2: Weaponization

At this stage, attackers create the attack vector that will be used in the cyberattack. This could include remote access malware, ransomware, or a virus or worm that can exploit a vulnerability identified during the reconnaissance phase. During the weaponization phase, attackers may also try to reduce the likelihood of being detected by any security solutions in place.

6.6.2.1 Example 1: Phishing email with exploit kit

After reconnaissance identifies a target user who might be susceptible to phishing, attackers develop a weaponized email. The email appears legitimate (e.g., mimicking a known company) and tricks the user into clicking a malicious link or downloading an attachment. The attachment or link delivers an "exploit kit" – a set of automated tools designed to exploit specific software vulnerabilities on the victim's machine.
Technique used:

- Attackers can use social engineering tactics to craft convincing emails, potentially including stolen user credentials or personal details gleaned from reconnaissance.
- The exploit kit itself might be purchased from the dark web or custom-coded for the specific vulnerabilities identified.

6.6.2.2 Example 2: Macro-enabled office document

Attackers can weaponize a seemingly harmless document like a Microsoft Word file. By embedding malicious macros (scripts) within the document, attackers can exploit vulnerabilities in the software or social engineer users into enabling macros. Once enabled, the macros can download and install malware, steal data, or establish a connection to a Command-and-Control server.
Technique used:

- Attackers can use readily available tools to embed malicious macros in documents.
- They might disguise the macros with legitimate-sounding names or leverage social engineering tactics to convince users to enable them.

6.6.3 Phase 3: Delivery

In the progression of a cyber intrusion, this phase marks the point at which the adversary actively initiates their offensive actions. After identifying a suitable target and crafting a specific method of attack, the attacker proceeds to deploy the chosen vector. This may involve exploiting vulnerabilities through direct access to the network or system, or indirectly by using deceptive techniques such as phishing emails to trick users into enabling unauthorized access. Irrespective of the method or the broader intent behind the intrusion – whether it be data theft, system disruption, or surveillance – this stage represents the formal commencement of the attack against the intended victim.

6.6.3.1 Example 1: Phishing email with malicious attachment

- Delivery Method: Email
- Technical Details: An attacker sends a phishing email that appears to be legitimate, such as from a bank or a colleague. The email contains a malicious attachment, often a document file (e.g., .docx, .pdf) or an archive (e.g., .zip, .rar). The email leverages social engineering tactics to trick the recipient into opening the attachment. This might involve urgency ("Urgent! Open Now to Verify Account") or exploit curiosity ("Top Secret Company Information Revealed").
- Payload: The attachment may contain a macro or embedded exploit that, once opened, downloads and installs malware on the victim's machine. This malware could then steal data, encrypt files for ransom, or establish a backdoor for further attacker access.

6.6.3.2 Example 2: Drive-by-download attack

- Delivery Method: Website
- Technical Details: The attacker compromises a legitimate website or injects malicious code into online advertisements. When a user visits the compromised website or clicks on the malicious ad, a script automatically downloads malware onto their device. The attacker might exploit vulnerabilities in the user's web browser, outdated plugins, or OS to bypass security measures and deliver the payload.
- Payload: Similar to the phishing email example, the downloaded file could be various types, designed to steal information, disrupt operations, or give the attacker control over the system.

6.6.4 Phase 4: Exploitation

Once the perimeter defenses of the target system have been compromised, the attacker proceeds to execute the malicious payload within the victim's infrastructure. This stage marks a critical escalation, as the intruder gains deeper access to internal systems. With this foothold, the attacker can deploy additional utilities, execute custom scripts to manipulate system behavior, or tamper with vital elements such as security certificates. These actions are typically intended to maintain persistence, escalate privileges, or facilitate further exploitation, thereby expanding the attacker's control and masking their presence within the compromised environment.

6.6.4.1 Example 1: Exploiting a buffer overflow vulnerability

- Vulnerability: A buffer overflow vulnerability occurs when a program tries to write more data into a memory buffer than it can hold. This can crash the program or, more importantly for attackers, allow them to execute malicious code.
- Technical Exploitation: The attacker delivers a payload (often through a phishing email or drive-by-download) containing malicious code specifically crafted to exploit the buffer overflow vulnerability.
- Exploit Impact: Once the attacker's code executes successfully, they can gain unauthorized access to the system, steal data, install additional malware, or take control of the machine.

6.6.4.2 Example 2: Escalating privileges with a local file inclusion vulnerability

- Vulnerability: A local file inclusion (LFI) vulnerability allows an attacker to trick a web application into executing code from a file on the server itself. This can be dangerous because the application might be running with higher privileges than a regular user.
- Technical Exploitation: The attacker might identify a web page or functionality that accepts user input. By crafting a specially formed URL that includes a path to a malicious file on the server, the attacker can exploit the LFI vulnerability.
- Exploit Impact: If the attacker's LFI exploit is successful, they might be able to elevate their privileges from a regular user to an administrator on the server. This would grant them significantly more control over the system and potentially the entire network.

6.6.5 Phase 5: Installation

Following the exploitation stage, the attack progresses into the installation phase, during which malicious software or code is embedded into the victim's system. This phase is critical for establishing a persistent foothold within the compromised environment. In many cases, attackers use this opportunity to set up covert access points, commonly referred to as backdoors. These hidden entryways allow them to maintain control over the system, even if the initial vulnerability used to gain access is discovered and patched. The installation phase thus plays a vital role in ensuring continued unauthorized access and lays the groundwork for future malicious activities.

6.6.5.1 Example 1: Dropper installing remote access Trojan (RAT)

- Delivery Method: Phishing Email with Attachment.
- Installation Technique: Dropper → seemingly harmless file (script) that executes and then downloads and installs the actual malicious payload.
- Technical Details: The attacker sends a phishing email with a doc file attached. Upon opening the doc file, a macro embedded within executes a dropper program also hidden within the document. This dropper then retrieves the actual malicious payload, a Remote Access Trojan (RAT), from a remote server controlled by the attacker and installs it on the victim's machine.
- Impact: Once installed, the RAT allows the attacker to remotely control the infected machine, steal data, spy on user activity, or deploy further malware laterally across the network.

6.6.5.2 Example 2: Living off the land (LOTL)

In some cases, attackers might not install entirely new software but instead abuse legitimate system utilities or tools for malicious purposes.

6.6.5.3 Example 3: Exploit kit installing ransomware

- Delivery Method: Drive-by-Download Attack.
- Installation Technique: Exploit Kit. An exploit kit is a pre-built set of tools that attackers use to automatically exploit vulnerabilities in a user's software.
- Technical Details: The victim visits a compromised website or clicks on a malicious ad. The website leverages an exploit kit to scan the user's system for vulnerabilities. If a vulnerability is found (e.g., unpatched web browser plugin), the exploit kit automatically downloads and installs the malicious payload, which in this case, is ransomware.
- Impact: Ransomware encrypts a victim's files, rendering them inaccessible. The attacker then demands a ransom payment in exchange for a decryption key.

6.6.6 Phase 6: Command and control

In the command-and-control (C2) stage of a cyberattack, adversaries leverage previously deployed malicious tools or compromised pathways to gain remote control over systems, user accounts, or networked devices within the targeted infrastructure. This remote access allows them to execute commands, exfiltrate data, or manipulate the environment without raising immediate suspicion. Often, during this phase, attackers engage in lateral movement across the network. This tactic enables them to deepen their infiltration, maintain persistence, and reduce the likelihood of detection by spreading their activities across various nodes and systems, ultimately securing multiple access points for sustained control.

6.6.6.1 Example 1: Domain generation algorithm (DGA) and C2 server

- Communication Method: DNS Requests
- Technical Details:
    - The attacker installs malware on a victim's machine.
    - This malware incorporates a Domain Generation Algorithm (DGA). A DGA is an algorithm that dynamically generates new domain names at regular intervals.
    - The malware periodically contacts these dynamically generated domains using DNS requests.
    - The attacker controls a network of C2 servers that constantly change their domain names to evade detection.
    - When the malware performs a DNS request for a generated domain, it attempts to connect to a C2 server controlled by the attacker.
- C2 Functionality: Once a connection is established, the attacker can send commands to the infected system through the C2 server. These commands might include instructions to steal data, deploy additional malware, or launch further attacks within the network.

6.6.6.2 Example 2: Peer-to-peer (P2P) network for C2

- Communication Method: Direct Communication Between Infected Devices
- Technical Details:
    - The attacker infects multiple devices within a network with malware.
    - This malware is designed to communicate directly with other infected devices within the network, forming a decentralized peer-to-peer (P2P) botnet.
    - One of the infected devices might be designated as a "controller" node within the P2P network.
    - The attacker communicates with the controller node, which then relays commands to other infected devices within the P2P network.

- C2 Functionality: Like the DGA example, the attacker can use the P2P network to issue commands to compromise devices, allowing them to control the botnet and carry out malicious activities.
  - Encrypted Communication: Attackers often encrypt communication between the malware and the C2 server to make it more difficult to detect.
  - C2 Server Obfuscation: Attackers use techniques like steganography or code obfuscation to hide malicious functionality within the C2 server itself.
  - C2 Detection and Disruption: Security teams can leverage network traffic analysis tools and threat intelligence feeds to identify and disrupt C2 communication channels.

6.6.7 Phase 7: Actions on objective

In the concluding stage of Lockheed Martin's CKC framework, threat actors execute the final components of their operation to achieve their ultimate aim. This stage is where the attack culminates in concrete action – whether that involves stealing sensitive information, corrupting or deleting critical data, encrypting files for ransom, or extracting valuable digital assets from the target environment. At this point, the attacker's presence, which may have remained covert throughout earlier stages, becomes most evident as the primary objective is fulfilled.

6.6.7.1 Example 1: Exfiltrating data with steganography

- Objective: Steal sensitive data (e.g., financial records, intellectual property)
- Technical Details:
  - The attacker gains access to a system containing sensitive data.
  - They then use steganography techniques to hide the stolen data within seemingly harmless files like images or videos.
  - Steganography embeds the stolen data within the carrier file in a way that's undetectable to the naked eye.
  - The attacker exfiltrates these modified files containing the hidden data through various channels, such as email attachments or cloud storage services.
- Impact: Steganography allows attackers to bypass traditional data exfiltration detection methods, making it more challenging to identify and prevent data theft.

6.6.7.2 Example 2: Disrupting operations

- Objective: Disrupt or disable critical network services
- Technical Details:
  - The attacker infects many devices (e.g., through compromised websites or malware) with botnet software.
  - This botnet software allows the attacker to remotely control the infected devices.
  - The attacker then coordinates the botnet to launch a DDoS attack against a target network.
  - In a DDoS attack, the botnet floods the target network with a massive amount of traffic, overwhelming its resources and causing service outages.
- Impact: A successful DDoS attack can prevent legitimate users from accessing critical services, leading to financial losses, reputational damage, and operational disruption for the targeted organization.

The sequence of steps referenced above originates from the CKC model initially introduced by Lockheed Martin in 2011. This framework was designed to map out the various stages of a cyberattack, offering a structured approach to identifying, understanding, and ultimately disrupting adversary actions. Over time, as threat landscapes evolved and attack methodologies became more sophisticated, cybersecurity researchers and practitioners recognized the need to adapt and extend the model. Consequently, an additional phase – monetization – was incorporated into the framework. This eighth stage reflects the attackers' endgame, where compromised systems or data are exploited for financial gain, whether through ransomware, data resale, or other illicit means. The inclusion of this phase underscores the growing emphasis on understanding not only how intrusions occur, but also the motivations driving them.

6.6.8 Phase 8: Monetization

In the monetization stage of a cyberattack, the primary objective of the adversaries shifts toward extracting financial gain from their malicious activities. This phase marks the culmination of earlier efforts, where attackers seek to convert their unauthorized access or stolen data into tangible profit. Although the strategies employed during monetization are not exclusively technical in nature, technical mechanisms often underpin or enhance the effectiveness of these illicit operations. For instance, the use of encryption in ransomware attacks, anonymization methods for cryptocurrency transactions, or secure communication channels for trafficking stolen data are all examples where technical components play a critical supporting role in facilitating financial exploitation.

6.6.8.1 Example 1: Cryptojacking with hidden mining script

- Monetization Technique: Cryptocurrency Mining
- Technical Details:
  - The attacker infects a victim's machine with malware that includes a hidden cryptocurrency mining script.
  - This script leverages the victim's computing power to mine cryptocurrency for the attacker's benefit.
  - The mining script might be obfuscated or designed to run only when certain conditions are met (e.g., during idle hours) to avoid detection.
- Impact: The victim's machine experiences reduced performance due to the additional processing power being consumed by the Cryptojacking script. This can lead to slower system response times and increased energy consumption.

6.6.8.2 Example 2: Ransomware with encrypted files and online payment portal

- Monetization Technique: Ransomware Attack
- Technical Details:
  - The attacker infects a victim's system with ransomware that encrypts important files, rendering them inaccessible.
  - The ransomware displays a message demanding a ransom payment in cryptocurrency in exchange for a decryption key.
  - The attacker might leverage a Tor hidden service to host a payment portal where the victim can anonymously send the ransom payment.
- Technical Aspects: While encryption and anonymization techniques are not strictly part of the kill chain itself, they play a crucial role in enabling this specific monetization method.

By understanding how attackers aim to profit from their intrusions, organizations can prioritize security measures and implement threat intelligence to mitigate these risks. Since its introduction, the CKC has undergone significant development in response to the changing landscape of cyber threats. Originally designed to model and anticipate the stages of a cyberattack, it has become a widely used framework among cybersecurity professionals and organizations to systematically analyze and respond to incidents. Despite its utility, the future trajectory of the CKC remains uncertain due to the rapidly evolving nature of threat actors, tactics, and technologies. In contemporary cybersecurity practice, the growing emphasis on extended detection and response (XDR) suggests a potential shift toward more dynamic and intelligence-driven models. One promising direction is the integration of the MITRE ATT&CK framework into a revised or alternative kill chain structure. Such an adaptation could provide security teams with a more granular and adaptable approach to threat detection and mitigation. Current limitations of the traditional kill chain model generally fall into two broad areas: an overreliance on perimeter-based defenses and insufficient accommodation of modern attack vectors that exploit system vulnerabilities beyond initial entry points:

- Perimeter Security: A major limitation frequently associated with Lockheed Martin's CKC framework lies in its treatment of the initial stages of a cyberattack – specifically, reconnaissance and weaponization. These early phases are typically conducted entirely outside the boundaries of the target organization's network, meaning they occur beyond the visibility and control of internal security systems. As a result, organizations often struggle to detect or respond to these preliminary actions, leaving a significant gap in their defensive posture. This externalized nature of the first two steps presents a challenge in developing a comprehensive and proactive security strategy, as potential threats may be well underway before any signs become apparent within the organization's monitoring scope.
- Attack Vulnerabilities: In contemporary cybersecurity discourse, a growing number of experts argue that existing methodologies tend to uphold outdated defense paradigms – particularly those rooted in perimeter-based protection and conventional malware prevention. These approaches, once foundational, are increasingly seen as insufficient in the face of today's rapidly evolving threat landscape, where attackers often bypass traditional security barriers through sophisticated, multistage techniques
- Further criticism is directed toward the continued reliance on the traditional CKC model, particularly regarding its applicability to insider threats. Detractors assert that the model, originally developed to describe external intrusion patterns, does not adequately capture the nuances of threats originating from within an organization. This misalignment may lead to significant vulnerabilities, as insider attacks often circumvent the very perimeters the kill chain assumes to be intact. While the CKC has been widely adopted in various sectors, its universal acceptance remains contested. Many cybersecurity professionals highlight inherent limitations in its structure and logic, advocating for more adaptable and comprehensive frameworks. Encouragingly, a number of alternative models have emerged that aim to address these perceived deficiencies, offering organizations new strategies to enhance their detection and response capabilities in the face of modern cyber threats.

6.7 DIAMOND MODEL

Designed for intrusion analysis, the Diamond framework [9] focuses on four key elements: Capability, Adversary, Infrastructure, and Target. By examining the relationships between these elements, security professionals can gain a better understanding of an attacker's motives

Adversary	Infrastructure	Capabilities	Victim
• Adversary is a person responsible for cyberattacks, keep track of Origin XYZ, Impacted area ABC	• Domain - Gmail.com, IP Address - 192.168.10.10, Email Address - akash@akash.com	• Different hacking tools used by adversaries - Worm, Trojan, Ransomware	• User: Akash, Asset: XYZ, Organization: ABC

Figure 6.28 Diamond model.

and techniques. This framework, created by Professor David Diamond, takes a broader view as illustrated in Figure 6.28 focusing on the motivations and capabilities of attackers.

It analyses threats through seven dimensions:

- **Capability**: What technical skills and resources do attackers possess?
- **Delivery**: How do they deliver the attack (e.g., phishing, malware)?
- **Infrastructure**: What infrastructure supports their attacks (e.g., botnets)?
- **Command and Control (C2)**: How do attackers control their tools and malware?
- **Activities**: What actions do they take during an attack (e.g., data exfiltration)?
- **Targets**: Who or what are they targeting (e. industries, specific organizations)?
- **Motivations**: Why are they attacking (e.g., financial gain, activism)?

6.7.1 Element #1: Adversary

Technical Details: This facet focuses on the attacker themself. Technical details you might examine include:

- Attacker Type: Are they a lone actor, a criminal organization, or a state-sponsored group?
- Technical Capabilities: What tools and techniques do they typically use? Do they have a history of exploiting specific vulnerabilities?
- Targeting Motivation: What is their goal? Financial gain, espionage, disruption, or something else?

Example: Let's say you identify a series of attacks targeting financial institutions. Technical analysis reveals the attackers use spear phishing emails with malicious attachments containing RATs. This suggests a financially motivated group with some technical knowledge, possibly leveraging pre-built exploit kits.

6.7.2 Element # 2: Capability

Technical Details: This facet explores the attacker's methods and tools. Here are some technical details to consider:

- Attack Techniques: What exploits, malware, or social engineering tactics do they employ?
- Delivery Methods: How do they initially gain access to systems (e.g., phishing emails, drive-by-downloads, software vulnerabilities)?
- Command and Control (C2): How do they maintain control over compromised systems (e.g., traditional C2 servers, peer-to-peer networks)?

Example: Continuing with the financial institution attacks, you discover a trend of phishing emails containing malicious macro-laden documents. Further investigation reveals the attackers use a specific exploit kit known to target vulnerabilities in outdated versions of a popular word processing application.

6.7.3 Element #3: Infrastructure

Technical Details: This facet examines the technical resources attackers use. Here are some technical details to consider:

- C2 Servers: Where are the attacker-controlled servers located? Do they use a single server or a network of distributed servers?
- Staging Servers: Do the attackers use intermediary servers to host malware or stolen data?
- Communication Channels: How do the attackers' tools communicate (e.g., standard ports, encrypted channels)?

Example: By analyzing network traffic, you identify suspicious connections to a server located in a known offshore hosting country. This server might be a C2 server used by the attackers to communicate with compromised systems within the financial institutions.

6.7.4 Element #4: Victim

Technical Details: This facet focuses on the targeted systems and networks. Here are some technical details to consider:

- Vulnerabilities: What weaknesses in the victim's systems or security posture might be exploited?
- Targeted Assets: What data or resources are the attackers most interested in?
- Security Controls: What security measures are in place to prevent or detect attacks (e.g., firewalls, intrusion detection systems)?

Example: The analysis of the financial institutions reveals outdated software and lax patch management practices, potentially creating vulnerabilities for the attackers to exploit. Additionally, you discover the attackers seem particularly interested in compromising user accounts with access to customer financial data. By analyzing each facet of the Diamond Model and the relationships between them, you can gain a comprehensive understanding of a cyber threat. This can inform the security posture by helping identify potential attacker motivations, prioritize vulnerabilities to patch, and implement appropriate detection and prevention measures. By analyzing these dimensions, security professionals can gain a deeper understanding of the "who" and "why" behind cyberattacks, allowing for more targeted defense strategies.

6.8 CONCLUSION

This chapter offers a comprehensive overview of CTI frameworks, highlighting their critical role in understanding and mitigating cyber threats through structured methodologies. By examining models such as the MITRE ATT&CK, CKC, and the Diamond Model, the chapter illustrates how organizations can systematically analyze adversary behaviors, identify vulnerabilities, and build targeted defense mechanisms. These frameworks serve not only as analytical tools but also as operational guides for mapping threat actor tactics, enhancing detection strategies, and aligning cybersecurity actions with organizational risk profiles. Practical use cases, such as ATT&CK Navigator and adversary emulation, further demonstrate how these models support red and blue team operations, strengthen incident response, and guide proactive threat hunting. Additionally, the emphasis on data normalization, TIP integration, and contextual intelligence extraction underscores the importance of transforming raw threat data into actionable insights. Collectively, these frameworks foster a common language for cybersecurity teams, improving collaboration, decision-making, and long-term security posture. As cyber threats evolve in complexity, adopting and adapting these CTI frameworks becomes essential for building resilient and responsive defense strategies tailored to organizational needs. This structured approach empowers security professionals to anticipate, prevent, and respond effectively to advanced and persistent cyber adversaries.

MULTIPLE CHOICE QUESTIONS

1. A SOC analyst observes unusual authentication attempts from multiple internal systems. The attempts originate from valid accounts but occur during non-working hours. Mapping the behavior in ATT&CK Navigator reveals techniques under Credential Access (T1555) and Valid Accounts (T1078). A review of recent threat intel shows activity resembling FIN6's known techniques. The SOC wants to determine whether this aligns with a more extensive intrusion set or a localized account compromise. What framework best supports correlating *adversary, capability, infrastructure*, and *victim*?

   A. Cyber Kill Chain
   B. MITRE ATT&CK Matrix
   C. Diamond Model of Intrusion Analysis
   D. ATT&CK Navigator Scoring

   Correct Answer: C
   Why correct: Diamond Model examines adversary → capability → infrastructure → victim, exactly what this multi-element pattern requires. Why others are wrong:
   - A: Kill Chain shows phases, not multi-entity relationships.
   - B: ATT&CK maps techniques, not relationships.
   - D: Navigator only visualizes technique patterns.

2. A financial institution notices increased scanning on its public-facing apps. Threat intel shows these scans come from cloud VPS instances previously tagged as part of APT41 infrastructure. The red team maps the activity to the Reconnaissance and Resource Development tactics in ATT&CK. They want to stop the attack before initial access occurs. According to CTI frameworks, where should defensive measures be prioritized?

   A. Cyber Kill Chain Phase: Delivery
   B. ATT&CK Tactic: Execution
   C. Cyber Kill Chain Phase: Reconnaissance
   D. Diamond Model Element: Motivation

   Correct Answer: C
   Why correct: Kill Chain emphasizes earliest disruption – blocking reconnaissance halts the attack before it starts. Why others are wrong:
   - A: Delivery comes later.
   - B: Execution is after initial access.
   - D: Motivation does not indicate a defense point.

3. A major corporation receives a well-crafted phishing email impersonating GitHub. The attachment contains a malicious macro that downloads a secondary payload and installs a RAT. Using ATT&CK Navigator, analysts map tactics across Initial Access, Execution, and Persistence. Leadership wants to know how the attack fits into the lifecycle of a cyberattack. Which model should be used for explaining the *sequence*?

    A. MITRE ATT&CK Navigator
    B. Cyber Kill Chain
    C. Diamond Model
    D. TIP-Driven IOC Normalization

    Correct Answer: B
    Why correct: Kill Chain explains sequential stages like delivery → exploitation → installation → C2. Why others are wrong:
    - A: Navigator does not explain order.
    - C: Diamond Model examines relationships, not sequence.
    - D: TIP normalization is unrelated.

4. A SOC team notices multiple logins from legitimate admin accounts from foreign locations. Using ATT&CK Navigator, they map T1078: Valid Accounts and observe heavy usage by multiple FIN groups. They want a defensive perspective to counter this technique using recommended controls. Which tool should they use?

    A. MITRE D3FEND
    B. ATT&CK Groups Page
    C. Cyber Kill Chain
    D. Diamond Model

    Correct Answer: A
    Why correct: D3FEND provides mapped countermeasures and defensive techniques for ATT&CK TTPs. Why others are wrong:
    - B: Shows group details, not defenses.
    - C: Gives attack phases, not mitigation controls.
    - D: Helps analyze motives, not defenses.

5. A bank compares FIN4 and FIN6 activity using ATT&CK Navigator's "Create Layer from Other Layers" and score expression options (a+b). The resulting heatmap shows overlapping techniques, especially in Credential Access and Discovery. Executives ask which framework supports such multigroup comparative analysis. Which option correctly identifies this?

    A. Diamond Model
    B. MITRE ATT&CK Framework
    C. TIP (Threat Intelligence Platform)
    D. Cyber Kill Chain

    Correct Answer: B
    Why correct: ATT&CK enables technique-based comparison of groups, software, and campaigns. Why others are wrong:
    - A: Not used to compare multiple groups' techniques.
    - C: TIP organizes data, not technique mapping.
    - D: Kill Chain is linear and not comparison driven.

6. A SOC receives IPs, emails, geolocation data, and malware hashes from different feed formats. Without normalization, correlation engine results are inconsistent. The CTI manager explains to leadership that the data must be standardized before use. Which component solves this?

   A. Cyber Kill Chain
   B. Threat Intelligence Platform
   C. ATT&CK Navigator
   D. Diamond Model

   Correct Answer: B
   Why correct: TIPs ingest diverse formats (emails, PDFs, IOCs, tweets) and normalize them. Why others are wrong:
   * A: Does not address data processing.
   * C: Only visualizes techniques.
   * D: Not a data ingestion framework.

7. An investigation finds a tool used in an intrusion. Public reports identify it as "CHOPSTICK," but other vendors label it differently. ATT&CK indicates it is associated software used by a known group. SOC analysts need clarity about overlaps and naming conventions. Which ATT&CK component provides this?

   A. Software → Associated Software
   B. Groups → Associated Groups
   C. Campaign → Associated Campaigns
   D. Tactics → Techniques

   Correct Answer: A
   Why correct: ATT&CK software entries show "associated software" names and overlaps. Why others are wrong:
   * B: Refers to group aliases, not software aliases.
   * C: Refers to campaign overlaps.
   * D: Irrelevant.

8. A SOC detects lateral movement via SMB and remote execution tools. Using ATT&CK, they map the behavior to Discovery and Lateral Movement tactics. They want to align this to a broader attacker lifecycle to design preventative controls earlier. What framework helps them identify where earlier disruption could occur?

   A. ATT&CK Navigator
   B. Cyber Kill Chain
   C. Diamond Model
   D. TIP Correlation

   Correct Answer: B
   Why correct: Kill Chain identifies pivot stages and defensive choke points. Why others are wrong:
   * A: Maps techniques but not lifecycle.
   * C: Analyzes adversary relationships, not stages.
   * D: Not lifecycle oriented.

9. CTI analysts identify multiple intrusions involving similar TTPs across several months, all targeting cloud infrastructure. MITRE documentation shows these as a named campaign. The SOC wants to understand how long the campaign ran and what groups it ties to. Which ATT&CK component provides this?

   A. Tactics
   B. Campaigns
   C. C2 Techniques
   D. Infrastructure Pages

   Correct Answer: B
   Why correct: Campaign pages show timeframes, associated groups, and techniques.
      Why others are wrong:
   - A: High-level goals, not attribution.
   - C: Only one tactic area.
   - D: Not a standalone ATT&CK component.

10. A red team prepares a simulation against a client. They use ATT&CK Navigator to map tactics for Reconnaissance, Initial Access, and Privilege Escalation, color-coding planned steps. They want to show executives which techniques align with real APT behavior. Which feature enables this?

    A. Technique Heat Mapping
    B. Create Layer from Other Layers
    C. Predefined Scoring Gradients
    D. Search and Multi-Select for Groups

    Correct Answer: D
    Why correct: Multi-select allows adding APT41/FIN6 etc. to emulate adversary behavior. Why others are wrong:
    - A: Heatmap helps visualize, not map actors.
    - B: Used for comparison, not selection.
    - C: Enhances visualization but not actor selection.

11. During analysis of a financial sector breach, the CTI team wants to identify whether attackers are financially motivated or conducting espionage. The framework must reveal who, why, and how they operate. Which CTI model provides motivation analysis?

    A. Cyber Kill Chain
    B. MITRE ATT&CK
    C. Diamond Model
    D. TIP Threat Feed Reports

    Correct Answer: C
    Why correct: Diamond Model includes *motivations*, unlike ATT&CK or Kill Chain.
       Why others are wrong:
    - A: Does not address motive.
    - B: Focuses on behavior, not intent.
    - D: Reports vary but lack structural motive analysis.

12. A cloud-heavy organization detects API enumeration, open bucket scanning, and DNS brute forcing. MITRE ATT&CK categorizes these under Reconnaissance and Resource Development. Leadership wants to know the attacker's next probable steps. What framework provides predictive insight?

    A. ATT&CK → Behavior cataloguing
    B. Kill Chain → Next attack stage prediction
    C. Diamond Model → Attack aftermath
    D. TIP → IOC scoring

    Correct Answer: B
    Why correct: Kill Chain predicts sequence → after recon → weaponization → delivery. Why others are wrong:
    - A: Catalogs behavior but not predict sequence.
    - C: Focuses on relationships, not next steps.
    - D: Not predictive.

13. During a CTI meeting, the team notices ATT&CK does not reveal when the attacker began preparing infrastructure or their psychological motives. They need a complementary framework. Which should they add?

    A. Kill Chain
    B. CVSS
    C. Diamond Model
    D. IOC-Only Tip Feed

    Correct Answer: C
    Why correct: Diamond Model covers adversary infrastructure, capability, and motivations. Why others are wrong:
    - A: Kill Chain doesn't cover motives.
    - B: CVSS is for vulnerabilities.
    - D: IOC feeds offer no strategic insight.

14. A CTI team receives thousands of emails, PDFs, OSINT tweets, and IOCs daily. They struggle because the formats differ and cannot compare threat patterns efficiently. Which solution best addresses this?

    A. Cyber Kill Chain
    B. TIP with normalization capability
    C. ATT&CK Navigator
    D. Diamond Model

    Correct Answer: B
    Why correct: TIPs ingest → normalize → correlate multiple data sources. Why others are wrong:
    - A: Not a data-processing tool.
    - C: Visualizes techniques only.
    - D: Not designed for ingestion.

15. Two intrusions targeting the same sector appear to share C2 infrastructure and malware families. Analysts check MITRE ATT&CK and find overlapping names under different vendors. Which ATT&CK component clarifies naming inconsistencies?

   A. Associated Groups
   B. Campaign Tactics
   C. Technique Sub-Techniques
   D. ATT&CK Navigator Layers

Correct Answer: A
Why correct: Associated Groups lists different names used for the same activity cluster.
   Why others are wrong:
   - B: Campaigns describe events, not naming overlaps.
   - C: Technique details, not group aliasing.
   - D: Navigator is just visual.

REFERENCES

1. Cortex, "What is a threat intelligence platform," *Palo Alto Networks*, 2026. https://www.paloaltonetworks.com/cyberpedia/what-is-a-threat-intelligence-platform
2. MITRE, "MITRE ATT&CK," *Mitre.org*, 2025. https://attack.mitre.org
3. "Matrix - Enterprise | MITRE ATT&CK®," *attack.mitre.org*, 2026. https://attack.mitre.org/matrices/enterprise
4. MITRE, "Groups | MITRE ATT&CKTM," *attack.mitre.org*, 2022. https://attack.mitre.org/groups
5. "Software | MITRE ATT&CK®," *attack.mitre.org*, 2026. https://attack.mitre.org/software
6. "Campaigns | MITRE ATT&CK®," *attack.mitre.org*, 2026. https://attack.mitre.org/campaigns
7. MITRE, "ATT&CK® navigator," *mitre-attack.github.io*, 2026. https://mitre-attack.github.io/attack-navigator
8. Lockheed Martin, "Cyber kill chain," *Lockheed Martin*, 2025. https://www.lockheedmartin.com/en-us/capabilities/cyber/cyber-kill-chain.html
9. D. Tidmarsh, "What is the diamond model of intrusion analysis in cybersecurity," *Cybersecurity Exchange*, Nov. 7, 2023. https://www.eccouncil.org/cybersecurity-exchange/ethical-hacking/diamond-model-intrusion-analysis

Chapter 7

Empowering threat detection through analytics

7.1 ACCESS DATA QUALITY

Throughout our exploration of Cyber Threat Intelligence (CTI), one recurring theme has been the critical need for clear, accurate visibility into an organization's digital assets. Without proper insight, teams may fall into a dangerous illusion of security. But there's another challenge that often gets overlooked even if visibility is achieved, what if the quality of the data being collected is subpar? Poor-quality data can be just as damaging, leading to flawed decisions, operational inefficiencies, misguided strategies, and potentially massive financial losses. Although data quality issues extend beyond threat hunting alone, cybersecurity professionals must still take them seriously.

Data quality is not binary; it lies on a spectrum. What qualifies as "acceptable" depends heavily on the use case. In essence, data can be considered high quality if it meets the needs of those relying on it. An effective data governance strategy should blend technological capabilities with an organization's cultural framework, ensuring that the insights generated align with core business goals. Timely and reliable data is essential for decision-makers to act effectively and confidently. Experts often describe data quality through various attributes, and while opinions differ on how many exist, six are almost universally accepted:

- Accuracy: The degree to which data reflects reality without error, enabling sound conclusions.
- Completeness: Ensures that datasets include all necessary attributes.
- Uniqueness: Each record should be distinct, avoiding redundancy.
- Validity: Information must conform to defined rules or standards.
- Timeliness: Data should be current and reflect recent conditions.
- Consistency: Data values should follow consistent formats and structures across datasets.

These core dimensions serve as a foundation for evaluating and improving trust in data. As data ecosystems evolve, additional dimensions, such as relevance, reliability, comparability, and retention, gain importance. For instance, consistency emphasizes that values remain standardized across various systems, often referencing a predefined data model or dictionary. A vital step in enhancing data integrity is data profiling, which involves two interconnected activities:

- Cleansing: This process addresses issues like duplicate entries, improper formats, and inconsistent data types. It also helps clarify relationships and definitions within the dataset.
- Monitoring: Involves continuously checking that the data adheres to established quality standards, ensuring compliance with predefined benchmarks.

DOI: 10.1201/9781003730583-7

Managing large volumes of data introduces several complications:

- Repurposing: Using the same dataset for different tasks can shift its meaning, leading to conflicting interpretations.
- Validation: Ensuring the data remains consistent with its original context or source.
- Rejuvenation: Attempting to extract new insights from outdated data often requires additional verification to maintain reliability.

7.2 IMPROVING DATA QUALITY

While the subject of data governance is both broad and specialized, this discussion will not delve into every responsibility typically handled by a data governance team to maintain data quality. Instead, we'll assume that the organization has already taken foundational steps – such as conducting a thorough inventory of its data assets and defining reference baselines for various data quality dimensions that will be evaluated. Additionally, we'll operate under the assumption that the organization has established a set of rules to validate data against these baselines. The data management team is also assumed to carry out routine evaluations to monitor data quality and implement improvements where needed. To aid in these efforts, consider exploring open-source tools designed for data quality assessment, including OSSEM Power-up, DeTT&CT, and Sysmon-Modular.

In 2024, a Managed Security Service Provider (MSSP) [1] adopted OSSEM Power-Up [2] to evaluate its log ingestion pipeline across enterprise clients. They began by loading OSSEM's Detection Data Model into their own security information event management (SIEM), defining data channels such as Windows Sysmon, application logs, and cloud audit streams. For each channel, they scored coverage (host/spread), timeliness (ingest latency), and retention via dcs.yml. OSSEM then evaluated structure and consistency by comparing log fields to canonical CIM entities (e.g., ensuring process_name, path, and command_line were captured). One client saw its structure score for Sysmon jump from 3 to 5 after confirming all relevant fields – especially EventID 1 – were mapped correctly. Consistency rose when malformed or inconsistent field names were normalized. By presenting these scores per data source, OSSEM helped the MSSP identify low-quality streams and prioritize enhancements, adding missing fields, tightening ingestion SLAs, and improving data normalization to achieve higher overall data quality.

In Q1 2025, a large European bank deployed DeTT&CT to assess its logging coverage against MITRE ATT&CK. Using the built-in CLI and editor, the security team defined dozens of data sources (Windows event logs, Azure AD, network flow logs) and scored them across five dimensions: device completeness, field completeness, timeliness, consistency, and retention. The team uploaded this data to ATT&CK Navigator to visualize coverage gaps. The heatmap revealed limited coverage for techniques like T1059 (Command and Scripting Interpreter) due to partial Sysmon deployment on servers. By comparing pre- and post-rollout states, they prioritized enabling Sysmon across Tier-0 servers and standardizing ingestion latency. Within weeks, visibility scores improved for over 40 techniques, and detection capabilities increased as new rules based on better data quality were implemented. Their DeTT&CT-driven approach ensured data investments directly enhanced security coverage.

A U.S. industrial control firm in mid-2024 revamped its Sysmon deployment using Sysmon-Modular configurations by Olaf Hartong. After ingesting logs into Azure Sentinel via an AMA agent, the analytics and incident response teams configured Sysmon-Modular to enable finest-grained telemetry – file creation, registry modifications, and network connections – only on branded ICS workstations. They tuned the configuration per environment: default balanced profile on general servers, and verbose including FileExecutable rules on SCADA systems, analyzing performance and ingestion cost against Sentinel's billing. Within two months, they observed a 30% increase in actionable telemetry without overwhelming storage. The structured and consistent fields mapped easily into their SIEM parsers, improving field completeness and consistency. This tuning ensured both high data quality and cost efficiency, enabling better detection of sophisticated threats targeted at critical operations.

7.3 THREAT INTEL ANALYTICS

In 2023, Chief Information Security Officers (CISOs) and cybersecurity teams are navigating an increasingly hostile digital environment. The rise in ransomware incidents has more than doubled compared to the previous year, while sensitive enterprise login credentials, including those tied to single sign-on (SSO), Active Directory, and cloud-based SaaS applications, are being widely circulated on platforms like Telegram. Moreover, initial access brokers (IABs) have become more active, regularly auctioning entry points into corporate networks to the highest bidder. Threat intelligence analytics is now a cornerstone in the fight against cyber-crime. It involves the structured process of gathering, examining, and interpreting threat-related data to produce actionable insights. Rather than passively defending against attacks, modern security teams are shifting toward a more offensive stance like tracking threat actors, identifying suspicious activities, and neutralizing risks before they escalate.

Amid this turbulent cyber landscape, the application of analytics to threat intelligence enables security operations to move beyond basic alerting. Sophisticated algorithms and analytical models help extract meaningful patterns from immense data streams, empowering decision-makers to predict, prevent, and respond to threats with greater precision. Unlike mere data collection, this analytical approach includes cross-referencing and interpreting diverse signals to expose hidden trends, understand adversary tactics, and identify novel threat vectors.

Advanced threat analytics equips defenders with a nuanced view of attacker behaviors. It reveals the motivations and methodologies of adversaries, helping organizations understand not just *who* is targeting them, but *how* and *why*. This includes profiling threat actors' tactics, techniques, and procedures (TTPs), enabling security teams to assess potential vulnerabilities, anticipated attack surfaces, and the likely consequences of a breach. For instance, cyber-criminal forums and dark web markets continue to be flooded with hacking kits, zero-day exploits, and custom malware, all easily accessible to bad actors. Keeping up with the speed and scale of these tools is daunting. Yet, with tailored analysis, organizations can focus their defenses on the most relevant threats. Notably, TTPs often vary by sector or vulnerability class. Organizations that continuously track these shifting tactics are better positioned to adapt their defenses and mitigate risks aligned with their specific industry.

A powerful advantage of threat intelligence analytics lies in its ability to uncover malicious activities at an early stage. By applying real-time analytics to incoming threat data, security teams can detect indicators of compromise (IOCs), observe the emergence of new malware strains, and identify unusual behaviors that signal an evolving attack. This early visibility allows for swift countermeasures such as:

- Fine-tuning intrusion detection systems
- Deploying updated threat signatures
- Sharing threat data with trusted partners to reinforce collective cyber defenses

One of the most pressing examples is the spread of *infostealer* malware [3]. These malicious tools harvest login credentials and browser-saved passwords from infected systems. The stolen data is compiled into "logs" and then posted or sold on Telegram channels and underground marketplaces like Genesis and Russian forums. As of August 2023, over 375,000 enterprise credentials had surfaced in such infostealer logs. More dangerously, these logs may include session cookies, granting unauthorized access to live user accounts.

Beyond identification and correlation, threat intelligence analytics provides crucial insights during live security incidents. By integrating external threat intelligence with internal security telemetry – such as logs from firewalls, IDS/IPS alerts, and endpoint data – organizations can better understand the full scope and impact of an intrusion. This interpretative power helps responders determine:

1. Which assets are affected
2. The severity and timeline of the attack
3. The optimal containment and remediation strategies

Furthermore, post-incident analysis using threat intelligence can trace back the root cause, highlight exploited vulnerabilities, and inform future hardening measures to prevent recurrence. By transforming fragmented threat data into cohesive, actionable intelligence, organizations can shift from reactive to proactive cybersecurity. In a year marked by surging cybercrime and sophisticated adversaries, such a strategic transformation is no longer optional; it is essential.

7.4 CYBER THREAT HUNTING

In the modern cybersecurity landscape, threat intelligence analytics plays a critical role in enabling proactive defense mechanisms. Instead of merely reacting to incidents, organizations are increasingly utilizing threat intelligence to actively scan their digital environments for subtle indications of compromise. This process, commonly referred to as proactive threat hunting, involves scrutinizing various forms of network telemetry, such as traffic patterns, event logs, and system behavior for early signs of malicious activity. These could range from covert advanced persistent threats (APTs) [4] to insider-driven anomalies that evade conventional security tools. By identifying these threats in their nascent stages, organizations can contain breaches before they escalate into significant security events. Beyond detection, threat intelligence analytics also transforms raw threat data into practical, context-rich insights. It supports a comprehensive understanding of potential threats, accelerates incident response, and contributes to predictive threat modeling. By fusing internal telemetry with external threat feeds, it elevates the effectiveness of CTI programs and fortifies an organization's defensive posture.

With sophisticated analytical tools and methodologies, organizations can gain a strategic edge in cyber defense, adapting faster to new threats and formulating informed, dynamic protection strategies for critical infrastructure and data. A well-rounded threat intelligence framework hinges on access to a wide array of credible and dynamic data sources. The strength of any threat analytics effort lies in its ability to extract meaningful intelligence from both internal and external feeds. To achieve a robust and adaptive CTI program, organizations must integrate and evaluate data across multiple dimensions of the threat landscape. Key sources that significantly enhance intelligence capabilities include:

- Open-Source Intelligence (OSINT): This includes freely available information from news portals, public forums, blogs, and social media channels. Monitoring such data allows analysts to keep pace with emerging threats, track adversary behaviors, and gain visibility into prevailing attack vectors and targets.
- Closed Source Channels: Proprietary threat intelligence sources – like dark web monitoring, commercial feeds, and restricted cybercriminal forums – offer privileged access to threat actor tactics and infrastructure. These sources are particularly valuable for industry-specific threats and supply chain vulnerabilities.
- Internal Security Telemetry: Corporate networks generate a rich repository of security-relevant data, including firewall logs, endpoint telemetry, and SIEM logs. Analyzing this internal data uncovers patterns of unauthorized access, privilege escalation, and abnormal activity that might indicate a breach.
- Historical Incident Data: Learning from previous attacks provides critical insights. Historical incident reports, including attacker techniques and exploited vulnerabilities, help refine threat models and incident response playbooks.
- Industry Collaboration Networks: By participating in information-sharing forums like ISACs or sector-specific alliances, organizations can benefit from peer insights and broaden their threat visibility. Shared intelligence often includes real-world attack data, mitigation strategies, and emerging risk trends.
- External Threat Feeds: Real-time integrations with external sources, such as malware repositories, blacklisted IP lists, and known IOCs, help automate threat detection and reduce reaction time during attacks.

Combining these data streams allows organizations to develop a nuanced and timely view of the threat ecosystem. Regular validation of data sources for relevance, freshness, and accuracy ensures continued efficacy and trustworthiness of the threat intelligence pipeline. Turning data into actionable intelligence requires more than just collection; it demands structured analysis. Employing analytical tools and proven techniques helps distil raw inputs into clear, decision-driving insights. Some critical approaches include:

- Aggregation and Correlation: This technique involves unifying threat information from various feeds to discover meaningful patterns and interdependencies among threat indicators. Tools like SIEMs and threat intelligence platforms automate this correlation, giving a comprehensive view of security risks.
- Contextual Data Enrichment: Raw data often lacks necessary depth. By enriching threat records with contextual attributes such as geolocation, attack history, or attacker profile which analysts can prioritize responses and reduce false positives. Automated enrichment services streamline this process.
- Machine Learning and Statistical Models: Predictive analytics allows systems to detect behavioral anomalies, categorize threats by severity, and forecast potential breaches. These models reduce the manual overhead involved in data interpretation and enable real-time threat detection with greater accuracy.
- Proactive Threat Hunting: Rather than waiting for alerts, skilled analysts use query-based hunting across system logs and behavioral data to unearth threats that evade standard detection. Advanced EDR tools, flow analytics, and behavioral modeling engines support this tactical approach.

Each of these techniques transforms scattered threat data into structured intelligence. When deployed systematically, they enhance both the strategic and operational aspects of cybersecurity, equipping organizations to stay agile and resilient in the face of evolving cyber adversaries.

7.4.1 Example: Canary tokens

Canary Tokens [5] serve as silent security alerts, much like digital tripwires for your systems and online environments. Attackers discreetly place them in files, directories, cloud storage, mobile devices, or anywhere sensitive data should remain untouched, as shown in Figure 7.1.

Their role is simple: if someone interacts with them, you will immediately know. These tokens are intentionally crafted to catch the eye of intruders; they appear valuable or intriguing, which boosts the chances of unauthorized access. Once triggered, they alert you instantly, signaling a potential breach. You don't need to monitor them constantly; just deploy them and carry on, confident they'll notify you only when it truly matters. What's more, they're incredibly efficient. There's no need to install heavy software or burden your system with extra background tasks. Lightweight and hassle-free, Canary Tokens offer a powerful, no-cost way to stay ahead of threats without interrupting your workflow, as illustrated in Figure 7.2.

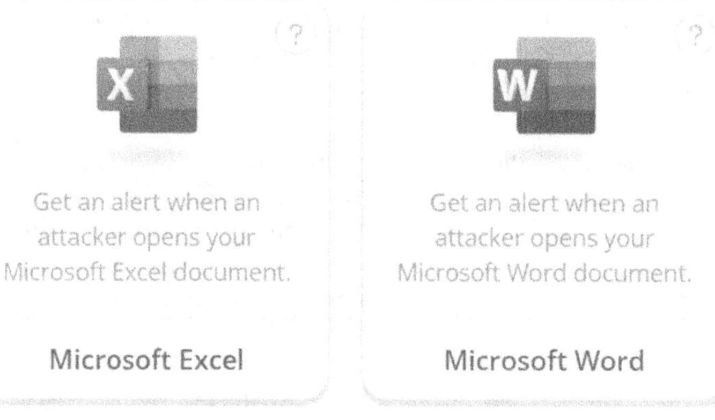

Figure 7.1 Canary tokens.

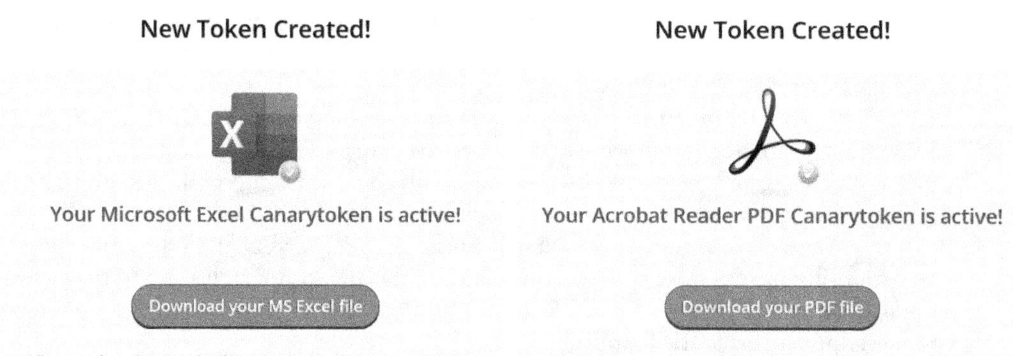

Figure 7.2 Token created (excel/PDF).

7.5 THREAT INTELLIGENCE PLATFORMS

Modern cybersecurity operations increasingly rely on dedicated platforms and intuitive dashboards that consolidate and organize threat-related data in one accessible location. These systems are designed to streamline the intake, analysis, and presentation of CTI. Through their robust functionalities, security teams can:

- Conduct deep, targeted investigations
- Interpret evolving threat patterns through visual analytics
- Develop tailored intelligence summaries
- Promote internal knowledge sharing and collaborative decision-making

Harnessing analytics in the realm of CTI is essential for translating raw data into strategic defense capabilities. When threat insights are applied purposefully, organizations are better positioned to anticipate malicious activity and respond with precision. The upcoming section outlines practical methods for turning threat data into actionable outcomes that support and strengthen your CTI initiatives. To generate meaningful outcomes from your intelligence efforts, the first step is narrowing your focus to the threats and indicators that are most pertinent to your specific environment. This involves understanding your organization's unique assets, sector-specific risks, and adversary behavior. By tapping into specialized intelligence sources – such as sector-relevant advisories, curated feeds, and technical reports, you can ensure that attention is directed toward the vulnerabilities and threat actors that matter most.

Raw threat indicators alone are often insufficient without the surrounding context. Enhancing threat data with information about known attacker groups, their methods, previous incidents, and operational objectives transform isolated signals into a clearer picture of risk. This contextual layering enables analysts to assess the relevance of threats in relation to ongoing campaigns or trends. Utilizing automated enrichment tools and intelligence platforms can significantly improve the efficiency and accuracy of this process, helping teams derive timely and strategic insights.

7.5.1 OSSEM Power-up

OSSEM Power-up is an open-source tool built using Python by Ricardo Dias, inspired by the foundational work of Roberto and Jose Rodriguez on the original OSSEM framework. This utility aims to assist users in identifying the most pertinent data sources for detecting specific MITRE ATT&CK techniques. It also serves as a framework for assessing the overall quality of the data sources available in a security environment. OSSEM Power-up evaluates data quality based on five essential dimensions: coverage, timeliness, retention, structure, and consistency. Each of these is scored on a scale from 0 to 5. To configure these scores, users must manually edit the relevant configuration files, as explained in the official documentation. Notably, the tool allows users to define multiple structural profiles depending on how the collected logs are intended to be analyzed or applied, adding flexibility to its evaluation approach.

After execution, the output can be exported in multiple formats, such as YAML, Excel spreadsheets, or directly to an Elasticsearch instance. This enables users to visualize the data through Kibana dashboards. Furthermore, OSSEM Power-up can generate a customized ATT&CK Navigator matrix that displays and highlights the evaluated data quality metrics for each ATT&CK technique, offering a visual perspective on where improvements or gaps may exist.

7.5.1.1 Example 1: Using OSSEM Power-up to evaluate credential dumping detection via data source quality scoring

In a mid-sized financial services organization with a hybrid IT infrastructure, the internal blue team was facing challenges in quantifying the effectiveness of their telemetry for detecting advanced threats. One such concern was the threat of credential dumping (MITRE ATT&CK T1003), where adversaries extract password hashes from memory or registry locations. Though the team had various log sources in place, ranging from Sysmon and Windows Event Logs to PowerShell transcript logging they lacked a cohesive mechanism to measure how well these sources covered specific ATT&CK techniques. This is where OSSEM Power-up was integrated as a methodical solution to improve the detection landscape. The project began with the identification of T1003 as a high-priority threat technique for evaluation. The team focused specifically on common behaviors within this technique, such as LSASS memory access, extraction of SAM registry hives, and PowerShell scripts interacting with credential-related APIs. These sub-techniques often signal the use of tools like Mimikatz or custom scripts to extract credentials post-compromise. The goal was to map these behaviors to available logs and then apply OSSEM Power-up to evaluate the quality of those sources across multiple data quality dimensions. These dimensions like coverage, timeliness, structure, retention, and consistency which allow for a well-rounded understanding of log effectiveness beyond just presence or absence.

To begin implementation, the OSSEM Power-up tool was cloned from its GitHub repository. It is a Python-based framework that leverages structured YAML configurations to link ATT&CK techniques with logging sources and assign scores to each based on quality metrics. In this case, the team prepared configuration files listing three critical log types: Sysmon Event ID 10 (process access), Windows Security Event ID 4673 (privileged service calls), and PowerShell logging (Event ID 4104). These were the most relevant data sources for tracing credential dumping activities. Each of these sources was rated manually. For example, Sysmon Event ID 10 was given a high coverage score because it captures memory access events, including those targeting lsass.exe, which is commonly abused in credential dumping scenarios. However, retention was rated slightly lower because Sysmon logs were configured to roll over every 7 days due to storage limitations. PowerShell logs were marked with moderate consistency since some endpoints had logging disabled due to performance issues during script execution. These evaluations were stored in structured YAML files under the / configs directory of the OSSEM Power-up installation.

Once the configuration was finalized, the Power-up tool was executed. It processed the configurations and produced output files summarizing the data quality metrics associated with each log source for the T1003 technique. The result was not only a tabular summary of quality scores but also a visually encoded ATT&CK Navigator matrix. This matrix used color gradients to indicate the level of confidence the team could place in their detection capability per technique, based on the scores given. For T1003, for example, Sysmon logs contributed to a dark green (high confidence) score due to their granularity and structure, whereas Security Event Logs showed an amber score due to inconsistencies across systems.

The team then exported the results in both Excel and YAML formats. These outputs were ingested into their Elasticsearch instance, allowing for the creation of a Kibana dashboard that reflected ATT&CK technique coverage by data source quality. This dashboard became a critical part of the team's weekly review process, enabling them to track not just detection logic, but the foundational data availability and structure that made such detections possible. They could now see, for instance, how changes in endpoint logging policy affected ATT&CK technique visibility. When a group of endpoints had PowerShell logging disabled, the matrix for credential dumping would automatically reflect a reduced quality score, warning the analysts that some detection rules might no longer fire as expected.

One of the most impactful outcomes of using OSSEM Power-up in this scenario was its influence on cross-department communication. Previously, discussions about logging improvements with the IT operations team were anecdotal or reactive. Now, with the color-coded ATT&CK coverage matrix and structured data quality breakdown, the cybersecurity team could present evidence-backed justifications for increasing retention policies, deploying Sysmon more broadly, or enabling PowerShell logging with minimal performance tradeoffs. In one case, the matrix helped detect a misconfiguration in a new batch of endpoints where LSASS access was not being logged due to a missing Sysmon rule – a gap that might have otherwise gone unnoticed until a real incident occurred.

The ability to define multiple profiles for evaluating structure also allowed the blue team to tailor quality assessments based on different detection goals. For instance, if logs were to be used for machine learning-based anomaly detection, structure would be scored higher if fields were normalized and enriched. Alternatively, for threat hunting, a looser structure might still suffice if raw telemetry was accessible and sufficiently verbose. OSSEM Power-up supported both use cases by allowing per-profile scoring in its configuration files, ensuring flexibility across various use cases.

OSSEM Power-up served as more than just a static evaluation tool. It created a feedback loop between visibility, logging infrastructure, and detection capability. For this enterprise, the tool enabled a more transparent and quantitative approach to evaluating telemetry – not just for compliance or audit purposes, but for improving real-time adversary detection. By focusing on one ATT&CK technique, the blue team built a scalable, repeatable framework that could be extended across the entire ATT&CK matrix, transforming detection engineering into a data-driven discipline rather than a reactive patchwork of rules and assumptions.

7.5.1.2 Example 2: Leveraging OSSEM Power-up to assess lateral movement coverage in a hybrid network

In a large university's cybersecurity operations center (SOC), the security team manages a hybrid environment with thousands of endpoints spread across multiple campuses. These include Windows-based labs, Linux research clusters, and a growing number of cloud-hosted services. In 2024, the SOC identified repeated attempts of lateral movement, particularly leveraging protocols like SMB, WinRM, and RDP to traverse the network post-compromise. While their SIEM rules had some alerting for anomalous RDP logins, the team struggled with verifying whether their log collection infrastructure offered meaningful visibility into the full scope of MITRE ATT&CK's T1021: Remote Services and T1071: Application Layer Protocol techniques.

To solve this, they introduced OSSEM Power-up into their detection engineering workflow, aiming to assess the data quality of their telemetry with respect to the techniques used during lateral movement. While tools like Elastic SIEM and Zeek were collecting logs, the security engineers wanted to systematically evaluate whether these sources offered reliable, timely, and complete data aligned with ATT&CK-relevant tactics. OSSEM Power-up's ability to map logs to ATT&CK techniques and assign qualitative scores across five core dimensions (coverage, timeliness, retention, structure, and consistency) offered a structured lens through which they could perform this assessment. The team began by identifying key data sources used to detect lateral movement behaviors. This included Windows Event Logs (especially Event IDs 4624, 4648, and 4672), Sysmon logs (Event IDs 3 for network connection and 1 for process creation), and Zeek logs from the border firewall and core switches. Additionally, telemetry from PowerShell (event ID 4104), WMI (Windows Management Instrumentation) tracing, and WinRM sessions were collected via custom logging configurations. These logs were parsed into an ELK stack and normalized using Elastic Common Schema (ECS) to maintain consistency across data platforms.

Using OSSEM Power-up, the team configured a new project profile focusing exclusively on Lateral Movement detection. In the data_quality_config.yaml file, they mapped the identified log sources to T1021 sub-techniques, such as:

- SMB/Windows Admin Shares (T1021.002)
- Remote Desktop Protocol (T1021.001)
- Windows Remote Management (WinRM)
- Remote Service Creation using WMI or PsExec (also related to T1569.002)

Each log source was evaluated manually using ground truth data from red team simulations conducted over the previous quarter. For instance, Sysmon Event ID 3 was highly valued due to its reliability in detecting outbound SMB/RDP connections, particularly when paired with parent-child process correlation using Event ID 1. However, due to an overly aggressive network log rotation policy, the retention of these logs was limited to just 3 days, which negatively impacted forensic readiness. Zeek logs, on the other hand, offered excellent coverage and retention but lacked field-level structure consistency when handling encrypted protocol metadata. The rating process followed OSSEM Power-up's expected structure from the configuration file is presented in Table 7.1.

With these scores defined, the team executed the OSSEM Power-up script. The tool ingested the configuration, mapped the relevant ATT&CK techniques, and produced a detailed output in YAML and Excel formats. These outputs were then loaded into Elasticsearch, allowing Kibana to visualize the data using bar graphs and a dynamically generated ATT&CK Navigator matrix. In this matrix, each technique related to lateral movement was color-coded based on the overall quality score. Techniques with full coverage and good log retention appeared green, while techniques dependent on less consistent logging sources appeared amber or red.

An important insight emerged when T1021.003 (Windows Remote Management) showed a particularly low consistency score. Upon investigation, it was revealed that while PowerShell script block logging was enabled on paper, some endpoint baselines had registry policies that disabled it silently. This created a false sense of visibility in detection rules. Using the matrix as a presentation tool, the SOC was able to brief system administrators with visual proof of data blind spots and secure buy-in to enforce centralized logging policies across campus machines.

The OSSEM Power-up framework also highlighted discrepancies between endpoints. The university's research department was running isolated, high-performance Windows 11 systems with advanced security configurations that broke logging compatibility with the main SIEM pipeline. As a result, Sysmon data from these machines never reached the SIEM, despite the assumption that these logs were flowing in. The inconsistency score for those data sources dropped, leading to an internal audit and eventual onboarding of these machines

Table 7.1 **OSSEM rating**

Sysmon_NetworkConnect:	WinEventLog_4624:	Zeek_ConnLogs:
Coverage: 5	Coverage: 4	Coverage: 5
Timeliness: 5	Timeliness: 5	Timeliness: 5
Retention: 2	Retention: 3	Retention: 4
Structure:	Structure:	Structure:
Default: 4	Default: 3	Default: 3
Consistency: 4	Consistency: 5	Consistency: 3

into the updated data pipeline. Beyond evaluating current detection coverage, the team used OSSEM Power-up's structure scoring profiles to support their machine learning efforts. They launched a project to analyze anomalous lateral movement behavior using a custom unsupervised model that relied on consistent field names and timestamp synchronization. Logs that scored low in the "structure" dimension were marked as unfit for ML pipelines, while high-scoring logs (e.g., Zeek's DNS and conn.log) were prioritized for model training. This capability, built directly into OSSEM Power-up's profiling features, saved hours of manual field inspection and data wrangling.

As a concluding effort, the SOC automated the export of OSSEM Power-up's output on a biweekly basis, allowing them to track trends over time. In one month, the average structure score for Sysmon logs increased by 1.2 points after tuning the endpoint configuration scripts to include missing fields. The ATT&CK Navigator visualization became a standing item in executive security reports, helping leadership understand the practical limitations of detection capability without relying solely on alert counts.

This use case proved that OSSEM Power-up is not just a static analysis tool, it serves as a strategic bridge between detection engineering, threat hunting, IT operations, and executive reporting. For large, distributed environments like universities, where device diversity and administrative autonomy can cause gaps in visibility, this framework introduced a disciplined way to measure, communicate, and enhance detection posture against advanced adversary behaviors like lateral movement. With its structured configuration, visual output, and integration into common SIEM workflows, OSSEM Power-up elevated the organization's threat detection maturity from reactive to data-driven and proactive.

7.5.2 DeTT&CT

Developed by the Cyber Defence Centre at Rabobank, the DeTT&CT framework is an impressive Python-based utility that plays a vital role in assessing the effectiveness of your organization's logging infrastructure. This tool is specifically designed to assist blue teams in rating the quality of their log sources and determining the extent of their visibility across various MITRE ATT&CK techniques. DeTT&CT helps teams visualize their detection landscape by mapping their existing detection capabilities against known adversary behaviors. Such mapping not only exposes visibility gaps but also guides improvements in monitoring and threat detection processes.

However, the process requires manual input, teams must first build an inventory of all available log sources and assign each a score ranging from -1 to 5. These values are determined using the predefined scoring criteria outlined in DeTT&CT's official reference tables (available in Excel format). Once the log sources are scored, the data can be used to construct a visibility matrix using the ATT&CK Navigator. This matrix makes it easy to pinpoint weaknesses in your monitoring setup. One of DeTT&CT's standout features is its ability to generate heatmaps, both general visibility maps and those tailored to specific adversary profiles enabling targeted threat detection enhancements. The tool includes a browser-based editor, accessible via a local web portal.

7.5.2.1 Example 1: Enhancing detection coverage in a financial institution's blue team operations

In a mid-sized financial institution with a growing digital footprint and heightened exposure to sophisticated threat actors, the Security Operations Center (SOC) team decided to evaluate the effectiveness of their current detection strategy. While they had deployed several tools and data collectors – ranging from endpoint detection agents to firewall and proxy logs – they lacked clarity on how well these sources mapped to known attack techniques, particularly those outlined in the MITRE ATT&CK framework. The team needed a way to align their log inventory with adversarial behaviors and ensure that their existing telemetry offered sufficient visibility. To address this challenge, the SOC initiated the integration of **DeTT&CT**, a Python-based open-source framework developed by Rabobank's Cyber Defence Centre. The objective was to systematically score log sources, map their detection capabilities, and identify blind spots across different attack surfaces.

The process began by creating a detailed inventory of all log sources available within their environment. This included Windows Event Logs, EDR telemetry, Sysmon logs, DNS queries, proxy logs, and network flow data from perimeter devices. For each data source, the team manually rated its capability to detect specific ATT&CK techniques, using DeTT&CT's scoring scale ranging from –1 (not applicable) to 5 (fully effective). For example, Sysmon logs provided moderate visibility (score 3) into lateral movement techniques such as "Remote Services: Remote Desktop Protocol (T1021.001)," whereas EDR provided stronger coverage (score 5) for credential access attempts like "LSASS Memory Dumping (T1003.001)." These scores were compiled into a structured spreadsheet format compatible with DeTT&CT.

After feeding the scored data into the DeTT&CT web client, accessible locally at http://localhost:8080, the team generated an interactive heatmap. This visual representation mapped log source coverage across different MITRE ATT&CK tactics and techniques. One critical observation was that while the institution had strong visibility over "Execution" and "Initial Access" tactics, there were major gaps in detecting "Persistence" and "Defense Evasion" techniques. For instance, the absence of registry audit logs or autorun key monitoring resulted in low scores for techniques like "Registry Run Keys / Startup Folder (T1547.001)." These findings were vital in helping the team prioritize where to allocate resources for log collection enhancement and rule development.

To provide leadership with actionable insights, the DeTT&CT-generated matrix was integrated into the ATT&CK Navigator, allowing stakeholders to filter by threat actor profiles. By selecting APT32, a financially motivated threat group known for targeting the financial sector, the SOC team could visualize which techniques used by this adversary were already covered and which were not. Techniques such as "Command and Scripting Interpreter: PowerShell (T1059.001)" showed high visibility, while others like "Hidden Files and Directories (T1564.001)" were virtually invisible in the current setup. This allowed the team to frame budget proposals and detection engineering roadmaps with objective data and clear justification.

DeTT&CT empowered detection engineers to rethink their alerting logic. For example, although PowerShell logs were collected, DeTT&CT made it clear that detection rules based solely on script execution events were insufficient without incorporating parent-child process lineage. This triggered a new detection development effort using Sigma rules that combined process tree analysis, command-line logging, and encoded PowerShell detection. Similarly, the visibility gaps in "Impair Defenses: Disable or Modify Tools (T1562.001)" led to the deployment of honeypot services and additional monitoring on service modification events.

The most transformative aspect of adopting DeTT&CT was not just its scoring system or heatmaps, but the mindset shift it brought. It allowed the SOC to transition from a reactive alert-based approach to a proactive, visibility-driven model. Rather than waiting for alerts to fire, analysts began looking at logs through the lens of adversary behavior, asking not just "Did we get an alert?" but "Do we even have visibility over this technique?" This behavioral framing helped senior blue teamers coach junior analysts on understanding the 'why' behind telemetry importance, bridging skill gaps and improving incident triage decisions.

In the subsequent quarterly red team assessment, the red team emulated a stealthy attacker leveraging living-off-the-land binaries (LOLBins) and registry-based persistence. Thanks to the improvements guided by DeTT&CT, many of these actions were flagged by newly developed detection rules. The red team noted that visibility had drastically improved compared to the previous assessment cycle. This feedback loop validated the framework's value not only as a planning tool but also as a driver of measurable detection maturity.

7.5.2.2 Example 2: Deploying DeTT&CT for incident readiness in a critical infrastructure environment

A large energy utility company operating in a critical infrastructure sector faced increasing pressure from regulatory bodies to demonstrate its cyber resilience against APTs. With expanding OT (Operational Technology) networks and convergence with IT environments, the cyber risk landscape had grown significantly. Recent intelligence reports highlighted that state-sponsored groups were increasingly targeting energy grids using lateral movement and privilege escalation techniques specific to ICS (Industrial Control System) environments. In this context, the company's cybersecurity division recognized a need to systematically evaluate how well their logging infrastructure could support detection of such attack vectors. The team adopted the DeTT&CT framework to gain a clear and measurable understanding of their visibility gaps and threat coverage.

The deployment began with the OT-IT integration team collaborating with cybersecurity analysts to inventory all available data sources. This included logs from ICS protocol monitoring tools, historian servers, HMI systems, network flow monitors, and Active Directory controllers. Once collected, each data source was evaluated against MITRE ATT&CK techniques applicable to ICS and IT domains. DeTT&CT's scoring rubric was used to assign values between –1 and 5 to indicate the depth of coverage. For instance, the company's asset inventory system provided partial insight into "System Owner/User Discovery (T1033)" and was scored a 2, whereas their HMI logs had zero visibility into "Screen Capture (T1113)" and were scored -1.

With these scores compiled into DeTT&CT's accepted format, the results were fed into the framework's web interface. Within minutes, a comprehensive heatmap was generated. The team could visually identify entire clusters of techniques with little to no visibility – especially under tactics such as "Lateral Movement," "Collection," and "Impact." For instance, techniques like "Remote Services: SMB/Windows Admin Shares (T1021.002)" and "Data Staged (T1074)" were almost completely unmonitored. This insight was a revelation, especially because prior incident readiness reports had indicated a high level of confidence in their coverage – a false sense of security.

One of the key outcomes of this DeTT&CT deployment was the realization that their perimeter-focused detection philosophy had left the internal network blind to lateral movements and privilege escalation activities. As a result, the cybersecurity team initiated several strategic changes. First, Sysmon was deployed across IT workstations and integrated with OT engineering workstations through secure data diodes. This allowed deeper visibility into process creation events and parent-child relationships essential for detecting techniques like "Abuse Elevation Control Mechanism: Bypass User Account Control (T1548.002)." Simultaneously, they enhanced logging from network segmentation appliances to capture unauthorized cross-zone communication attempts.

Using DeTT&CT's ATT&CK Navigator compatibility, the team simulated potential attack chains from known threat groups like Xenotime and Sandworm. By overlaying the group-specific techniques on their heatmap, they could trace which steps in an attack path would go undetected. These simulations directly influenced their threat hunting queries and alerting rules. For example, they developed correlation rules to flag unusual use of PsExec and modified Windows Defender exclusions – two known techniques used in OT attacks.

DeTT&CT heatmap also helped demonstrate compliance progress to external auditors. Regulators appreciated the transparency and methodical approach to logging strategy. The heatmap was included in board-level presentations, where senior leadership could see a red-to-green transformation over time, quantifying the effectiveness of their cybersecurity investments. This was instrumental in securing funding for more advanced visibility tools, including deception technologies and cross-domain SIEM enrichment. The incident response team further used DeTT&CT's visibility matrices during tabletop exercises. For example, during a ransomware simulation targeting OT assets, the team relied on the visibility map to decide which logs to query and which behaviors were expected to be visible. This led to faster response times, more informed decisions, and a structured post-incident analysis that fed back into detection engineering.

DeTT&CT not only enhanced the utility's security posture but also embedded a culture of evidence-based visibility assessment across departments. It turned log coverage into a measurable asset rather than an assumed capability. The regular update of log scoring every quarter ensured that as new systems were introduced or legacy systems retired, the visibility picture stayed current. In a domain where downtime can have national repercussions, this systematic approach to detection maturity made all the difference.

7.5.3 Sysmon-Modular

Sysmon-Modular, created by Olaf Hartong, offers a flexible way to build and manage Sysmon configurations. Designed with adaptability in mind, this tool is especially useful for consultants who manage security setups across multiple clients. Rather than dealing with a single, complex configuration file, Sysmon-Modular allows users to break it down into smaller, easier-to-maintain components. One of its standout features is the ability to align each configuration module with the MITRE ATT&CK framework. This mapping allows users to clearly understand which specific adversarial techniques are being monitored or detected. Additionally, it supports the creation of custom ATT&CK Navigator layers, offering a visual representation of coverage based on the selected Sysmon configuration rules.

7.5.3.1 Example 1: Enterprise threat detection in a financial organization using Sysmon-Modular

In today's threat landscape, financial institutions remain among the top targets for cybercriminals due to the high value of financial data, customer records, and transactional access. In this case study, we explore how a cybersecurity consultant used Sysmon-Modular to transform endpoint detection and visibility in a large financial enterprise with five branch offices and over 700 Windows-based endpoints. The deployment aimed to detect credential theft, lateral movement, unauthorized PowerShell execution, and persistence techniques without overloading the SIEM pipeline. The solution delivered measurable improvements in detection capability, log clarity, and incident response efficiency, all while aligning with the MITRE ATT&CK framework.

The organization in question was a medium-sized national financial institution with critical infrastructure spread across multiple locations. It maintained centralized services in its head office, including domain controllers, file servers, an Exchange mail server, and core banking systems. Most employees worked on Windows 10 systems, while IT and security staff operated Windows Server 2016 and 2019 platforms. Logging existed through a basic Windows Event Forwarding (WEF) system and Microsoft Defender ATP; however, the security team lacked visibility into advanced attacker behaviors, such as credential access or process injection.

While existing antivirus systems could detect known malware signatures, the real challenge was detecting attacker TTPs (Tactics, Techniques, and Procedures) before they triggered antivirus or reached domain controller access. The organization contracted a cybersecurity consultant to review their current endpoint logging and deploy a more advanced, yet scalable and maintainable detection strategy. That's where Sysmon-Modular came in. Sysmon, or System Monitor, by Microsoft Sysinternals, provides detailed logs about process creation, network connections, file modifications, and more. However, writing a single monolithic Sysmon configuration file can quickly become a maintenance burden, especially when changes are needed frequently to respond to new threat intelligence. This is where Sysmon-Modular, developed by Olaf Hartong, shines.

Sysmon-Modular enables configuration in a modular way, breaking rules into smaller, categorized sections (modules) such as process_create, dns_query, powershell, and image_load. Each module contains rules tailored to a specific logging goal, such as detecting remote execution or tracking PowerShell usage. Even more powerfully, each rule is mapped to MITRE ATT&CK techniques, allowing organizations to see exactly which adversary behaviors are being monitored. This alignment with MITRE ATT&CK provided a clear value proposition to management and security leadership. By building a modular Sysmon configuration aligned to attacker techniques, the consultant could offer a well-documented, scalable, and threat-driven logging policy.

The consultant began by auditing the existing Windows Event Log structure and identifying noise-heavy logs versus high-fidelity ones. Sysmon v13.34 was chosen as the baseline version. A centralized Sysmon deployment strategy was proposed using GPO (Group Policy Object), which would install Sysmon with the modular configuration via script. The consultant used Sysmon-Modular's PowerShell build script, which dynamically generates the sysmon.xml from individual rule files found in the GitHub repo. Each module was reviewed and tuned for relevance based on the environment. For example, since the organization didn't use Sysinternals PsExec regularly, that detection module was kept active, but modules involving software installers were trimmed to reduce false positives. Modules were categorized under:

- Execution Monitoring (T1059): process_create, powershell, and script_block
- Credential Access (T1003): image_load with filters for lsass.exe and known dumping tools
- Lateral Movement (T1021, T1071): network_connect, named_pipe, and remote_thread
- Persistence (T1547): registry_event, file_create, and driver_load

In the image_load module, rules were included to alert if DLLs were injected into lsass.exe, winlogon.exe, or explorer.exe, which commonly indicates credential dumping or session hijacking. Additionally, the powershell module logged base64-encoded commands or encoded execution flags (-enc, -nop), which are red flags for obfuscated malware or reverse shells. Logs generated by Sysmon were forwarded via Winlogbeat to the organization's Elastic SIEM (part of the ELK stack). The consultant customized dashboards to tag incoming logs by their module origin. For example, process creations from the lateral_movement module would be grouped under the ATT&CK category T1021. This visual alignment helped analysts quickly trace suspicious activity back to ATT&CK tactics and sub-techniques.

To demonstrate coverage, the consultant generated an ATT&CK Navigator layer file using Sysmon-Modular's built-in mappings. The layer showed 24 sub-techniques being covered across 8 primary ATT&CK tactics. This helped justify future funding for additional detection initiatives and earned positive response from leadership.

7.5.3.1.1 Use Case 1: Detecting credential dumping

Two weeks post-deployment, an alert fired from the image_load module, showing a suspicious DLL injected into lsass.exe – a hallmark of credential dumping. The event log, enriched with metadata such as ImageLoaded, Hash, and ParentImage, showed that a renamed mimikatz.exe (named winhelper64.exe) was executed from a temp directory. Sysmon's logging showed the process lineage from a user profile directory, confirming privilege escalation. The logs were instrumental in reconstructing the timeline: the attacker gained access via phishing, executed the binary with local admin rights, and attempted to dump credentials. Defender had not yet flagged it, but Sysmon did. This event was contained quickly, thanks to the high-fidelity logs generated by the image_load and process_create modules. A deeper audit later revealed the phishing origin, and compensatory controls were added.

7.5.3.1.2 Use Case 2: Monitoring unauthorized powershell execution

In another instance, an intern mistakenly ran a PowerShell command that attempted to download a file from an external domain using Invoke-WebRequest. While not malicious, this raised compliance concerns. The powershell and script_block logging modules captured the encoded command line, decoded it, and logged the entire script execution in clear text. Since this activity was mapped to T1059.001, an alert was automatically raised. This example highlighted the tool's value beyond just catching malicious behavior, it also supported policy enforcement and user behavior monitoring.

After initial deployment, the modular configuration proved easy to maintain. When new threats emerged, such as Raspberry Robin USB infections the consultant added a new module for removable_media and autorun.inf detection, without touching the existing core config. This made the policy adaptable without regression errors. Monthly updates were scheduled to pull the latest from the GitHub repo and manually review rule changes. Testing was done in a sandbox environment before pushing updates via GPO. Additionally, to minimize log overload, certain benign paths (like C:\Program Files\Adobe) were whitelisted in the file_create and process_create modules, reducing noise in the SIEM by over 35%. The deployment of Sysmon-Modular brought several key lessons to light:

- Modularity Enhances Scalability: Breaking down the configuration into categorized rule sets meant easier updates, better documentation, and reduced error rates.
- ATT&CK Alignment Drives Visibility: Mapping rules to ATT&CK gave the security team confidence in what they were detecting and what needed improvement.
- False Positives Must Be Tuned: Even good rules can generate noise; tuning and whitelist management are essential to keep SIEM signals valuable.
- Logs are Gold During Incident Response: The rich telemetry captured by Sysmon was pivotal in quickly identifying and isolating malicious activity that would have otherwise gone unnoticed.

Sysmon-Modular empowered the financial organization with a mature, scalable endpoint detection configuration aligned to adversary behavior. Through thoughtful module selection, ATT&CK integration, and SIEM visualization, the solution enabled fast response to credential theft attempts, PowerShell abuse, and suspicious file modifications. The modular architecture proved future-proof, with easy customization, regular updates, and minimal overhead. For security teams and consultants aiming to enhance Windows endpoint visibility without drowning in log volume, this case study demonstrates that Sysmon-Modular is not just a tool; it's an operational enabler.

7.6 UNDERSTANDING THREAT DATA AND RESULTS

Throughout the units and exercises covered so far, a common limitation exists: all activities were conducted within a controlled lab setting. This introduces a form of bias, as the dynamics of a lab differ greatly from those in a real-world production environment. For example, the scale of systems in a lab is typically much smaller, fewer endpoints, users, and less unpredictable activity or "background noise" caused by everyday interactions with the system. When we transition from testing in a lab to deploying detections in a live environment, the shift in scale and complexity often requires us to fine-tune our detection logic. The objective in threat hunting isn't just to sift through false positives (though they do occur), but to surface the threats that evade detection altogether, our goal is to uncover false negatives. This means focusing on malicious activity that our current security measures may have overlooked.

Before we rely on any detection rule, it's essential to test it against actual production data. When we do so, three possible outcomes may arise:

- Zero Matches: If no results appear, it suggests that the behavior observed in the lab isn't occurring in the live system. This might indicate that our detection logic is specific and reliable.
- Limited Matches: A small number of results means we must examine each instance carefully to rule out false positives and ensure that no genuine threat has been missed.
- Excessive Matches: If we get an overwhelming number of results, our query may be too broad and will need refinement to accurately pinpoint malicious activity without being flooded by irrelevant data.

This leads us to an important question – what steps should we take when our detection method generates too many results? To address this, we need to consider how different types of data influence our ability to provide meaningful context. Data varies significantly in form depending on how it's collected, who or what generates it, and the systems used to store it. Understanding these characteristics is key to enriching our detection strategies and enhancing their precision in real-world applications. Two primary levers to classify data are structured and unstructured data.

Structured data has the following features:

- Is clearly defined
- Is easily searchable
- Is easy to analyze
- Is clearly formatted in text and numbers
- Is usually quantitative
- Resides in fixed field within a file or record
- Is related to a data model
- Requires less storage space

Unstructured data has the following features:

- Is raw, unformatted data
- Is not easy to process
- Is usually qualitative
- Is not related to a data model
- Requires more storage space
- Can convert image to audio, video, email, and so on

In most cases, unstructured data significantly exceeds structured data in volume. While structured data is typically organized within relational databases like SQL, unstructured data is commonly managed through non-relational databases such as MongoDB. Since unstructured data lacks a predefined schema, it requires advanced analytical methods to extract meaningful insights. There is also a hybrid form known as semi-structured data, sometimes referred to as self-describing data. This type blends characteristics of both structured and unstructured formats. Although it doesn't adhere to the rigid structure of relational models, it employs tags or metadata to make the data searchable and classifiable. Common formats in this category include JSON, XML, and CSV files, and they account for a substantial share of data produced across systems today. Each data type like structured, unstructured, and semi-structured, calls for specific analytical approaches. The analysis can also be classified based on whether the data is quantitative (numerical) or qualitative (descriptive).

For quantitative data, three main analytical strategies are employed:

- Classification involves determining the likelihood that a particular data point belongs to a predefined category.
- Clustering groups similar data points based on shared characteristics or patterns.
- Regression focuses on identifying the relationship or dependency among variables to make predictions.

For qualitative data, which usually consists of textual or categorical information, two key analysis techniques are often used:

- Narrative analysis, which interprets stories or information derived from various sources such as interviews, articles, or transcripts.
- Content analysis, which involves organizing and interpreting data based on themes or patterns within the content itself.

To sum up, qualitative analysis often guides the development or refinement of hypotheses, while quantitative analysis supports measuring and validating them. Qualitative data usually consists of text or labels, whereas quantitative data is numerical – either as whole numbers (discrete) or decimals (continuous).

7.7 DETERMINE SUCCESS OF THREAT HUNTING PROGRAM

To effectively measure the impact and success of a threat hunting initiative, the team must first develop a robust data model accompanied by a well-defined process for ensuring the integrity and reliability of the data.

- The team should base all hunting activities on threat intelligence that is specifically aligned with the organization's risk profile and threat landscape.
- Part of the hunt should include identifying areas where there is insufficient visibility or where telemetry is lacking.
- Any detections that arise during the hunt must be automated efficiently to support timely responses and reduce manual overhead.
- Additionally, each hunting activity, regardless of whether it results in a detection should be thoroughly documented for future analysis and reference.

Beyond these foundational practices, the effectiveness of the threat hunting program can also be gauged by tracking how the team's capabilities evolve over time, reflecting their growth in expertise, methodology, and operational maturity. One of the most effective ways to evaluate the impact and efficiency of a threat hunting initiative is by actively seeking input from others involved in or affected by the process. Engaging team members in reflective discussions can uncover practical insights like what aspects are functioning well, where bottlenecks exist, and what adjustments might enhance the program. It's also valuable to approach cross-functional teams and ask whether inter-team coordination feels smooth and whether there's potential for deeper collaboration. Input from senior leadership is equally important, as their perspective often captures strategic alignment and broader organizational impact. To guide these conversations, consider using thoughtful and open-ended questions such as:

- What improvements would you recommend for this initiative?
- Are there any flaws you perceive in the current structure or methodology?
- Have you encountered any inefficiencies while interacting with our workflow?
- Are we adequately fulfilling the objectives we set out to achieve?
- If you were leading this, what approach might you consider?
- How would you evaluate the cooperation between our team and others?
- What transformations should we aim for over the next few months?
- Are we effectively highlighting our contributions to the organization's security posture?
- What are your ideas for enhancing our threat detection and response methods?
- Could we present our results in a clearer or more impactful way?
- What do you feel we're doing particularly well? What could use refinement?
- Is there anything unclear or incomplete about our reported outcomes?
- What's one practical change we could adopt to boost our overall effectiveness?

By fostering these feedback loops, you not only strengthen the threat hunting operation but also promote a culture of continuous improvement and shared accountability.

7.8 CONCLUSION

This chapter underscores the transformative power of analytics-driven threat intelligence in shaping modern cybersecurity strategies. By emphasizing data quality, structured telemetry, and the practical use of tools such as OSSEM Power-up, DeTT&CT, and Sysmon-Modular, the chapter illustrates how organizations can enhance their threat detection capabilities and align closely with adversary techniques defined by frameworks like MITRE ATT&CK. It advocates for a data-centric approach that blends contextual intelligence with operational insights, enabling more precise detection, faster incident response, and better-informed decision-making. The importance of structured and unstructured data, and how they influence detection efficacy, is thoroughly examined, providing practical strategies for analysis and enrichment. Through real-world examples, the chapter demonstrates how high-fidelity telemetry, when properly collected and evaluated, not only closes visibility gaps but also boosts an organization's readiness against advanced threats. Lastly, the chapter emphasizes the need for continuous validation, feedback loops, and performance measurement as critical elements of a mature threat hunting program. These efforts empower security teams to shift from reactive defense to proactive threat anticipation, fostering a resilient cybersecurity posture capable of adapting to evolving threats in real time. Overall, the chapter provides a pragmatic blueprint for operationalizing threat intelligence to achieve measurable security outcomes.

MULTIPLE CHOICE QUESTIONS

1. A global MSSP deploys OSSEM Power-up across multiple clients to score data quality. During review, a major client shows excellent coverage for Sysmon but very low scores for structure and consistency. Analysts discover that several endpoints use different field names for process_path and command_line due to outdated custom parsers. OSSEM marks these inconsistencies in the ATT&CK Navigator output, resulting in amber and red patches. Leadership wants to know which data quality attribute is most responsible for detection gaps.

   A. Timeliness
   B. Structure
   C. Coverage
   D. Retention

   Correct Answer: B – Structure
   Why correct: The chapter explains that structure problems arise when field names or
       data formats are inconsistent, causing detection rules to fail. Why others are wrong:
   • A: Timeliness relates to ingest latency.
   • C: Coverage was already high.
   • D: Retention deals with log duration, not field uniformity.

2. A financial organization deploys Sysmon-Modular across all endpoints. After deployment, analysts notice that credential dumping behavior on some systems is not detected, even though all modules are enabled. On inspection, they find missing Sysmon Event ID 10 entries due to MSI script failure on 18% of machines. OSSEM Power-up scoring reveals coverage = 5 for most systems but = 0 for misconfigured hosts. What explains the false negatives?

   A. Inconsistent data source completeness
   B. SIEM ingestion error
   C. Incorrect MITRE ATT&CK mapping
   D. Outdated threat intelligence feed

   Correct Answer: A – Inconsistent data source completeness
   Why correct: The chapter emphasizes coverage gaps when some endpoints do not
       produce
   required events (e.g., Sysmon Event ID 10 → LSASS access). Why others are wrong:
   • B: Logs are missing before SIEM.
   • C: ATT&CK mapping doesn't affect raw detection.
   • D: Threat feed age doesn't block Sysmon logs.

3. A university SOC uses DeTT&CT to evaluate lateral movement visibility across thousands of endpoints. The generated heatmap reveals that T1021.003 (WinRM) has a visibility score of -1 across all servers. The team knows WinRM logs *should* be available but finds that PowerShell script block logging is disabled through a mis-applied GPO. What best describes this scenario?

   A. Lack of structured data
   B. Lack of logging completeness
   C. Broken ATT&CK technique mapping
   D. Retention failure

Correct Answer: B – Lack of logging completeness
Why correct: DeTT&CT scoring shows techniques not covered when a log source is
  missing entirely. Why others are wrong:
- A: Structure refers to field formats, not missing logs.
- C: Mapping is irrelevant when logs don't exist.
- D: Retention concerns old logs, not absence.

4. A threat hunter develops a query for detecting abnormal PowerShell use on production systems. When run, the query returns more than 20,000 events daily, making triage impossible. Reviewing telemetry, analysts realize most events come from verbose script block logging on developer machines. According to the chapter, what is the first tuning step?

   A. Disable PowerShell logging
   B. Narrow the query using context-enriched fields
   C. Switch to unstructured log parsing
   D. Only ingest PowerShell logs weekly

   Correct Answer: B – Narrow the query using context-enriched fields
   Why correct: Chapter emphasizes refining broad detections using contextual and struc-
     tured data (e.g., parent process, encoded command flag). Why others are wrong:
   - A: Disabling logs removes visibility.
   - C: Unstructured data increases noise.
   - D: Weekly ingestion kills real-time detection.

5. A SOC receives a threat-Intel alert showing hundreds of corporate credentials in infoste-aler logs leaked on Telegram. Internal SIEM logs show no alerts for credential dumping. OSSEM Power-up scoring shows low retention and timeliness for browser credential logs. What core issue enabled the compromise?

   A. Poor uniqueness
   B. Poor retention and freshness of telemetry
   C. Poor structure of log fields
   D. Poor consistency across log sources

   Correct Answer: B – Poor retention and timeliness of telemetry
   Why correct: Chapter highlights that stale or poorly retained credential logs result in
     blind spots
   exploited by infostealers. Why others are wrong:
   - A: Uniqueness refers to duplicates.
   - C: Structure issues cause parsing problems but not absence.
   - D: Consistency affects uniformity, not missing telemetry.

6. During an ongoing ransomware incident, analysts collect massive amounts of unstruc-tured data – PDF reports, email screenshots, OSINT forum dumps, JSON blobs, and chat transcripts. They struggle to correlate patterns. The team realizes they need a method to extract themes and meaning quickly. What technique does the chapter recommend?

   A. Regression analysis
   B. Content analysis
   C. Clustering
   D. Quantitative correlation

Correct Answer: B – Content analysis
Why correct: The chapter states content analysis is ideal for interpreting qualitative or unstructured data (emails, transcripts, screenshots). Why others are wrong:
- A: Regression applies to numerical data.
- C: Clustering is for quantitative behavior grouping.
- D: Quantitative correlation requires structured numeric data.

7. A consultant deploys Sysmon-Modular on a large enterprise network. After rollout, the SIEM becomes overloaded with benign file creation logs. Investigation shows that the file_create module logs everything, including activity from software update agents. What solution aligns with the chapter?

   A. Remove the file_create module entirely
   B. Tune Sysmon-Modular by adding path exclusions
   C. Reduce log retention to save storage
   D. Turn off network connection logging

Correct Answer: B – Add path exclusions
Why correct: Chapter emphasizes tuning Sysmon-Modular with whitelists to reduce noise without losing visibility. Why others are wrong:
- A: Removes important detection ability.
- C: Retention reduction solves storage, not noise.
- D: Removes lateral movement visibility.

8. A SOC heatmap exported from DeTT&CT shows strong visibility across T1059, T1003, and T1547, but retention scores are often 1 or 2. Analysts note logs are overwritten after only 48 hours. What risk does this create?

   A. Increased false positives
   B. Inability to conduct historical analysis or delayed hunts
   C. Decrease in structured data
   D. Loss of enriched threat intelligence

Correct Answer: B – Inability to perform long-term detection or forensics
Why correct: Retention limits historical visibility, harming threat hunting and incident response. Why others are wrong:
- A: Retention does not increase FP.
- C: Structure unaffected.
- D: Enrichment is independent of retention.

9. A senior analyst reviews an ATT&CK Navigator layer generated from OSSEM Power-up. They assume green cells mean detection rules are functioning correctly. However, a junior points out that green indicates high-quality data, not detection logic accuracy. Which statement reflects the chapter's guidance?

   A. Data quality scores directly prove rule accuracy
   B. Data quality is separate from detection accuracy and must be validated in production
   C. OSSEM Power-up automatically tests detections
   D. ATT&CK Navigator layers always reflect true detection capability

Correct Answer: B

Why correct: Chapter explains the difference between high-quality telemetry vs. validated

detection logic; real-world testing is essential. Why others are wrong:

- A & C: OSSEM does not validate rules.
- D: Navigator is only visualization.

10. A company places Canary Tokens inside sensitive shared folders. A triggered token reveals that an internal workstation accessed a decoy Excel file at 3 AM. Sysmon logs show correlated network connections to external IPs. The team wants to enrich both external TI and internal telemetry to understand the breach scope. Which process is recommended?

  A. Pure IOC matching
  B. Contextual data enrichment
  C. Unstructured regression
  D. Disable Sysmon to reduce noise

Correct Answer: B – Contextual data enrichment

Why correct: Chapter emphasizes combining TI + telemetry for deeper incident interpretation. Why others are wrong:

- A: IOC matching lacks context.
- C: Regression is quantitative only.
- D: Disabling Sysmon reduces visibility.

11. A SOC improves logging quality using Sysmon-Modular. However, SIEM costs suddenly spike because verbose network connection logs are pouring in from thousands of endpoints. The SOC needs to maintain detection value while controlling log volume. What reflects the chapter's recommended strategy?

  A. Disable Sysmon network modules entirely
  B. Tune Sysmon-Modular to balance granularity and cost
  C. Shorten retention to 24 hours
  D. Replace Sysmon with OSINT feeds

Correct Answer: B – Tune Sysmon-Modular

Why correct: The chapter describes tuning for "balanced profile" vs "verbose profile" depending on environment. Why others are wrong:

- A: Completely losing network visibility is unacceptable.
- C: Retention solves cost but ruins detection.
- D: OSINT cannot replace endpoint telemetry.

12. A threat hunter receives JSON, XML, and CSV logs from a cloud app. Another teammate incorrectly labels them as structured logs. What classification is correct?

  A. Structured data
  B. Semi-structured data
  C. Unstructured data
  D. Narrative data

Correct Answer: B – Semi-structured
Why correct: Chapter explicitly defines JSON/XML/CSV as semi-structured with
metadata tags. Why others are wrong:
- A: Structured logs require rigid schema.
- C: They clearly have structure.
- D: Narrative is qualitative storytelling text.

13. A detection team builds an ML model for anomaly detection using endpoint telemetry.
The model repeatedly fails due to inconsistent field types (string vs integer) and missing
normalization. According to the chapter, which data quality dimension is the biggest
problem?

   A. Accuracy
   B. Consistency
   C. Timeliness
   D. Uniqueness

Correct Answer: B – Consistency
Why correct: ML requires consistent formats; chapter notes consistency ensures stan-
dardized field values. Why others are wrong:
- A: Accuracy is correctness, not uniformity.
- C: Timeliness irrelevant.
- D: Uniqueness relates to duplicates.

14. During an active intrusion, analysts ingest 20+ threat feeds. Many feeds contain overlapping IOCs, different naming conventions, and conflicting severity ratings. They need
a way to standardize inputs before correlation. Which tool or concept aligns with the
chapter?

   A. OSSEM Power-up
   B. Threat Intelligence Platform (TIP)
   C. Sysmon-Modular
   D. Canary Token

Correct Answer: B – TIP
Why correct: TIPs normalize, deduplicate, and unify disparate threat intelligence for-
mats. Why others are wrong:
- A: Evaluates data quality, not TI normalization.
- C: Endpoint logging only.
- D: Deception, not data management.

15. A threat hunting manager wants to assess program maturity. Alerts generated during
hunts are automated, hunts are documented, and visibility gaps are recorded. The team
also gathers feedback from IR, SOC, IT, and leadership to refine strategy. What does
this represent?

   A. Detection engineering
   B. Continuous improvement and feedback loops
   C. IOC pivoting
   D. OSINT correlation

Correct Answer: B – Continuous improvement and feedback loops
Why correct: Chapter stresses feedback-driven maturity evaluation as a core element of successful hunting programs. Why others are wrong:
- A: Detection engineering is separate.
- C: Not related to maturity measurement.
- D: OSINT correlation is only one input.

REFERENCES

1. "What is a managed security service provider (MSSP)?," *Fortinet*, 2026. https://www.fortinet.com/resources/cyberglossary/what-is-mssp
2. Hxnoyd, "GitHub - hxnoyd/ossem-power-up: A tool to assess data quality, built on top of the awesome OSSEM," *GitHub*, 2019. Accessed Jul. 15, 2025. https://github.com/hxnoyd/ossem-power-up
3. "What is InfoStealer malware and how does it work?," *Packetlabs*, 2014. https://www.packetlabs.net/posts/what-is-infostealer-malware-and-how-does-it-work
4. Imperva, "What is APT (advanced persistent threat) | APT security | imperva," *Imperva*, 2019. https://www.imperva.com/learn/application-security/apt-advanced-persistent-threat
5. Thinkst Applied Research, "Know. Before it matters," *Canarytokens*, 2024. https://canarytokens.org/nest

Chapter 8

Conclusion

This book has traversed the essential pillars of Cyber Threat Intelligence (CTI), beginning with a foundational introduction that demystified the concept and outlined its relevance in safeguarding modern digital infrastructures. Starting with a clear understanding of CTI, the initial chapters explained how intelligence is gathered, categorized, and transformed into actionable insights. Readers were guided through layers of the internet surface, deep, and dark web, and how they serve as key information sources for intelligence collection. Through various real-world scenarios, the book demonstrated how CTI supports strategic planning, risk forecasting, and incident response across diverse sectors. The role of CTI analysts was given due attention, emphasizing not only the skills required but also the practical tools and environments they operate within. Moving into the global cyber threat landscape, the book highlighted the evolution of adversarial techniques, motives, and the expanding range of threat actors, including state-sponsored groups, cybercriminals, and insiders.

The discussion on threat actors' tactics, such as the use of Command-and-Control (C2) servers, further illustrated how persistent threats are executed and maintained. Moreover, the Threat Intelligence Lifecycle served as a backbone for many chapters, guiding readers on how raw threat data is processed, verified, and disseminated for action. By integrating theory with practical applications, the first few chapters laid a strong foundation for readers to understand CTI as both a discipline and a practice that enhances cybersecurity operations.

The middle chapters shifted focus toward actionable threat detection strategies through advanced analysis methods and real-time intelligence. Readers were introduced to the art and science of threat hunting, where techniques such as static and dynamic malware analysis are used to uncover threats that evade automated systems. Static analysis offered insight into file structures and signatures, while dynamic analysis helped in behavioral profiling by observing malware in a sandboxed environment. These approaches, when combined with high-quality telemetry and endpoint data, gave security professionals a comprehensive view of attack vectors and system vulnerabilities. Furthermore, the book emphasized the integration of CTI into operational defense models. This included a detailed discussion on clustering, attribution, and adversary tracking, tools that transform intelligence from reactive reports into proactive threat disruption. Case studies and toolsets such as VirusTotal, Cuckoo Sandbox, Sysmon-Modular, and DeTT&CT were explained not just theoretically but through their operational relevance.

The chapters pulled together the threads of data collection, enrichment, analysis, and strategic decision-making by showing how CTI is operationalized in real environments. Emphasis was placed on aligning intelligence workflows with industry standards such as the MITRE ATT&CK framework. Techniques like detection mapping using OSSEM and DeTT&CT were highlighted as practical methods for ensuring that detection rules are comprehensive and coverage gaps are minimized. The deployment of Sysmon-Modular for telemetry enrichment showcased how even basic logging tools, when properly configured, can offer profound

DOI: 10.1201/9781003730583-8

insights into attacker behavior. At the core of this operational journey was the idea that effective CTI is not just about data, but about context, correlation, and clarity.

Whether it's a SOC analyst responding to alerts or a CISO making high-level strategic decisions, the actionable nature of intelligence becomes the bridge between detection and prevention. Moreover, the book stressed that collaboration between internal teams, external partners, and global intelligence communities is vital for dismantling adversarial campaigns. The evolution of CTI is continuous, and this book underscores that intelligence should not be viewed as a static report but as a dynamic process. By blending technical precision with strategic intent, organizations can shift from reactive defenses to anticipatory security, building resilience against the sophisticated threats of tomorrow.

Chapter 1 delves into the multifaceted domain of CTI, beginning with a clear explanation of what CTI entails in modern cybersecurity practice. It introduces readers to essential terminologies and concepts that form the basis of threat intelligence frameworks. The structure of the internet is then examined through the lens of the surface web, deep web, and dark web, shedding light on how each layer contributes to the landscape of cyber threats and intelligence gathering. Moving beyond definitions, the chapter outlines practical use cases, illustrating how CTI supports areas such as vulnerability assessment, predictive defense, and strategic planning. The narrative emphasizes the significance of CTI in today's digital security infrastructure, highlighting its transition from reactive measures to proactive threat anticipation. Finally, the role of the CTI Analyst is explored, detailing their core functions, analytical skills, and the tools commonly used to transform raw data into actionable insights. This chapter is structured to bridge theoretical understanding with practical applications, offering readers a holistic view of how CTI operates as a cornerstone in identifying, analyzing, and mitigating emerging cyber risks across diverse sectors.

Chapter 2 explores the evolving landscape of cyber threats, offering readers a comprehensive understanding of current digital risks faced by individuals, organizations, and nations. It begins by examining prevailing cyber threats, such as ransomware, data breaches, phishing campaigns, and supply chain attacks, emphasizing their sophistication and widespread impact. The chapter then delves into the various threat actors behind these incidents, including state-sponsored groups, cybercriminal organizations, hacktivists, and insider threats, detailing their motives, capabilities, and tactics. To support foundational knowledge, it defines and explains critical cybersecurity terms, ensuring clarity for readers new to the field. A focused section on Command and Control (C2) servers illustrates how attackers maintain remote access to compromised systems, often evading detection for extended periods. The chapter also outlines the Threat Intelligence Lifecycle, highlighting the structured process of collecting, analyzing, and disseminating actionable threat data to enhance cyber defense mechanisms. To bridge theory with practice, a case study analyzing a real-world cyberattack is presented, dissecting each phase of the attack and the corresponding defensive measures. Through this structured agenda, the chapter provides both a strategic and technical lens on CTI, equipping readers with the tools to understand, detect, and respond to modern cyber adversaries.

Chapter 3 introduces the foundational elements of proactive threat detection in cybersecurity. It begins by outlining the core concept of the threat hunting process aimed at uncovering stealthy threats that evade conventional security systems. Unlike automated detection tools, threat hunting leverages human intuition, contextual understanding, and iterative investigation to uncover hidden indicators of compromise (IOCs). A critical phase in the process involves hunting for samples, where potentially malicious files or executables are collected from various sources such as honeypots, network sensors, endpoint logs, and sandbox environments. Once collected, these samples undergo static feature extraction, a method that analyzes code structure, metadata, and file signatures without execution. This phase helps identify suspicious traits, such as obfuscated strings, rare imports, or malicious API calls. The chapter further delves into dynamic behavior extraction, which involves executing the sample in a controlled environment to observe real-time actions such as process creation, registry changes, and network connections. This behavioral analysis is key to detecting zero-day threats and understanding attacker tactics, techniques, and procedures (TTPs). Together, these methods create a holistic threat profile, equipping analysts with deeper insights to strengthen security posture.

Chapter 4 delves into the advanced components of proactive cyber defense, focusing on the strategic use of threat intelligence to uncover and disrupt adversary activity. It begins with a comprehensive overview of CTI sources and feeds, emphasizing the importance of integrating open-source, commercial, and internal telemetry to enhance situational awareness. The chapter then explores clustering and correlation techniques, enabling analysts to group similar attack patterns and identify links across disparate incidents, ultimately improving detection accuracy and reducing response time. The concept of attribution is analyzed next, detailing methods for uncovering the identity or origin of an attack through behavioral signatures, infrastructure analysis, and threat actor profiling. Further, the chapter discusses tracking adversaries across infrastructure and time, leveraging persistent indicators and behavioral analytics to follow threat actor movements and tactics. Finally, takedown strategies are examined, where collaboration with law enforcement, hosting providers, and industry coalitions can dismantle malicious infrastructures and disrupt ongoing campaigns. This chapter combines theory with operational insights, offering practical guidance for defenders to move beyond detection and into active threat disruption, forming a vital part of modern cyber defense architecture.

Chapter 5 presents a comprehensive introduction to the practical aspects of malware analysis, focusing on both traditional and modern approaches used by cybersecurity professionals. It begins by establishing foundational knowledge about malware types, behavior patterns, and the significance of malware analysis in identifying, understanding, and mitigating threats. The discussion then progresses into setting up isolated and secure environments using virtual machines (VMs), a critical step for safely analyzing malicious software without compromising host systems. Various open-source and commercial tools used in static and dynamic analysis are introduced, enabling readers to dissect malware samples, monitor behavioral changes, and extract IOCs. Furthermore, the chapter explores the growing trend of utilizing cloud-based malware analysis portals such as VirusTotal, Any. Run, and Hybrid Analysis, which offer scalable, collaborative, and intelligence-driven platforms for rapid threat assessment. Through this hybrid approach – combining local VM analysis with cloud intelligence – readers gain hands-on insight into how modern malware is investigated in real-world scenarios. The chapter emphasizes a methodical workflow that balances safety, accuracy, and speed in analysis, equipping learners with the essential skills to engage in malware research, threat hunting, and incident response. This foundational knowledge lays the groundwork for more advanced reverse engineering and threat intelligence gathering.

Chapter 6 delves into the foundational frameworks that guide modern CTI operations, offering a structured approach to understanding, analyzing, and mitigating cyber threats. It begins by exploring the core principles of CTI frameworks, highlighting their role in transforming raw threat data into actionable insights. Special attention is given to the MITRE ATT&CK Framework and its CTI-specific utilities, including the ATT&CK Navigator, which enables visual mapping of adversary behaviors for targeted defense strategies. The chapter also introduces the Cyber Kill Chain (CKC), a model developed to understand the stages of a cyberattack, aiding defenders in identifying and disrupting attacks at each phase. In addition, the Diamond Model of Intrusion Analysis is discussed as a methodology for correlating adversary infrastructure, capabilities, victims, and motivations. Collectively, these models serve as critical tools for threat attribution, pattern recognition, and decision-making. Through an integrated understanding of these frameworks, readers will gain the ability to contextualize threats more accurately, prioritize responses effectively, and align intelligence efforts with organizational risk. This chapter not only presents theoretical foundations but also emphasizes practical application, making it essential for analysts, security architects, and decision-makers aiming to enhance their CTI maturity and resilience against evolving threats.

Chapter 7 explores the practical implementation of modern threat intelligence and cyber threat hunting methodologies, with a focus on enhancing detection capabilities through high-quality data and specialized tools. It begins by emphasizing the importance of assessing data quality, as reliable and well-structured data forms the foundation of effective threat analysis. The chapter delves into the role of threat intelligence analytics in identifying, correlating, and prioritizing security threats. Techniques such as OSSEM (Open-Source Security Event Metadata) and tools like DeTT&CT are examined for their contributions to structuring threat data, mapping detection coverage, and aligning with the MITRE ATT&CK framework. Sysmon-Modular is also introduced as a customizable configuration that enriches telemetry collection for Windows environments, enabling detailed process and behavior tracking. The chapter further explores how cyber threat hunting leverages these tools and frameworks to proactively identify adversary behaviors that evade traditional detection. It concludes with insights into interpreting threat data and transforming raw information into actionable intelligence. Through this integrated approach, combining data validation, tool optimization, and analytical reasoning, this chapter offers a blueprint for building robust and responsive threat detection systems that empower security teams to detect, analyze, and respond to threats with greater precision and confidence.

Based on these book chapters, here are multiple-choice questions (MCQs) to test your understanding.

8.1 CHAPTER 1

1. A senior threat analyst is examining malware that was delivered via an Excel file attached to an email. Upon opening, the malware installed a service that restarts upon system reboot and established a hidden communication channel with a remote server using DNS tunneling. Days later, unusual outbound traffic was observed from the system during off-hours. Which stage of the malware lifecycle was most likely actively ongoing when the outbound traffic was detected?

   A. Initial Access
   B. Execution
   C. Command-and-Control
   D. Persistence

   Correct Answer: C. Command-and-Control
   Explanation: The outbound traffic during off-hours suggests the malware was actively communicating with the attacker's infrastructure – this aligns with the *Command-and-Control (C2)* stage, where instructions and data exfiltration occur.

2. You are correlating login failure events from geographically improbable locations across multiple employee accounts. These logs were initially raw data from multiple firewalls. You visualized login anomalies using a SIEM dashboard and identified patterns suggesting credential stuffing attempts. Which stage of the DIKW framework have you achieved once you've identified this pattern and its significance?

   A. Data
   B. Information
   C. Knowledge
   D. Wisdom

   Correct Answer: C. Knowledge
   Explanation: Recognizing attack patterns and interpreting their context (e.g., credential stuffing) represents *knowledge*. You've moved beyond organizing data (*information*) to applying analytical insights.

3. Your organization recently faced multiple suspicious registry edits and software installations after midnight. Analysts reviewed the logs but found no actual breach yet. The security team wants to configure alerts to catch such behaviors early in the attack lifecycle. Which type of indicator should be prioritized for setting up alerts in this scenario?

   A. Indicator of Compromise (IoC)
   B. Indicator of Attack (IoA)
   C. Malware Hashes
   D. DNS Sinkhole

   Correct Answer: B. Indicator of Attack (IoA)
   Explanation: IoAs reflect *behaviors* and *intent* during the early stages of an attack. Registry changes and unusual timings are signs of a possible attack in progress – making IoAs the right choice for real-time detection.

4. A financial institution is undergoing a cybersecurity audit. The compliance officer requests proof that their cybersecurity framework is capable of identifying and mitigating industry-specific threats proactively. Which CTI feature best aligns with regulatory compliance in this context?

   A. Collection of open-source threat feeds
   B. Use of hash calculators for integrity checks
   C. Deployment of general antivirus software
   D. Intelligence-driven detection of targeted threats

   Correct Answer: D. Intelligence-driven detection of targeted threats
   Explanation: Regulatory frameworks often expect organizations to use *proactive, intelligence-led security practices* tailored to their threat landscape, which goes beyond basic detection tools.

5. During a threat actor investigation, your team needs to access a hidden forum suspected of trading ransomware kits. The site cannot be found via Google and requires a .onion address. Which technology must be used to safely access and monitor this platform?

   A. DNS Resolver
   B. Tor Browser
   C. Proxy Server
   D. VPN Gateway

Correct Answer: B. Tor Browser

Explanation: Accessing .onion domains on the dark web requires the *Tor Browser*, which routes traffic through encrypted relays to maintain anonymity, essential for dark web investigations.

6. You are reviewing a threat intelligence report regarding a persistent threat group targeting healthcare infrastructure. The report includes attack timelines, malware families used, and infrastructure IPs. You are tasked with determining what security measures to take next. Which CTI Analyst responsibility is most applicable here?

   A. Developing encryption protocols
   B. Conducting forensic data recovery
   C. Translating threat data into strategic decisions
   D. Patching vulnerable applications

   Correct Answer: C. Translating threat data into strategic decisions

   Explanation: A CTI Analyst's primary duty is to *analyze threat data* and *translate it into actionable intelligence*, informing what defensive actions or priorities the organization must adopt.

7. Your threat team identifies a malware sample that matches signatures found in both Lazarus Group and a lesser-known cybercriminal syndicate's past activities. It uses public exploit kits and obfuscates C2 communication. Why is it difficult to accurately attribute this malware to a specific group?

   A. It's written in a non-standard programming language
   B. It lacks an encryption module
   C. It's based on open-source code reused by multiple actors
   D. It uses IPv6 addressing

   Correct Answer: C. It's based on open-source code reused by multiple actors

   Explanation: Attribution is difficult when *open-source malware tools* are involved, as they can be used by different threat actors, making behavioral and origin analysis ambiguous.

8. You are testing a suspicious executable within a banking SOC. The environment must ensure total control, data privacy, and full observability. The institution has strict offline policies due to compliance. Which type of sandboxing should you deploy?

   A. Cloud-based sandbox with AI integration
   B. Appliance-based VM sandbox
   C. Public online malware analysis tool
   D. Browser sandbox plugin

   Correct Answer: B. Appliance-based VM sandbox

   Explanation: An *appliance-based sandbox* provides complete *local control and privacy*, making it ideal for sectors like banking that operate under *strict regulatory and data isolation policies*.

9. An intern claims they accessed the darknet using a Tor browser to visit underground hacking forums. You realize they're conflating terminology. What is the most accurate correction to clarify their misunderstanding?

   A. The darknet is only accessible using VPNs
   B. The dark web is the encrypted tunnel, not the content
   C. The Tor browser accesses the dark web which exists *within* the darknet
   D. The deep web and darknet are the same

Correct Answer: C. The Tor browser accesses the dark web which exists *within* the darknet

Explanation: The *dark web* is a *subset* of the *darknet*, accessed via tools like Tor. The darknet refers to the *underlying network infrastructure*, not just the content.

10. You received a suspected malware file during an investigation. The file's MD5 hash differs from the one listed in a known malware repository. However, behavior analysis still shows strong similarity to that family. What might explain this discrepancy in hash values?

 A. The file is safe and not malware
 B. The file was corrupted during transfer
 C. The malware uses polymorphism to evade detection
 D. The hash is irrelevant for malware classification

Correct Answer: C. The malware uses polymorphism to evade detection

Explanation: Polymorphic malware *modifies its code* upon each infection, changing the hash value while retaining malicious behavior, making signature-based detection challenging.

8.2 CHAPTER 2

1. Your organization just migrated to a hybrid-cloud model. Security leaders have mandated Zero Trust implementation to prevent lateral movement. During an internal audit, a consultant flags that identity verification is only performed at initial login. Which fundamental principle of Zero Trust is being violated in this case?

 A. Network micro-segmentation
 B. Continuous verification of access
 C. Role-based access control
 D. Phishing-resistant MFA

Correct Answer: B. Continuous verification of access

Explanation: Zero Trust mandates that every access request is verified based on identity, location, device, and behavior – even after initial login. A static login approach contradicts this principle.

2. While reviewing outbound traffic logs, your team finds encrypted DNS requests occurring at irregular intervals from a workstation. The device shows no performance anomalies and passes antivirus checks. Which attacker technique does this activity most likely represent?

 A. Data exfiltration via clipboard injection
 B. Lateral movement via SMB
 C. C2 beaconing using DNS tunnelling
 D. Brute-force SSH attack

Correct Answer: C. C2 beaconing using DNS tunnelling

Explanation: The use of encrypted DNS requests at irregular intervals is characteristic of stealthy beaconing behavior, where malware checks in with its C2 server disguised as legitimate DNS traffic.

3. An oil and gas company suffers a ransomware attack where the attackers encrypted systems and also threatened to leak gigabytes of safety inspection reports if ransom wasn't paid. Incident responders find the data exfiltrated days before encryption. Which ransomware tactic best categorizes this attack?

   A. Triple extortion
   B. Locker ransomware
   C. Double extortion
   D. DDoS ransom

   Correct Answer: C. Double extortion
   Explanation: The attackers exfiltrated data and then encrypted systems, threatening to leak sensitive information – a hallmark of double extortion tactics.

4. You notice that a senior engineer downloaded large volumes of source code to an external drive during a midnight session. The user had legitimate access but deviated from usual work patterns. Which tool or technique is best suited to flag this activity in real-time?

   A. Static malware scanner
   B. SIEM with IOC feeds
   C. User and Entity Behavior Analytics (UEBA)
   D. Firewall access control list (ACL)

   Correct Answer: C. User and Entity Behavior Analytics (UEBA)
   Explanation: UEBA detects anomalous user behavior such as time-based deviations and abnormal data movement, ideal for catching potential insider threats.

5. A threat Intel team publishes a report identifying a phishing domain used in multiple attacks. Days later, another analyst discovers the same domain had expired and been parked prior to its use. Which stage of the intelligence lifecycle failed in this case?

   A. Collection
   B. Feedback
   C. Processing
   D. Analysis

   Correct Answer: D. Analysis
   Explanation: The domain's previous ownership and registration history should have been examined during the analysis phase. Failing to contextualize raw indicators is an analytical shortcoming.

6. During a red team simulation, defenders failed to detect communications between infected hosts and the C2 server. Forensic analysis revealed the use of a domain generation algorithm (DGA) to vary command domains hourly. Which C2 evasion technique was successfully used by the adversary?

   A. Beacon throttling
   B. Fast flux hosting
   C. DGA-based domain obfuscation
   D. Protocol downgrading

   Correct Answer: C. DGA-based domain obfuscation
   Explanation: DGAs dynamically generate numerous domain names, allowing malware to rotate through domains and evade detection or blacklisting efforts.

7. A cybersecurity team detects unauthorized API requests accessing billing data from cloud-based infrastructure. The logs reveal these calls originated from a misconfigured microservice without authentication controls. What best describes the exploited vulnerability in this incident?

    A. Server-side request forgery (SSRF)
    B. Cross-tenant attack
    C. API abuse due to misconfiguration
    D. Credential stuffing

    Correct Answer: C. API abuse due to misconfiguration
    Explanation: The attacker exploited exposed API endpoints lacking proper authentication, a common form of cloud-native API abuse.

8. An APT group launches a long-dwell-time campaign targeting telecom infrastructure across Asia. Their techniques include using PowerShell scripts, living-off-the-land binaries, and disguising payloads as legitimate updates. Which threat actor tactic is this campaign most closely aligned with?

    A. Hacktivist DDoS attack
    B. Nation-state advanced persistent threat
    C. Credential phishing scam
    D. Cybercrime-as-a-service

    Correct Answer: B. Nation-state advanced persistent threat
    Explanation: The use of stealthy, persistent, and contextually targeted techniques over extended periods characterizes a nation-state APT operation.

9. A global retail company integrates SOAR into its SOC. After 3 months, analysts report reduced alert fatigue and faster triage but note difficulty adjusting playbooks during novel threats. What is a known challenge of automation in CTI-based SOC workflows?

    A. Excessive memory consumption
    B. Over-reliance on machine learning alone
    C. Static playbooks that lack adaptive context
    D. Lack of regulatory approval

    Correct Answer: C. Static playbooks that lack adaptive context
    Explanation: Automated SOAR systems often depend on predefined playbooks. Without dynamic threat modeling, novel or evolving attacks may be mishandled or missed.

10. A CISO prepares a board presentation on emerging threats from Chinese APT groups targeting global semiconductor firms. The presentation will inform future investment in cybersecurity and risk posture. Which type of threat intelligence should the CISO rely on?

    A. Technical
    B. Tactical
    C. Operational
    D. Strategic

    Correct Answer: D. Strategic
    Explanation: Strategic intelligence offers high-level, long-term insight into geopolitical threat actors and their motivations, supporting executive decision-making.

8.3 CHAPTER 3

1. A security analyst examines a malicious JavaScript file obtained from a phishing campaign. The code appears obfuscated with base64 encoding and multiple layers of string concatenation. Before any runtime behavior is observed, the analyst tries to deconstruct the code. Which approach best supports this type of analysis?

   A. Running the file in a sandbox
   B. Checking memory dumps for IOCs
   C. Using a deobfuscation script and viewing the code statically
   D. Observing system logs for registry changes

   Correct Answer: C. Using a deobfuscation script and viewing the code statically
   Explanation: This is a classic static analysis use case – understanding malicious code without executing it. Deobfuscation tools help decode and inspect the code safely.

2. During dynamic analysis in a virtual machine, a malware sample fails to execute fully. Upon examining the API calls and behavior logs, the analyst notices a sudden termination after querying system hardware and processes. What is the most likely explanation for this behavior?

   A. The VM lacked internet access
   B. The malware was missing a critical DLL
   C. The malware detected the analysis environment
   D. There was a hash mismatch during execution

   Correct Answer: C. The malware detected the analysis environment
   Explanation: Malware often includes anti-debugging or anti-VM techniques to avoid detection. Detecting virtualization or analysis tools can trigger premature termination.

3. A threat hunter receives a suspicious .exe from a suspected phishing incident. Before executing it, they extract the PE (Portable Executable) header to examine metadata like compilation time and imported DLLs. Why is PE header analysis useful during static investigation?

   A. It confirms encryption keys used
   B. It reveals runtime stack traces
   C. It helps identify artifacts like compiler, timestamp, and imports
   D. It runs the binary in a safe container

   Correct Answer: C. It helps identify artifacts like compiler, timestamp, and imports
   Explanation: The PE header contains valuable static metadata that can help attribute malware, detect packing, or check for unusual compile times and dependencies.

4. During an endpoint compromise assessment, an investigator launches tools like Process Explorer, Autoruns, and TCPView to monitor live processes, startup entries, and open network connections from the suspected machine. Which type of analysis is this workflow associated with?

   A. File carving
   B. Static string extraction
   C. Dynamic behavioral analysis
   D. Signature matching

Correct Answer: C. Dynamic behavioral analysis

Explanation: These tools observe live, runtime behavior – which is at the core of dynamic analysis in threat hunting workflows.

5. An EDR alert indicates that svchost.exe initiated outbound traffic, but the original parent process shows no such behavior historically. Further analysis reveals injected shellcode in the memory of svchost.exe. Which technique is most likely being used by the attacker?

   A. DLL sideloading
   B. Process hollowing
   C. Port scanning
   D. Log poisoning

Correct Answer: B. Process hollowing

Explanation: Process hollowing involves replacing the memory of a legitimate process (like svchost.exe) with malicious code while preserving its appearance – enabling stealthy operations.

6. You reverse engineer a ransomware executable and identify hardcoded domains, IP addresses, and specific filenames used for ransom notes. No network behavior was observed yet. What type of threat intelligence are these findings best classified as?

   A. Tactics and procedures
   B. Indicators of attack (IoA)
   C. Indicators of compromise (IoC)
   D. Exploitation vectors

Correct Answer: C. Indicators of compromise (IoC)

Explanation: These hardcoded artifacts – like filenames and domains – are static IoCs that can be used in signatures and detection rules.

7. A suspicious file is executed in a controlled lab. Within seconds, several child processes are spawned, and then an unexpected attempt is made to modify the boot configuration of the host system. Which threat behavior does this most likely indicate?

   A. Fileless malware using macros
   B. Reconnaissance activity
   C. Inhibit system recovery (T1490)
   D. Exploit of printer spooler service

Correct Answer: C. Inhibit system recovery (T1490)

Explanation: Attempts to modify boot configuration or delete backups often map to the MITRE ATT&CK technique T1490 – used to prevent system recovery after ransomware attacks.

8. An organization uses automated sandboxing for dynamic malware analysis. However, multiple malware samples are returned with "No activity detected," even though analysts suspect the files are malicious. What is a common cause for this failure in sandbox-based analysis?

   A. The sandbox was low on disk space
   B. The malware checks for sandbox artifacts before executing
   C. The sandbox has outdated antivirus definitions
   D. The malware is hardware-bound and won't run anywhere else

Correct Answer: B. The malware checks for sandbox artifacts before executing

Explanation: Many malware variants are designed to detect sandbox environments and suppress malicious behavior if such conditions are identified – commonly through hardware, timing, or registry checks.

9. During a triage exercise, an analyst encounters a .exe file that shows minimal readable strings and an unusually small import table, despite a large file size. What is the most plausible reason for this discrepancy?

    A. The file is corrupted
    B. It is an archive file, not an executable
    C. The executable is packed or compressed
    D. It uses a 64-bit encoding scheme

    Correct Answer: C. The executable is packed or compressed

    Explanation: Malware often uses packing to obfuscate contents and avoid signature-based detection. Packed files hide strings and APIs by compressing or encrypting the code.

10. After a phishing attack, a user's machine behaves erratically but antivirus tools report no infections. A memory dump reveals an injected process holding a decoded payload that is absent from the disk. What advantage does memory analysis provide in such scenarios?

    A. It bypasses sandbox emulation.
    B. It highlights unreachable backup sectors
    C. It uncovers in-memory execution missed by file-based scanning
    D. It allows for registry key modifications

    Correct Answer: C. It uncovers in-memory execution missed by file-based scanning

    Explanation: Memory forensics reveals fileless or in-memory malware that doesn't exist on disk – bypassing traditional detection and making dynamic analysis essential.

8.4 CHAPTER 4

1. Your SOC is tracking a phishing campaign targeting utility sector employees. Several endpoints have shown suspicious DNS-over-HTTPS activity. To automate detection and response via SOAR, your team needs to ingest structured threat feeds directly into the response engine. Which integration method best enables this automated orchestration?

    A. Manual JSON extraction and signature application
    B. Scheduled Excel-based IOC imports from vendors
    C. STIX/TAXII-enabled feed consumed directly by the SOAR platform
    D. Direct email alerts to analysts with domain lists

    Correct Answer: C. STIX/TAXII-enabled feed consumed directly by the SOAR platform

    Explanation: STIX/TAXII enables standardized and machine-readable CTI ingestion. It supports real-time threat feed integration, essential for triggering SOAR-driven automated response workflows.

2. During a red team operation, your team is tasked with emulating the behavior of a known APT that leverages DLL sideloading and dual-use tools. You want to replicate the attack realistically based on current adversarial tradecraft. What element of operationalized CTI is most useful for this simulation?

   A. Clustering IP addresses based on physical geography
   B. MITRE ATT&CK-aligned TTPs from contextualized threat feeds
   C. Random malware hashes from dark web forums
   D. Expired DNS records from public blacklists

   Correct Answer: B. MITRE ATT&CK-aligned TTPs from contextualized threat feeds
   Explanation: Enriched CTI with ATT&CK-aligned TTPs provides behavioral context necessary for red teams to emulate adversaries with high fidelity.

3. A suspicious document is attached to a spear-phishing email targeting finance executive. When analyzed, it appears structurally encoded and encrypted to bypass static scanners. Which CTI tool best enables detection of such techniques via structural disassembly?

   A. VirusTotal
   B. DOCGuard
   C. OpenCTI
   D. AlienVault OTX

   Correct Answer: B. DOCGuard
   Explanation: DOCGuard specializes in deep inspection of document internals, identifying evasive features such as encoding, embedded payloads, or encryption layers used in phishing campaigns.

4. Aerospace firms are reporting repeated intrusion attempts. CTI reports show multiple overlapping domains across different attack phases. Analysts need to track changes in infrastructure used by the attacker. What method best supports this investigation?

   A. Static hash matching across samples
   B. OSINT-based keyword searches in phishing databases
   C. Passive DNS correlation across historical records
   D. Registry inspection of local endpoints

   Correct Answer: C. Passive DNS correlation across historical records
   Explanation: Passive DNS allows analysts to trace domain-to-IP changes and uncover reused infrastructure over time – a critical component of campaign-level CTI.

5. Security telemetry shows that ransomware operators are registering new domains shortly before DNS lookup spikes and attack deployment. You want to detect such behavior in advance. Which type of CTI feed is best suited for this purpose?

   A. Botnet sinkhole telemetry
   B. Behavioral CTI feed based on DNS anomalies
   C. Antivirus signature-based IOC feed
   D. Manually updated blacklists

   Correct Answer: B. Behavioral CTI feed based on DNS anomalies
   Explanation: Behavioral threat intelligence enables early warning based on how threats behave, like sudden DNS resolution spikes – often a precursor to ransomware activity.

6. Your agency needs to gather intelligence on a nation-state actor's malware propagation without interacting with their C2 infrastructure to avoid tipping them off. Which CTI approach supports this covert data collection?

   A. Trigger-based alerts from SIEM
   B. Active probing of known malicious domains
   C. Passive DNS monitoring
   D. Public disclosure of attacker IPs

   Correct Answer: C. Passive DNS monitoring
   Explanation: Passive DNS allows the observation of DNS queries and responses without active interaction, making it ideal for stealthy intelligence gathering.

7. Multiple politically motivated intrusions against NGOs reveal a recurring set of file hashes. You need to determine if these indicators point to a common actor or campaign. What CTI technique should be used?

   A. AV signature log review
   B. Clustering and TTP correlation via OpenCTI
   C. Community comment comparison on VirusTotal
   D. Internal phishing simulations

   Correct Answer: B. Clustering and TTP correlation via OpenCTI
   Explanation: OpenCTI allows linking indicators to campaigns through TTP mapping and clustering, helping uncover underlying patterns and threat actor attribution.

8. Your malware lab detects a sample with known imphash and ssdeep similarity to previously documented espionage malware. You want to assess if it's a variant from the same family. What should be the next analytical step?

   A. Launch brute-force attacks for more indicators
   B. Search social media platforms for opinions
   C. Correlate static features through clustering analysis
   D. Format the drive for full remediation

   Correct Answer: C. Correlate static features through clustering analysis
   Explanation: Clustering helps group malware samples based on shared code characteristics, enabling attribution to known malware families or campaigns.

9. Your team identifies a new C2 domain used in a banking impersonation attack. The malware uses SSL tunnels to exfiltrate data. You aim to neutralize the threat and preserve forensic evidence. What is the best response?

   A. Block all SSL connections from the enterprise
   B. Sinkhole the domain by contacting the hosting provider
   C. Format all impacted machines
   D. Notify users via internal messaging

   Correct Answer: B. Sinkhole the domain by contacting the hosting provider
   Explanation: Sinkholing safely redirects C2 traffic, prevents further data loss, and enables ongoing observation of compromised systems for evidence.

10. An adversary updates their malware payload weekly on a public GitHub repository, subtly changing strings and filenames. Your goal is to monitor and track these changes efficiently. Which strategy should be employed?

    A. Weekly GitHub snapshotting
    B. DNS brute forcing
    C. YARA rules and OSINT queries for reused strings and filenames
    D. VPN blocklist automation

    Correct Answer: C. YARA rules and OSINT queries for reused strings and filenames
    Explanation: YARA rules help detect malware based on byte patterns or reused code, while OSINT helps identify attacker fingerprints in public repositories.

8.5 CHAPTER 5

1. You're analyzing a suspicious .jpg file found in an employee's download folder. On running it through a hex editor, you see it starts with 4D 5A. What should be your first conclusion?

    A. The file is a corrupt image
    B. It is a renamed executable with PE structure
    C. The file is a valid JPEG
    D. The file contains encrypted ZIP data

    Correct Answer: B
    Explanation: The hex signature 4D 5A corresponds to "MZ", which is the signature of a Portable Executable (PE) file. The .jpg extension is likely a disguise.

2. You are using FakeNet on a Windows VM to analyze malware with network behavior. After initiating the analysis, you see outbound DNS and HTTP requests being redirected to 127.0.0.1. What is the purpose of this setup?

    A. To allow malware to exfiltrate data safely
    B. To simulate legitimate domain resolution
    C. To block malware's outbound traffic and simulate C2
    D. To forward the traffic to antivirus software

    Correct Answer: C
    Explanation: FakeNet intercepts and loops back traffic to the localhost, simulating a command-and-control (C2) environment so malware remains active without leaking data externally.

3. While conducting static analysis, you hash a suspicious file and upload it to VirusTotal. It shows a 2-year-old detection and 58 AV hits. What's your next step?

    A. Consider the threat neutralized due to age
    B. Execute it in the production environment
    C. Conduct behavioral analysis to verify current impact
    D. Discard the file without further review

    Correct Answer: C
    Explanation: Despite its age, the malware could still be active or repurposed. Dynamic analysis helps observe current behavior and any new IOCs or persistence mechanisms.

4. A malware sample attempts to run InternetOpenA and URLDownloadToFileA. What does this imply about the malware's behavior?

    A. It's trying to establish persistence
    B. It's collecting hardware information
    C. It's attempting to download additional payloads
    D. It's encrypting local files

Correct Answer: C
Explanation: These functions are commonly used to connect to a remote server and download files, typical in droppers or staged payload delivery malware.

5. During a live packet capture in Wireshark, you apply the filter tls.handshake.type eq 1 and inspect the 'Client Hello' message. What critical detail can this reveal?

    A. Public IP of sandbox
    B. CPU architecture
    C. Domain name the malware attempts to connect to
    D. File hash of the payload

Correct Answer: C
Explanation: The TLS 'Client Hello' packet often contains the Server Name Indication (SNI) field, which reveals the domain the client (malware) wants to connect to.

6. You use NetworkMiner to analyze a .pcap file from a ransomware attack. What advantage does this tool provide over raw Wireshark analysis?

    A. It decrypts ransomware binaries
    B. It automatically extracts credentials and files
    C. It modifies DNS settings for sandbox
    D. It converts binary into readable assembly

Correct Answer: B
Explanation: NetworkMiner extracts artifacts like files, credentials, and metadata from PCAPs, offering a forensic summary that is faster to interpret than raw packet inspection.

7. You're using ANY.RUN to analyze malware. Why is enabling a Man-in-the-Middle (MITM) proxy for HTTPS traffic critical in this environment?

    A. To bypass sandbox detection by malware
    B. To improve the speed of malware execution
    C. To analyze decrypted HTTPS traffic
    D. To obfuscate sandbox IP address

Correct Answer: C
Explanation: Enabling MITM allows interception and analysis of encrypted HTTPS traffic, which is crucial for understanding modern malware communication with its C2.

8. You're reverse engineering a dropper using FLARE-VM. What benefit does using Chocolatey and Boxstarter provide in this environment?

    A. Compresses malware into base64 format
    B. Obfuscates assembly code for stealth
    C. Automates repeatable malware lab setup
    D. Detects zero-day vulnerabilities

Correct Answer: C

Explanation: Chocolatey and Boxstarter automate tool installations and configurations, ensuring consistent and repeatable setups for malware analysis labs.

9. You have executed a suspicious file in a sandbox and observed rapid creation of .tmp files in C:\Users\Temp\. Which malware behavior does this suggest?

   A. Ransomware encryption keys being stored
   B. Steganography
   C. Payload unpacking or evasion techniques
   D. SQL injection logs

Correct Answer: C

Explanation: Temporary files often indicate runtime unpacking, a behavior used by malware to extract its payload dynamically and avoid static detection.

10. While analyzing an executable file, you run the strings command and find URLs, registry paths, and Win32 API calls. What type of analysis are you conducting?

   A. Behavioral
   B. Static
   C. Network
   D. Cryptographic

Correct Answer: B

Explanation: strings reveal static, human-readable content without executing the file, helping identify indicators like C2 addresses and behaviors statically.

8.6 CHAPTER 6

1. Your SOC is mapping adversary behavior using the MITRE ATT&CK matrix. An attacker uses Mimikatz to dump LSASS credentials. Where would this activity be placed within ATT&CK?

   A. Initial Access
   B. Execution
   C. Credential Access
   D. Exfiltration

Correct Answer: C

Explanation: Mimikatz is commonly used for extracting credentials from memory, aligning directly with the Credential Access tactic in the MITRE ATT&CK framework.

2. While conducting CTI enrichment, you pull IOCs from a threat report and correlate them to MITRE TTPs. Which framework provides adversary behavior mapped to real-world campaigns?

   A. OWASP
   B. Cyber Kill Chain
   C. MITRE ATT&CK
   D. STRIDE

Correct Answer: C

Explanation: MITRE ATT&CK is a knowledge base of adversary tactics and techniques based on real-world observations and mapped to known threat actor behaviors.

3. An analyst observes initial phishing, followed by malware execution, privilege escalation, and data exfiltration. Which framework provides a sequential flow of these activities?

   A. MITRE ATT&CK
   B. Diamond Model
   C. Cyber Kill Chain
   D. D3FEND

   Correct Answer: C

   Explanation: The Cyber Kill Chain offers a linear sequence of attacker activities from Reconnaissance to Actions on Objectives, making it useful for high-level detection modeling.

4. You're asked to visually chart how adversaries moved from lateral movement to C2 channels. Which of the following tools best integrates with ATT&CK Navigator for this purpose?

   A. Nessus
   B. BloodHound
   C. MITRE ATT&CK Navigator
   D. Wireshark

   Correct Answer: C

   Explanation: MITRE ATT&CK Navigator allows visualization of TTPs in an interactive grid format, supporting overlays for adversary mapping and detection coverage analysis.

5. You receive STIX/TAXII feeds and want to import them into your threat intelligence platform for structured analysis. Which CTI concept are you applying?

   A. Indicator pivoting
   B. Threat hunting
   C. Threat intelligence normalization
   D. Threat intelligence ingestion

   Correct Answer: D

   Explanation: Ingestion refers to consuming structured threat intelligence data from feeds (e.g., STIX/TAXII), enabling automation in CTI processing pipelines.

6. You're designing defenses using MITRE D3FEND to complement ATT&CK. If you're focusing on hardening credentials and monitoring login attempts, what category are you in?

   A. Execution Blocking
   B. Credential Hardening
   C. Lateral Movement Inhibition
   D. Threat Actor Attribution

Correct Answer: B

Explanation: D3FEND includes specific techniques like Credential Hardening, which counter ATT&CK's credential access vectors via mitigations like MFA and audit logging.

7. You're building threat actor profiles and want to classify them based on capability, motivation, and intent. Which model helps you best with such contextual adversary profiling?

   A. MITRE ATT&CK
   B. Cyber Kill Chain
   C. Diamond Model
   D. D3FEND

Correct Answer: C

Explanation: The Diamond Model focuses on four core components: adversary, infrastructure, capability, and victim, making it ideal for adversary profiling and analysis.

8. A ransomware campaign is detected using known TTPs. Which benefit of MITRE ATT&CK is most relevant when prioritizing SOC alert response?

   A. Mapping exploits to CVEs
   B. Tracking business continuity
   C. Contextualizing alerts with tactics and techniques
   D. Preventing SQL injection

Correct Answer: C

Explanation: MITRE ATT&CK helps SOCs contextualize raw alerts by linking them to known tactics and techniques, improving triage and incident response efficiency.

9. While analyzing an APT report, you notice the attacker reused the same C2 infrastructure from a previous campaign. Which CTI concept does this illustrate?

   A. Threat modeling
   B. Attribution
   C. Intelligence pivoting
   D. Campaign overlap

Correct Answer: D

Explanation: Reuse of infrastructure or tools across operations by the same actor indicates campaign overlap, a valuable CTI pattern for tracking persistent threats.

10. You are tasked with communicating adversary techniques to executive leadership. Which representation is most effective in this context?

    A. Hex dumps from the malware sample
    B. Detailed packet captures
    C. ATT&CK Navigator heatmaps
    D. Assembly-level instruction flow

Correct Answer: C

Explanation: ATT&CK Navigator heatmaps provide a visual, executive-friendly summary of detected or mitigated adversary techniques across different kill chain phases.

8.7 CHAPTER 7

1. You're building a threat intelligence dashboard and want to display indicators that include suspicious IP addresses, malicious domains, and rogue URLs. Which data type are you primarily visualizing?

   A. Tactical threat data
   B. Strategic threat data
   C. Operational threat data
   D. Indicator of Compromise (IOC)

   Correct Answer: D
   Explanation: IPs, domains, and URLs are classic Indicators of Compromise (IOCs) used for threat detection and blocking at the tactical level.

2. Your team pulls a threat report highlighting how a threat actor exploits CVE-2023-12345 in Apache servers. The report includes MITRE TTPs and recommended patches. What kind of intelligence is this?

   A. Operational Intelligence
   B. Strategic Intelligence
   C. Tactical Intelligence
   D. Incident Response Playbook

   Correct Answer: C
   Explanation: The information is Tactical Intelligence – focused on specific vulnerabilities, TTPs, and immediate actionable guidance relevant to defenders and SOC teams.

3. You receive a MISP feed containing structured intelligence in STIX 2.1 format. What is one major benefit of consuming threat intel in this format?

   A. Enables encrypted email exchanges
   B. Facilitates unstructured IOC extraction
   C. Supports automation and data interoperability
   D. Prevents system compromise during parsing

   Correct Answer: C
   Explanation: STIX is a structured format that enhances machine-readable interoperability and automation, making it ideal for integrating into SIEMs and threat platforms.

4. While reviewing a phishing campaign, you notice that emails use newly registered domains with slight character alterations like "google.com". Which CTI technique helps detect this?

   A. Exploit chaining
   B. DNS sink holing
   C. Domain permutation analysis
   D. SSL certificate pinning

   Correct Answer: C
   Explanation: Domain permutation or typo squatting analysis detects lookalike domains used in phishing or impersonation by evaluating character substitutions and alterations.

5. A threat intelligence platform (TIP) auto-ingests feeds from AbuseIPDB, PhishTank, and AlienVault OTX. What challenge might arise if no deduplication process is used?

   A. Overhead from encryption algorithms
   B. Redundancy and conflicting context for IOCs
   C. Incomplete attack lifecycle mapping
   D. Misclassification of CVEs as zero-days

   Correct Answer: B
   Explanation: Without deduplication, multiple feeds may report the same IOC differently, causing redundancy, noise, and inconsistent IOC context in your platform.

6. An executive asks for a summary of ransomware threats impacting the logistics sector over the past year. Which level of threat intelligence is most appropriate?

   A. Tactical
   B. Operational
   C. Strategic
   D. Threat hunting report

   Correct Answer: C
   Explanation: Strategic intelligence is designed for non-technical stakeholders and provides high-level insights about trends, threat actors, and sector-specific impacts.

7. You're configuring your SIEM to alert on TTPs related to lateral movement. Which component of the MITRE ATT&CK framework should you use to create detection rules?

   A. Capabilities
   B. Techniques and Sub-Techniques
   C. Campaigns
   D. CVEs

   Correct Answer: B
   Explanation: Techniques and Sub-Techniques in ATT&CK directly describe adversarial behavior and are essential for building SIEM correlation rules for detection.

8. Your red team simulates a known APT group by using its documented TTPs. Which type of intelligence enables this simulation?

   A. Strategic intelligence
   B. Threat behavior profiling
   C. Technical indicators
   D. Automated IOC sandboxing

   Correct Answer: B
   Explanation: Threat behavior profiling maps adversary activities across the kill chain, helping emulate real APT behaviors during red team assessments.

9. In your CTI process, you integrate threat intelligence into incident response workflows. What is the main advantage of this integration?

   A. Faster domain registration for alerts
   B. Real-time IOC obfuscation
   C. Accelerated incident triage and remediation
   D. Simplified SOC hiring processes

Correct Answer: C

Explanation: Integrated CTI supports faster decision-making during incidents, enabling more accurate triage, threat containment, and remediation.

10. You are validating CTI sources and evaluating an open-source feed. What metric would be most important to assess its reliability?

    A. The number of indicators provided per hour
    B. Its adherence to STIX/TAXII formats
    C. IOC false positive rate and historical accuracy
    D. The amount of dark web data included

Correct Answer: C

Explanation: False positives and historical accuracy are key in evaluating a threat feed's reliability. High-quality intel reduces noise and alert fatigue in defense systems.

For Product Safety Concerns and Information please contact our EU
representative GPSR@taylorandfrancis.com
Taylor & Francis Verlag GmbH, Kaufingerstraße 24, 80331 München, Germany